Muslim Schools, Communities and Critical Race Theory

Damian Breen

Muslim Schools, Communities and Critical Race Theory

Faith Schooling in an Islamophobic Britain?

Damian Breen
De Montfort University
Leicester, UK

ISBN 978-1-137-44396-0   ISBN 978-1-137-44397-7   (eBook)
DOI 10.1057/978-1-137-44397-7

Library of Congress Control Number: 2017949540

© The Editor(s) (if applicable) and The Author(s) 2018
The author(s) has/have asserted their right(s) to be identified as the author(s) of this work in accordance with the Copyright, Designs and Patents Act 1988.
This work is subject to copyright. All rights are solely and exclusively licensed by the Publisher, whether the whole or part of the material is concerned, specifically the rights of translation, reprinting, reuse of illustrations, recitation, broadcasting, reproduction on microfilms or in any other physical way, and transmission or information storage and retrieval, electronic adaptation, computer software, or by similar or dissimilar methodology now known or here-after developed.
The use of general descriptive names, registered names, trademarks, service marks, etc. in this publication does not imply, even in the absence of a specific statement, that such names are exempt from the relevant protective laws and regulations and therefore free for general use. The publisher, the authors and the editors are safe to assume that the advice and information in this book are believed to be true and accurate at the date of publication. Neither the pub-lisher nor the authors or the editors give a warranty, express or implied, with respect to the material contained herein or for any errors or omissions that may have been made. The publisher remains neutral with regard to jurisdictional claims in published maps and institu-tional affiliations.

Cover illustration: Hongqi Zhang / Alamy Stock Photo

Printed on acid-free paper

This Palgrave Macmillan imprint is published by Springer Nature
The registered company is Macmillan Publishers Ltd.
The registered company address is: The Campus, 4 Crinan Street, London, N1 9XW, United Kingdom

For Nyle

Acknowledgements

This book marks the culmination of a decade's work on a path that might easily have never been trodden. Initially, I have to express my gratitude to the participants in the research that informs this monograph, in particular those that facilitated access so that the research could take the form that it ultimately did. Assurances of anonymity make it impossible to directly acknowledge several individuals whom I will always feel indebted to as a result of their encouragement and their roles in the research. However, I am able to acknowledge those in the academic world who have been instrumental in supporting and helping me to realise my aspirations. There is no question that without the support and guidance of Chris Pole, throughout my studies at the University of Leicester, I would not have made the transition from optimistic student to viable PhD candidate. His guidance led me to successfully attain an ESRC+3 studentship at the Institute of Education, University of Warwick. It was at Warwick that my doctoral research on Muslim schools developed and came to fruition. I am proud to have completed my PhD in the Warwick Religions and Education Research Unit (WRERU) under the supervision of Eleanor Nesbitt and Bob Jackson. I will always be grateful for the time I spent in Eleanor's office, simultaneously working out how to be a researcher on the one hand and how to present myself within this newly accessed world on the other. I also enjoyed the company of Natasha Leahy, Nick Lee, Alan Prout, Julia Ipgrave, Elisabeth Arweck and Stephen Parker during my time at the Institute of Education, and in particular I enjoyed the stimulating conversations we shared. I am of course also grateful to the ESRC for their funding of the research that would ultimately inform this monograph.available to teachers in Chap

As alluded to in Chaps. 4 and 5, I also feel that it is important to acknowledge a shift in my own politics which occurred somewhere between the final year of the PhD and the first year in my first permanent academic post at Keele University. Discussions with Farzana Shain not only ensured that I set about developing the doctoral research with a view to writing a monograph but also led me to reconsider the academic positioning of the work. In addition to professional support and guidance, she introduced me to several individuals who have been influential in recent years including Kalwant Bhopal, Chris Allen and Nasar Meer. In this period, I came to a realisation that my research increasingly revealed parallels with emerging work on Critical Race Theory. Parallel to this process, I have been fortunate enough to work collaboratively with Nasar Meer, and he has proven to be a valuable mentor, appearing at exactly the right time and offering practical as well as professional guidance. I am grateful for the discussions we have shared around my work and the book in particular, as these have allowed me to identify and resolve conceptual problems that may have otherwise evaded detection. During this time, I was also fortunate enough to cross paths with David Gillborn and share my aspirations to apply CRT in the study of British Muslim communities. I will always be grateful for the first in-depth conversation that we shared, during which I felt like much was hanging in the balance, only to be met with encouragement, support and practical guidance. I am also grateful for your guidance on the book, which again allowed me to resolve issues which otherwise may have been overlooked. In particular, I would like to thank you for our discussions on the practice of being a white researcher and the implications of occupying space, the politics of 'speaking for', and strategies for using whiteness against itself in the field of ethnic and 'racial' studies. I learnt an awful lot from those conversations, and they have had a lasting impact. Those who have had less direct academic input but who invariably kept me sane along the way would include Stacey Pope, who has intermittently vetted the contents of my mind over the last decade, and Richard Courtney, who has offered much in the way of amusement.

Of course, academics are real people, and there is no way that I would have been able to produce this work without the support of my family. First and foremost, I would like to thank my partner-in-everything Sabrina Salmon for believing in me and giving me support, contentment and endless happiness to offset the ludicrous stresses of completing a work such as this. And of course, thank you for our son Nyle. The relentless charm and cheeky smile you both share is my inspiration to keep on pushing forward—I hope I have made you both proud. I would also like to thank the wider family that I have inherited through Sabrina—aside from the fun and games, you have welcomed me into a world which has connected the ivory tower with real life in a way that has made me increasingly personally invested in the politics around my research—thank you. There is also no question that I would not have made it along the academic path without the encouragement of my mum and dad, Breda and Patrick Breen. Their constant encouragement and emphasis on the importance of education has allowed me to navigate this academic world with some kind of purpose. In particular, recent events have given us all reason to feel closer than ever, and I hope this is felt by both of you as much as it is by me.

Finally, Chaps. 3, 6, 7 and 8 develop ideas and data that have appeared to some degree previously, and so I very gratefully acknowledge the copyright holders of the following:

Breen, D. (2009). A Qualitative Narrative of the Transition from Independent to Voluntary Aided Status: A Problem for the Concept of the Muslim School. In A. A. Veinguer, G. Dietz, D. Jozsa, & T. Knauth (Eds.), *Islam in Education in European Countries Pedagogical Concepts and Empirical Findings* (pp. 95–112). Münster: Waxmann.

Breen, D. (2013). State-funded Muslim Schools and the Public Sphere: Stakeholders and Legitimacy in the UK Context. In J. Miller, K. O'Grady, & U. McKenna (Eds.), *Religion in Education: Innovation in International Research* (pp. 41–57). London: Routledge-Falmer.

Breen, D. (2014). British Muslim Schools: Institutional Isomorphism and the Transition from Independent to Voluntary-Aided Status. In R. Race (Ed.) 2013: *Advancing 'Race' and Ethnicity within Education* (pp. 32–46). Hampshire: Palgrave Macmillan.

Breen, D. (2016). Critical Race Theory, Policy Rhetoric and Outcomes: The Case of Muslim Schools in Britain. *Race Ethnicity and Education.* doi 10.1080/13613324.2016.1248828.

Dr Damian Breen (May 2017)

Contents

1 British Muslim Communities, 'Faith' Schooling and Critical Race Theory   1
CRT and British Muslims?   4
References   7

2 Exploring the Application of Critical Race Theory to Muslims in Britain   9
Critical Race Theory: 'Roots'   9
Tacit Intentionality   15
CRT, Education and Interest Convergence   16
Whiteness?   17
Counter-Narratives   19
Islamophobia: Premises and Possible Limitations   21
From Islamophobia to CRT   24
Anti-Muslim Racism?   26
A Meaningful Application of CRT in the Study of Muslim Communities in Britain   31
References   32

3 Critical Race Theory, Policy Rhetoric and Outcomes: The Case of Muslim Schools in Britain   35
Prevent: Implications for Political and Educational Equity   37
Fundamental British Values   39

xi

xii CONTENTS

Muslim Schools in England and Wales	41
New Labour: A Sustained Interest in State-Funded Minority Religious Schooling?	42
Anxiety Following 2010?	43
Numbers of British Muslim Schools	46
Issues Around Faith Schooling and Muslim Schools Post-2010	49
Gains Made in the Post-2010 Era	51
In Conclusion: Identifying Master-Narratives Around British Muslims and Implications for State-Funded Islamic Schooling in Britain	54
References	57
4 Applying CRT in Research on Muslim Schools	61
Critical Race Theory: and Method	63
Voice and Counter-Storytelling in CRT	64
Whose Voice?	65
The Research Design	66
The Rationale for Ethnography	68
The Insider/Outsider Debate: Preparation, Ethics, Practice	70
Ethnic Diversity and British Muslims	70
Gender in the Context of Research in Muslim Schools	72
Conducting Research Among Muslim Women: Reality in the Field	73
Moving from Methodology to Method	75
References	75
5 Researching Muslim Schools in Practice	79
Ethnographic Interviews	79
Participant Observation	84
Using Grounded Theory for Data Analysis	87
Conclusion	90
References	92
6 Muslim Schools as Mobilisations of Interests: How Islamic Schools Come into Being	95
The Independent Sector: A Site for Islamic Schooling	96
Introducing Medina Primary: Positioning the School Within the Independent Sector	99

Introducing Hiqmah School: Location, Community and Intake	100
Medina Primary and Hiqmah School: Origins	101
Introducing 'Nasira', Al-Falah and Al-Iman	105
Muslim Schools as a Response to 'Need'	109
Muslim Schools as Mobilisations of Community Interests	112
References	112

7 Community, Connectivity and Nuanced Needs 115

Introducing the Primary Stakeholders: Families and Intake at Medina Primary	116
Families and Intake at Al-Falah and Al-Iman	119
The Role of Staff in Provision: Profiles of Staff and Implications for the School Environment	123
Profile of the Staff at Medina Primary	123
Employing Staff in the Voluntary-Aided Sector: Non-Muslim Staff at Al-Falah	127
Profile of Staff at Al-Iman: Structural Changes and the Voluntary-Aided Sector	128
Grant-Maintained or Voluntary-Aided Status: Staff and Intake at Hiqmah School Over Time	130
Reconciling Diversity, Muslim Schools and Stakeholder Interests?	135
References	136

8 Manifesting Educational and Islamic Interests in Independent and State-Funded Contexts 137

Practices and Values	138
Islamic Practice in Protected Spaces	141
Islamic Voices, Autonomy and Empowerment	143
Learning Practices by Example	144
Autonomy in Denominational Provision: Delivering Islamically Focused Content	146
Arabic in Everyday School Life	150
Approaches to Providing an 'Islamicised Curriculum': The Independent Context	152
Islamicising the Curriculum: The State-Funded Context	155
Muslim Schooling and Connections to Community	157

xiv CONTENTS

In Conclusion: In What Ways Do the Above Examples of Provision Serve the Interests of Muslim Stakeholders?	159
References	164

9 In Conclusion: Distilling an Effective Counter-Narrative Around British Muslim Schools

	167
Muslim Schools, Tacit Intentionality and Interest Convergence	167
Strategies and Smokescreens	171
Muslim Schools, Diversity and Community Needs	172
A Note on the Future for State-Funded Muslim Schools	175
In Conclusion: So What?	176
References	178

Glossary of Islamic Terms	179
Notes on the Use of Arabic	183
Islamic Arabic Definitions Are Taken From	185
References	187
Index	197

CHAPTER 1

British Muslim Communities, 'Faith' Schooling and Critical Race Theory

Muslims living in Britain in the twenty-first century represent an increasingly substantive and yet ethnically and culturally diverse community. At the centre of public and political debates around cultural diversity, there has been a sustained focus on Muslim communities and their relationships with the state. Following the advent of the first state-maintained Muslim schools in 1998, the emergence of Islamic schools in the state sector represents one of the key ways in which Muslim communities have been enfranchised in terms of polity. Whilst the emergence of these schools represents a step towards clearer institutional partnerships with the state, concerns around Muslim communities in contemporary Britain have been sustained at the centre of public political debates. Discussions around Islam in the public space have been positioned against a backdrop of media narratives around global events such as the attack on the World Trade Center on 11 September 2001, and at the national level, the London bombings of 7 July 2005 and more recently the death of drummer Lee Rigby in May 2013 (Bignall 2013) and the knife attacks at Leytonstone underground station (London) in December 2015 (Dodd and Addley 2015). Furthermore, tensions around Islam in the public space in Europe have recently been fuelled by anxieties following a series of terrorist attacks including those on the *Charlie Hebdo* offices in Paris in January 2015 (Henley and Willsher 2015) and a series of coordinated attacks in the French capital in November of the same year (Henley and Chrisafis 2015). The following year saw media reports of two suicide bombs being detonated at Brussels Airport, Belgium in March 2016 and also the 'truck

© The Author(s) 2018
D. Breen, *Muslim Schools, Communities and Critical Race Theory*,
DOI 10.1057/978-1-137-44397-7_1

1

attacks' (Borger and MacAskill 2016) in Nice (July 2016) and Berlin (December 2016) and most recently the Westminster attack (March 2017). Alongside this sustained political and media attention, at the national level we have seen the rise of the British National Party and the English Defence League in the UK—political organisations which are both openly sceptical of the ability of Muslim and British/English communities to coexist peacefully. Within these political discourses Muslim communities are viewed as responsible by proxy with regard to anxieties around Islamic extremism and terrorism articulated in the tabloid media. Thus, the development of state-funded Muslim schools in England and Wales has taken place against a backdrop of public anxiety around the appropriateness of Islamic schools, particularly in the state sector.

In the light of the above, this monograph will explore the realities of Muslim schooling in both independent and state-funded contexts as a means of providing a counter-narrative which challenges anxieties around Islamic schooling in contemporary Britain. Specifically, this work will offer distinctive insights into the ways in which Critical Race Theory (CRT) can be used in the analysis of British state-funded Muslim schools. Existing bodies of work on Islamophobia will serve as a starting point for exploring the social conditions around Muslim communities in the British context. However, the book will set out the rationale for using CRT as a means of gaining a more nuanced analysis of the conditions around the emergence of British state-funded Muslim schools. Primarily, ethnographic research conducted inside Muslim schools will inform the original contribution of the book. This will allow for a critical analysis of the lived experiences of key stakeholders in both independent and state-funded Muslim schools in an unrivalled depth. Whilst debates around Muslim schools remain at the centre of public, political and academic debates around faith schooling, these exchanges have not yet been informed by ethnographic research in any substantive way. Thus the monograph will be the first of its kind to apply CRT in the study of Muslim schools, whilst drawing on in-depth ethnographic research to inform the analysis. The book will primarily draw on the author's PhD thesis, which comprised a comparative case study of Muslim primary schools. The doctoral research from which the book is derived took the form of a comparative ethnographic case study of an independent Muslim primary school and a voluntary-aided Muslim primary school. In addition, interviews were also carried out with a key informant to offer historical narratives of two further Muslim schools which had made the transition from independent to voluntary-aided status. The historical narratives of these two schools provide a context study and a point of reference for findings in the comparative ethnography. Whilst publications are currently available which draw on qualitative research with stakeholders in Muslim schooling, there is no existing published monograph which draws on ethnographic research carried out inside these institutions. It is worth noting that there are currently only 21 state-funded Muslim schools in England and Wales, with 12 being voluntary-aided, eight being free schools and one operating as an academy. With such small numbers, the comparative case study (including an ethnographic case study in a voluntary-aided Muslim school) offers an opportunity to gain insights into the lived experiences of stakeholders in unrivalled depth and detail. This approach to researching the lived experiences of key stakeholders in both maintained and independent Muslim schooling has not been demonstrated in a monograph elsewhere. Furthermore, the proportion of Muslim schools in the independent sector relative to the maintained sector also indicates a need for a critical enquiry into outcomes regarding the state funding. Whilst the are 21 state-maintained schools, the number of independent Muslim schools is far higher at approximately 158 (AMS 2014). These figures demonstrate that, whilst Muslim communities are clearly engaged in developing faith schools, the proportion which have actively pursued and/or been successful in securing state funding have been relatively few. As a means of offering an explanation for the trend in outcomes detailed above, the first-hand ethnographic research informs a critical analysis of institutional changes, specific to Muslim schools, which occur in the transition from operating in the independent to the state-funded sector. Furthermore, the narrative of one Muslim school making the transition from the independent to the state-maintained sector is documented in real time.

The ethnographic research also gives critical insights into the ways in which provision is manifested specific to independent and state-funded contexts. These insights have important implications for understanding the relationships between the state, the school as an institution, staff and the parent body. Highly qualitative accounts of how these relationships are manifested will inform critical debates around the position of British Muslims as stakeholders in the emergent partnerships between communities and the state, which are manifested in the development of state-maintained Muslim schools. The key focus of the monograph is to marry first-hand experiences of Muslim schooling with a critical consideration of debates around the enfranchisement of Muslim communities in terms of polity and the nation state. Within this context, education serves as a key site within which Muslim communities have made some objective economic gains. It is the synthesis of these wider debates around the position of Muslim communities in contemporary political context and highly qualitative insights from within Muslim schools which will constitute the distinctive and original contribution of the monograph. Further to the above, the conceptual contribution will also provide an analysis of emergent policy frameworks and associated pathways which shall inform the future of state-funded Muslim schools. Specifically this includes exploring the implications of the Academies Act 2010, and the regulations around free schools, as likely frameworks for the future of state-funded Muslim schooling in England and Wales.

CRT and British Muslims?

The insights offered from the ethnographic research that informs this monograph is situated within a CRT framework. A key objective that this monograph sets out to achieve is to make a contribution to developing CRT which allows a meaningful application of the theory to Muslim communities in Britain. This is achieved through drawing on established work on Islamophobia as a quasi-intersectional theoretical framework. CRT is increasingly emergent in British academic discourse. However, traditionally the roots of CRT lie in American legal discourse and have been centred on the position of African Americans in the wider American social context. Thus, CRT emerged out of concerns around the historical, political and socio-economic position of African Americans relative to wider white American society. Within this tradition, CRT has developed as a critical analysis of the historical relationships between white and black people and is therefore fundamentally concerned with issues of 'race' and power. Central to its purpose is the core objective of providing counter-narratives to challenge, undermine and expose the implicit and explicit forms of racism manifested in the everyday acceptance of power relations between black and white people as they function in contemporary context. As documented by Ladson-Billings (1998: 15), contemporary American society was founded on white European concepts of status which related power and influence directly to property. Not only were black people absent in decision making in the founding of the American nation state, but African slaves were actually part of the property used to identify the status of white settlers (Ladson-Billings 1998: 15). American

CRT theorists have traditionally been fundamentally concerned with the implications of this historic relationship between African Americans and white American society. Therefore, at its very roots, CRT was fundamentally concerned with the plight and purpose of a very specific 'racial' minority in a very specific historic, social, economic and political context.

As CRT has become more informed and developed as an academically (rather than legal) centred discourse over time, there have been insightful applications which go above and beyond solely focusing on the position of African Americans. Although less prominent, variations of CRT have indeed been applied in the analysis of inequalities across various 'racial' identities. This has happened most notably with the development of LatCrit theory as a mechanism for drawing on themes manifested in CRT but with a view to analysing the marginalisation of Latin Americans (see Delgado 1997; Solorzano and Delgado-Bernal 2001). The emergence and continuing development of LatCrit theory indicates that applications of CRT do not necessarily need to be confined to the analysis of African Americans. Furthermore, the ways in which CRT has been used to address issues of inequality which apply to political rather than ethnic ideas around 'race' will be considered in more detail in Chap. 2. The real question at the centre of the discussion is the extent to which CRT can be meaningfully applied in the analysis of Muslim communities in the UK context. Answering this question is not as simple as constructing the argument that CRT is applicable for the analysis of marginalisation across minority ethnic Muslim communities. If we are to come to a resolve about the applicability of CRT to Muslim communities, then we need to come to resolve that CRT can be applied meaningfully in the analysis of inequalities which go across religious as well as ethnic and/or 'racial' lines. The argument across Chaps. 2 and 3 will be centred around demonstrating the extent to which CRT can be meaningfully applied in the analysis of processes of marginalisation and the ways that this might be experienced within Muslim communities in the British context.

Further to the above, the monograph offers insights into the relationship between Muslim communities and denominational Islamic schools in the wider faith schools debate through a CRT lens. Whilst CRT has traditionally been focused on the plight of African Americans in the American context, in more recent years CRT has been adopted and adapted to explore the position of black Caribbean and black African groups in British educational contexts. Furthermore, CRT in the British context is starting to be applied to gain insights into a wider range of marginalised groups. More specifically, scholars such as Housee (2012) have already applied CRT to the analysis of British Muslim communities. These initial applications of CRT are focused around minority ethnic Muslim groups. Whilst these insights represent an important step forward for CRT in Britain, the coming chapter will aim to explore how existing bodies of work on Islamophobia may offer a mechanism for reconciling religious marginalisation with racialised processes of discrimination. In line with the foundations laid out in bodies of work on Islamophobia, this monograph will aim to explore the extent to which CRT can be used to conceptualise racialised anti-Muslim (rather than exclusively minority ethnic Muslim) discrimination. The analysis draws on the apparatus of CRT as a strategy for providing a counter-narrative around Muslim schools in the British public space, which exposes the ways in which tacit intentionality and interest convergence are inherently manifested in policy frameworks around state funding for denominational faith schools.

The state funding of Muslim schools has recently been a topical issue within the context of a media climate which has seen sustained public political anxiety around Islam in the public space, most notably manifested in the government's *Preventing violent extremism* agenda (these issues are explored in depth in Chap. 3). With regard to education specifically, the recent inquiry into the 'Trojan Horse letter' in Birmingham (UK), where an alleged 'Islamic takeover plot' (Mackie 2014) was reported to be in process in a series of schools, demonstrates a clear example of the ways in which increased Islamic influence in education has become equated with concern. Within this climate, state funding for Muslim schools remains a contentious issue. Although Muslim schools may find themselves at the centre of critics' concerns about state funding for faith schooling in England and Wales more generally, published empirical studies carried out within state-funded Muslim schools are limited to one or two cases (see Walford 2003; Thorley 2008). Academics have highlighted the need for further research into Muslim schools (see Berglund 2009; Tinker 2009). Specifically, there is a void in the highly qualitative ethnographic studies synonymous with traditions in the sociology of education. Therefore, although it may appear that Muslim schools are prominent in academic debates concerning faith schools, such debates are not consistently informed by research which garners insights into the lived experiences of Islamic schooling. At the theoretical level, subsequent chapters will explore the ways in which CRT can be used as a conceptual framework that can be suitably applied to the plight of Muslim communities in the British educational context. Situated within this theoretical framework, findings from the author's doctoral thesis will inform the original contribution to research. The first-hand research comprises a comparative ethnographic case study of an independent Muslim primary school and a voluntary-aided Muslim primary school, along with further qualitative insights from two Muslim schools which have successfully made the transition from the independent to the state-maintained sector.

References

AMS. (2014). Data from the Association of Muslim Schools UK. Website as of 6 October 2014. Available at: http://ams-uk.org/muslim-schools/

Berglund, J. (2009). *Teaching Islam: Islamic Religious Education at Three Muslim Schools in Sweden*. Uppsala: Universitetstryckerie.

Bignall, P. (2013, May 23). 'He Was Always Smiling': Lee Rigby Named as Woolwich Victim. *The Independent*. Available at:http://www.independent.co.uk/news/uk/crime/he-was-always-smiling-lee-rigby-named-as-woolwich-victim-8628583.html. Accessed 1 Dec 2016.

Borger, J., & MacAskill, E. (2016, December 20). Truck Attacks in Berlin and Nice Reflect Change in Islamic State Tactics. *The Guardian*.Available at:https://www.theguardian.com/world/2016/dec/20/truck-attacks-in-berlin-and-nice-reflect-change-in-isis-tactics. Accessed 21 Dec 2016.

Delgado, R. (1997). Rodrigo's Fifteenth Chronicle: Racial Mixture, Latino-Critical Scholarship, and the Black-White Binary. *Texas Law Review, 75*, 1181–1201.

Dodd, V., & Addley, E. (2015, June 8). Leytonstone Knife Attack: Man Convicted of Attempted Murder'. *The Guardian*. Available at:https://www.theguardian.com/uk-news/2016/jun/08/leytonstone-knife-attack-man-convicted-of-attempted. Accessed 10 Aug 2016.

Henley, J., & Chrisafis, A. (2015, November 14). Paris Terror Attacks: Hollande Says ISIS Atrocity Was "Act of War". *The Guardian*. Available at:https://www.theguardian.com/world/2015/nov/13/paris-attacks-shootings-explosions-hostages. Accessed 2 Dec 2016.

Henley, J., & Willsher, K. (2015, January 7). Charlie Hebdo Attacks: "It's Carnage, a Bloodbath. Everyone is Dead. *The Guardian*. Available at: https://www.theguardian.com/world/2015/jan/07/charlie-hebdo-shooting-paris-magazine-target-raid. Accessed 21 Aug 2015.

Housee, S. (2012). What's the Point? Anti-racism and Students' Voices Against Islamophobia. *Race Ethnicity and Education, 15*(1), 101–120.

Ladson-Billings, G. (1998). Just What is Critical Race Theory and What's it Doing in a *nice* Field Like Education? *International Journal of Qualitative Studies in Education, 11*(1), 7–24.

Mackie, P. (2014). Islamic Takeover Plot in Birmingham Schools Investigated. *BBC News.* Available at: http://www.bbc.co.uk/news/uk-englandbirmingham-26482599. Last accessed 7 Aug 2017.

Solorzano, D. G., & Delgado-Bernal, D. (2001). Examining Transformational Resistance Through a Critical Race and LatCrit Theory Framework: Chicana and Chicano Students in an Urban Context. *Urban Education, 36*(3), 308–342.

Thorley, S. (2008). Learning Together: Christian and Muslim School Exchanges. In M. Tory & S. Thorley (Eds.), *Together and Different: Christians Engaging with People of Other Faiths* (pp. 7–19). Norwich: Canterbury Press.

Tinker, C. (2009). Rights, Social Cohesion and Identity: Arguments for and Against State Funded Muslim Schools in Britain. *Race, Ethnicity and Education, 12*(4), 539–553.

Walford, G. (2003). Muslim Schools in Britain. In G. Walford (Ed.), *British Private Schools: Research on Policy and Practice* (pp. 158–176). London: Woburn Press.

CHAPTER 2

Exploring the Application of Critical Race Theory to Muslims in Britain

This monograph utilises a novel application of Critical Race Theory (CRT) to explore issues around Islamic schooling in Britain. Whilst there are relationships between 'race' and religion in the case of British Muslim communities, the enquiry here goes far beyond a potentially narrow focus on any one Muslim group of any particular 'racial' background. In the same token, it is not possible to simply conflate 'race' with religion. This chapter sets out to transcend the problems in both positions identified above by providing a rationale for a meaningful application of CRT to Muslim communities in Britain. Achieving this requires a complex exploration of the characteristics of CRT, its premises and what emerging work on Islamophobia reveals about the parallels between racism as it is understood in CRT and anti-Muslim discrimination.

CRITICAL RACE THEORY: 'ROOTS'

Whilst this chapter is focused on developing a meaningful rationale for applying CRT in the analysis of British Muslims, it is important to first acknowledge other relevant works which have explored the positioning of Muslims and have arguably been contextually significant for the development of CRT. For example, the work of Fanon, most notably his critique of French colonisation in Algeria, explores contradictions inherent within colonialism which include the ways in which apparently universal 'Western' ideals play out in highly racialised ways (see Fanon 1963). Fanon's critique of colonialism draws attention to the brutality of the 'civilising' mission

© The Author(s) 2018
D. Breen, *Muslim Schools, Communities and Critical Race Theory,*
DOI 10.1057/978-1-137-44397-7_2

9

and its dehumanising effects, in particular through the aggressive repression of the Algerian anti-colonialist movement in the 1950s (Go 2013: 217). Of course, Fanon's work is expansive, and it would be ambitious to attempt to summarise his substantive contribution here. However, there are specific aspects of his contribution which are of central relevance not only for CRT but also for the ways in which CRT can be applied to understand the contemporary marginalisation of Muslims in Western European contexts. For example, Fanon demonstrates the misalignment between ideals of 'shared humanity' manifested in colonial rhetoric and the outcome of its practice which inevitably results in divided spheres, a twofold citizenship of existence for the coloniser and colonised (Fanon 1963: 45). The Algerian example is particularly significant here, as it embodies a dichotomous dynamic where the public space becomes fractured across the lines of the coloniser and colonised. Most significantly, this separation represents something of an ideal type with the principles of *laïcité* and secularism manifested in the 'universal' principles of the coloniser. The extent of the Western European interests manifested in these 'universal' principles becomes exposed when considering that at the opposite end of the dynamic (both in terms of the juxtaposition of religious and secular principles, but also in terms of power relations), the colonised happen to be a Muslim-majority society. This fracturing of the social space is significant not only due to its implications for oppression, assimilation and marginalisation of the colonised but also because of the irreconcilable nature of the dichotomy of secular and religious principles and how these are distributed across the power dynamic between the coloniser and the colonised. Whilst Fanon's contribution is far more substantive than we are able to account for here, including extensive discussions around decolonisation, this insight alone is clearly relevant for understanding contemporary relations between Muslims and Western European states (this point will be developed more substantively in Chap. 3), even in the absence of tangible colonial relations. Furthermore, we are also presented with a historic example which demonstrates how the Islamic becomes identified as in opposition to, or at least other than, that which is European.

It is perhaps possible to understand more of how this positioning of Islam in contemporary European settings has unfolded when considering Said's (1978) critique of 'Orientalism'. As with Fanon, the totality of Said's contribution is too extensive to meaningfully summarise here. However, the notion of Orientalism and its critique offers interesting insights into perceptions of Islam and Arab nations. For Said, Orientalism only exists as a primarily Western European discursive construction which serves the dual purpose of (a) categorically identifying that which is 'the Orient' in broadly geographic terms; and (b) limitations on thought and action around 'the Orient' (Said 1978: 3). Said's discussion of Islam within this dynamic allows us to take Fanon's insights around colonialism and develop them further, in the process drawing attention to the ways in which Eurocentric views of Islam are embedded with power relations. For example, Said argues that even relatively inert examples of European literary texts (Shakespeare is Said's chosen example) routinely gain part of their identity from interaction with the reader and are therefore reconstituted every time they are read (Said 1985: 92). However, in Said's analysis this privilege was rarely extended to 'the Orient, the Arabs or Islam which separately or together were supposed by mainstream academic thought to be confined to the fixed status of an object frozen once and for all time in the gaze of Western percipients' (Said 1985: 92). Orientalism thus embodied a set of power relations which imposed and then reinforced notions of 'Islam' and 'Muslim' to the extent that neither existed, except as communities of interpretation which gave them existence (Said 1985: 93). For Said, these imposed interpretations mean that the labels of 'Arab' or 'Muslim' are so saturated with meanings and so overdetermined by history, religion and politics that 'no-one today can use them without attention to the formidable polemic mediations that screen the objects, if they exist at all, that the labels designate' (Said 1985: 93). The invariably disempowering imposition of notions of Islam described by Said in his critique of Orientalism parallels some of the ways in which Islam and Muslims are positioned within contemporary master-narratives in British and European public discourse. For our purposes, a multidimensional model of master-narratives around British Muslims is identified at the end of Chap. 3.

The above discussion invariably demonstrates the ways in which Islam has been constructed as other to that which is European or 'Western'. Furthermore, through Said's work on Orientalism, we also gain insights into how 'Western' perceptions of Islam are formulated and the power relations manifested in the ways in which these are negotiated. A recurring theme in the above examples has been the tendency for Muslim groups to be identified by reference to the 'Western' gaze within which that which is Muslim is constructed only within the constraints of Eurocentric ideological suppositions. Contemporary anxieties around Islam in the European public space indicate that the aftermath of colonialism retains residual and arguably racialised (this *will* be argued more substantively later on) processes of marginalisation which continue to disenfranchise Muslim groups. As the discussion progresses, we will explore parallels between both explicit and less tangible ways in which anti-Muslim discrimination has come to be manifested in Britain specifically. It is through these parallels that we can begin to explore the ways in which CRT can be meaningfully applied to understand anti-Muslim discrimination.

As noted above, the analysis in this work seeks to apply what has been principally a theory of 'race' (which has its substantive roots in exploring racism as it is experienced by African Americans) to garner insights into marginalisation across religious lines. The complex rationale for this application is set out throughout the remainder of the chapter. However, before we explore the complexities of this application of CRT, it is important to recognise some of the ways in which the political mobilisation of black consciousness has been manifested and organised across specifically religious lines. The Nation of Islam (NOI) represents a highly relevant example of the ways in which the political mobilisation of black consciousness has been informed by clear intersections with a very specific interpretation of Islam. Furthermore, the NOI has played a central role in the development of understandings around 'white supremacy', a concept central to the political mobilisation manifested through the movement and also to CRT. Of course, the foundations for black political mobilisation had previously been well established through the work of W. E. B. Du Bois and Marcus Garvey. For example, in his public address *The conservation of races* (1897), Du Bois posited that the default strategy for those of African descent attempting to achieve 'salvation' in the USA had been to aspire to losing one's 'race identity' (Du Bois 1897: 10). Du Bois contests this, arguing that salvation lies in the collective mobilisation of that which is culturally 'black'. Du Bois advocated the mobilisation of 'Negro' colleges, business organisations, newspapers, schools of art and literature, the institutionalisation of intellect—all across 'race' lines (Du Bois 1897: 13), with each of the above representing a mobilisation of black interests. These mobilisations would be not only necessary for positive advancement but are also imperative for negative defence (Du Bois 1897: 13). Garvey also advocated for such mobilisation, although he was more radical than Du Bois in his separatist rhetoric (Terrill 2001: 28). Garvey's convictions around the mobilisation of black interests was manifested in the establishment of the *Universal Negro Improvement Association*, founded in 1914 by Garvey (Garvey 1927: 47), which grew to encompass several million followers with 700 branches in 38 states, the Caribbean and Africa by 1925 (Gavins 2016: 50). The mobilisation manifested in the Nation of Islam invariably grew from the influence of Du Bois and Garvey; however, there are interesting dynamics around religion that are relevant here. Whilst Garvey's narratives were heavily influenced by Christian rhetoric, Du Bois considers a much more complex relationship between religion and 'black folk' (see Du Bois 1903). As part of his seminal conceptualisation of 'double consciousness' (Du Bois 1903), Du Bois outlines the manifestation of mobilisation among black Americans through sectarian Churches in the USA. On the one hand, Du Bois explores the ways in which the embedding of Christianity, and its institutionalisation through the establishment of Churches by and for black American communities, represent examples of autonomous black mobilisation (Du Bois 1903: 131). The inherent concern for Du Bois is the origin of first access to the particular faith (through white American slave owners), and the implications of Christian premises for the obedient compliance of black Americans to an overtly white supremacist organisation of power relations (Du Bois 1903: 134). For Du Bois, the Christian qualities of obedience, deferred gratification and salvation in the next world serve dual functions of virtuousness on the one hand, whilst facilitating racialised oppression through advocating unquestioning obedience on the other (Du Bois 1903: 134). Arguably, the mobilisation against white supremacy manifested in the Nation of Islam (NOI) clearly demonstrates a step towards addressing Du Bois' concern about the function of Christianity in the oppression of black Americans. The NOI also represents a historically significant example of how a particular manifestation of Islam has been integral for the purposes of racialised political resistance. In the tradition of Garvey, during his time with the NOI Malcolm X arguably represents their most recognisable voice, articulating an anti-white-supremacist narrative that has been undeniably relevant for CRT and its interrogation of power relations across 'race' from the late twentieth century to date.

CRT has its roots in American Critical Legal Studies and has been most commonly applied to analyse racism as experienced by African Americans. As noted by Warmington (2012), CRT is an emergent phenomenon in the British context, which has its roots in the work of American scholars such as Ladson-Billings (1998), Bell (1990), Delgado (1995), and Delgado and Stefancic (2000). The Foundations of CRT are rooted in the conviction that experiences of racism have become normalised in wider American society (Delgado 1995: xiv). Furthermore, the normalisation of racism serves the interests of white supremacy through maintaining the structural, political and socio-economic position of African Americans in American society. Central to this process is the notion of a wider social desensitisation to racism and the effects and outcomes of discrimination across 'racial' grounds. It is this concern over desensitisation which is laid as the foundation stone for CRT as an analytical framework. Delgado and Stefancic articulate their concerns clearly through arguing that racism has become 'normal and not aberrant in American society' (Delgado and Stefancic 2000: xvi). Arguably the most powerful feature of this process is the notion that racism is ingrained and a 'normal' aspect of American society as it has come to be (Delgado and Stefancic 2000: xvi). Although policies which are centred around promoting equal opportunities do exist, they are simply focused on addressing explicit forms of racism. However, a fundamental tenet of CRT is the conviction that there are many more 'business as usual' (Delgado and Stefancic 2000: xvi) types of racism which occur in unseen ways and yet permeate individuals' lives. It is the anxiety that resides around the failure to address such forms of racism which informs the rationale behind CRT. Put simply, if such instances of racism are left unchecked then the problem never becomes manifested within a wider public consciousness.

CRT is centred around the conviction that these more intangible forms of racism are the principal mechanism whereby white supremacy is maintained. The problem is not simply that these forms of racism are normalised. Rather, they serve as the root of all power to maintain race inequality. Policy developments which are focused on addressing explicit discrimination serve as a smokescreen to hide the more pervasive, tacit forms of racist intentionality. Activities at the surface level of policy development may therefore indicate that much work is being done to challenge issues around racism. This encourages wider public faith in the status quo, with publics safe in the knowledge that mechanisms are in place to address racism outright. In the rhetoric of public and political narratives, racism is unacceptable and is being addressed. However, the complexities of tacit racist intentionality, and the ineffectuality of policies to combat these less obvious forms of racism, ensure that the existing dynamics of power relations are maintained.

The notion of a 'smokescreen' such as that outlined above has been a long-established concept within CRT. This is illustrated through the work of Crenshaw et al. (1995), who argue that racial justice is 'embraced in the American mainstream in terms that excluded radical and fundamental challenges to status quo institutional practices' (Crenshaw et al. 1995: xiv). Thus, within a CRT framework, racism exists beyond the narrow interpretation of overt racist incidents but rather is focused on a 'more powerful form of white supremacy which is normalised and taken for granted' (Gillborn 2005: 486). It is for this reason that a number of Critical Race Theorists have argued that failure to question and acknowledge the presence and powerful influence of more implicit forms of racism equates to acting in the interests of maintaining the marginalised position of racialised minorities (Preston and Chadderton 2012). It is the invisibility of increasingly indirect and pervasive forms racism which serves as the root of the power relations which maintain the marginalised positions of racialised minorities.

Tacit Intentionality

In line with the above, CRT has been applied within the field of education as a strategy for revealing tacit intentionality which may be manifested in policies aimed at challenging racial inequality. One of the central tenets of CRT is the notion that *tacit intentionality* serves as a key mechanism in reinforcing white supremacy in the social context. The maintenance of power relations across 'race' in contemporary contexts does not occur simply as a result of racism becoming more unseen or normalised. The reinforcement of existing power relations across 'race' occurs as a by-product of the outcomes of policies designed and implemented by white power holders (Gillborn 2005). This continuation of racial domination and inequity represents a form of *tacit intentionality* on the part of policy makers (Gillborn 2005). In practice, this is manifested through the sustaining of policies which have a proven record of producing detrimental outcomes for racial minorities. For example, high-stakes testing, school performance tables and selection by 'ability' have remained within the British educational system for sustained periods of time in spite of the fact that research indicates that these policies have detrimental outcomes for black students (Gillborn 2005). Alleviating these conditions within educational contexts requires that teachers develop an awareness and acknowledgement of the ways in which they may participate and promote, albeit tacitly, white privilege (Ryan and Dixson 2006: 4). However, this tacit intentionality embedded in the educational system goes deeper than the individual-level practice of educational professionals. The very policy frameworks within which those professionals operate are founded upon a tacit intentionality which privileges the position of whites over racialised minorities. Thus, a total solution to 'race' inequity in education cannot be achieved by deflecting responsibility down to the individual level as pre-scribed within existing neoliberal educational frameworks. The problem here is that policy makers have decided, either actively or tacitly, to place 'race' equity at the margins, and therefore 'race' inequality at the centre of education policy (Gillborn 2005). Thus, tacit intentionality is manifested through attitudes towards policy making that either fail to prioritise or appropriately cater to the interests of racialised minorities. Clearly, this is a process which is not necessarily actively or overtly implemented but rather has its roots in long-established cultural, economic and historical struc-tures of racial domination which inevitably result in the promotion and implementation of policies and practices that are known to be racially divi-sive (Gillborn 2007: 499). These attitudes are inevitably informed by a normative reading of the politics of democracy within which political interests are fairly represented, and the history of colonial relations is a thing of the past.

CRT, Education and Interest Convergence

Derrick Bell (1980) offers a well-documented critical analysis of initiatives aimed at promoting desegregation which were implemented in the American educational context. Bell argues that the wider rationale given for desegregation strategies was centred around a concern over schools which had an intake of 80% or more of black or white pupils, even though these communities were living side-by-side. Part of the desegregation strategy involved strategically locating magnet schools that were designed to attract parents and families from both white and black communities. The intention was that these schools would also have a particular academic specialism aimed at improving educational attainment for all attendees. Part of the problem with these desegregation strategies was that white families stood to gain an additional advantage in education over their African American counterparts. Therefore, although on the surface African Americans are given an opportunity for educational advantage, this was only relative to the same advantages being extended to the group against which they are identified as being underachieving. Thus, as Bell argues, it is clear that desegregation has only been promoted in ways which advan-tage whites (Bell 1980: 94). This example demonstrates the concept of 'interest convergence' (Bell 1980: 94) whereby the marginalisation of minority groups is addressed only where gains are also facilitated for white groups. The impacts of interest convergence are demonstrated further through Lomotey and Staley's (1990) analysis of Buffalo County, heralded as the benchmark of success in desegregation strategies. Lomotey and Staley's research revealed that under these benchmark desegregation strategies, African American families continued to be poorly served by educational provision. Specifically, attainment rates failed to rise, and suspension, expulsion and dropout rates actually continued to steadily increase among African American pupils (Lomotey and Staley 1990).

Furthermore, evidence to support this illusion of progress extends beyond the active implementation of strategies which fail to fulfil the objective of benefitting African Americans. As argued by Ladson-Billings, it is the benefits as experienced by white families and their apparent support for these strategies which informs the public narrative that desegregation in Buffalo County represented a benchmark for success (Ladson-Billings 1998). This 'interest convergence' serves as the rationale behind strategies which are apparently focused on benefitting racialised minorities, whilst policies which exclusively prioritise the interests of minority racialised groups remain few and far between (see Bell 1990; Ladson-Billings 1998; Gillborn 2005). From this position, such policies and strategies are therefore illusory and merely serve to enfranchise white groups whilst sustaining the relative marginalisation and disadvantage experienced by racialised minorities.

WHITENESS?

The discussion above necessarily leads us to consider what we mean by the terms whiteness and also leads us to consider what is meant by 'white supremacy' within CRT. Critical White Studies is a facet of CRT which aims to unpack ideas around what is meant by the term 'whiteness'. As CRT is concerned with identifying tacit processes of racism which might otherwise remain absent in the wider public consciousness, it is important to consider what is meant by whiteness with an appropriately critical eye. The distinction between whiteness and white individuals has most famously been articulated in the frequently cited works by Bonnett (1997) and Leonardo (2002). Leonardo outlines that 'whilst whiteness represents a racial discourse, the category of white people represents a socially constructed identity usually based on skin colour' (Leonardo 2002: 31). Bonnett (1997) highlights both the distinction and relationship between white people and whiteness further. For Bonnett, it is not necessarily the case that white people as individuals inevitably reinforce whiteness any more than heterosexuals are necessarily homophobic or men are necessarily sexist (Bonnett 1997: 189). However, the likelihood is that most homophobic individuals are heterosexual, and most sexist discrimination occurs against women (Gillborn 2005). This point identifies that white people are not necessarily *always* acting in the interests of reinforcing whiteness. Furthermore, it also indicates that individuals do not have to be 'white people' to actively reinforce and act in the interests of whiteness (Ladson-Billings 1998).

Consistent with the distinction between white people and whiteness, Preston and Chadderton argue that white positionality is informed by intersectionalities across social class, gender, sexuality and ability/disability (Preston and Chadderton 2012: 92). Thus, temporary ambiguities may occur where white people are positioned on the margins of whiteness (Preston and Chadderton 2012: 92). If this is the case, then the critical focus on whiteness in CRT is not an assault on white people per se; it is an assault on the socially constructed and constantly reinforced power of white identifications and interests (Gillborn 2005: 488). Furthermore, Preston and Chadderton condense extensive inquiry into the distinction between whiteness and white people through arguing that the many and various ways in which the white working classes, white immigrants and white women have been positioned on the fringes of white respectability are key examples where these groups are given a liminal position within whiteness (Preston and Chadderton 2012: 92). The distinction between white people and whiteness serves as a crucial part of the rationale for applying CRT to Muslim communities in contemporary Britain. British Muslims may be a religious rather than racial group, yet expansive work on Islamophobia (to be discussed in more detail later on in this chapter) clearly demonstrates the ways in which Muslims have systematically and discursively been posited in opposition to white British society. Therefore, although there are white Muslims, a CRT lens indicates that such individuals are likely to be positioned on the fringes of whiteness, if not racialised as the Muslim 'other'. Thus, simply bearing white skin does not free these individuals from the discursive effects of whiteness, which result in the explicit and implicit forms of racism as experienced by Muslim communities. Rather, drawing on Preston and Chadderton, it is conceivable that for white Muslims, Islamic identification may offset the protection from racist marginalisation that white privilege ordinarily affords 'white' people.

Counter-Narratives

One of the key purposes of CRT is to offer critical narratives which expose the tacit nature of racism and marginalisation. This is achieved through an emphasis on constructing 'counter-narratives', which are central to CRT. Counter-narratives do not merely describe a methodological preference amongst academics with an interest in CRT; there is also an epistemological purpose to counter-narratives which is inherently tied into the convictions that underlie CRT. It is important to draw a distinction between counter-narratives and counter-storytelling in CRT contexts. Drawing on the work of Stanley (2007), counter-narratives within CRT are understood to embody 'perspectives that run opposite or counter to the presumed order of control' (Stanley 2007: 14). These 'counter-narratives' challenge and deconstruct 'master-narratives' and offer alternatives to dominant discourses (Stanley 2007: 14). Indeed, the key purpose of this monograph is to explore how far policies concerned with facilitating state-funded Muslim schools have actually offered feasible strategies for British Muslims to negotiate substantive outcomes. Under the former New Labour political rhetoric, and more recently the Coalition/Conservative advocation of 'Free Schools', the 'master-narrative' seemingly indicates that accessible strategies are openly available to Muslim communities looking to develop state-funded religious schools. The comparative numbers of independent Muslim schools and state-funded Muslim schools, 158 and 21 respectively (AMS 2014), indicate that processes are at work which result in Muslim schools primarily residing in the independent sector. Applying CRT in the analysis of state-funded Muslim schools therefore allows for the construction of a counter-narrative which, contrary to policy narratives, exposes processes of tacit intentionality which serve to sustain the exclusion of Muslim communities from enfranchisement through state faith schooling (Breen 2016).

Counter-narratives should be distinguished from the process of 'counter-storytelling' whereby participants offer insights into tacit experiences of exclusion or racist experiences. The process of counter-storytelling is best understood as a methodological tool for gaining access to and documenting experiences of racism as experienced by participants. Epistemologically speaking, the purpose of counter-storytelling is to give voice to those who experience these tacit processes of racism and marginalisation. From a methodological viewpoint, the epistemological rationale behind counter storytelling gives the process a particular methodological validity. If it is impossible to account for more intangible processes of racism unless they are experienced first-hand, then individual accounts of these experiences hold an unrivalled weight in terms of the overall purpose of CRT. One important point to maintain here is that the purpose of counter-storytelling is rooted in informing more widely constructed counter-narratives directed at challenging public or master-narratives within which tacit processes of racism are largely absent. The rationale for counter-storytelling is inherently tied to both the focus on tacit racism and critical inquiry around whiteness in CRT. As argued by Gillborn, a powerful and dangerous dynamic of whiteness is that many (possibly the majority) of white people have no awareness of whiteness as a construction, let alone their own role in sustaining and playing out inequities at the heart of whiteness (Gillborn 2005: 490). It is this lack of awareness which serves to cloud the tacit processes of marginalisation which are manifested in phenomena such as interest convergence. Given the complexity of the relationship between white people and whiteness, passivity, in and of itself, can be seen to be a political act (Preston and Chadderton 2012: 92). Preston and Chadderton posit this argument from the position of viewing whiteness as property and argue that protecting whiteness requires the daily tacit choices by whites in accepting white privilege (Preston and Chadderton 2012: 92). The purpose of counter-storytelling as a research tool, and counter-narratives constructed from utilising a CRT analytical framework, is to expose and challenge this passivity. Both of these processes serve to reveal the tacit processes of racism and marginalisation which lie hidden from those who do not experience them first-hand.

Within CRT, counter-narratives have also traditionally been more widely informed through an analysis of policy and practice. The purpose of this chapter is to establish a critical rationale for applying CRT to analyse the position of Muslim communities within the UK context. The complexity of the distinction between whiteness and white people serves as the first foundation stone for exploring the capacity to apply CRT to this context. British Muslims are not a homogeneous group, and so the rationale for applying CRT cannot exclusively be informed by the assumption that the term 'Muslim' can be applied as a proxy for 'minority ethnic'. Rather, instances of anti-Muslim discrimination are likely to impact across the spectrum of ethnic identities comprising British Muslim communities in nuanced ways. The ways in which this might play out at the conceptual level are explored through a critical consideration of work on Islamophobia in the coming section. Thus, it is posited here that the ways in which *tacit* processes of marginalisation may be manifested in the British Muslim experience, and the insights that might be gained through pursuing counter-narratives and counter-storytelling in this regard, serve as a further part of the rationale for adopting CRT as a suitable analytical framework for studying Muslim communities.

ISLAMOPHOBIA: PREMISES AND POSSIBLE LIMITATIONS

Whilst media attention around Islam has increased in the media following 9/11 and the London bombings of 2005, contemporary discussions around Islamophobia precede these global events by several years. Arguably one of the most influential documents of its kind (Allen 2010a: 52), the Runnymede Trust published *Islamophobia—a challenge for us all* in 1997. Concurrently, an emerging body of coherent academic work has developed in recent years exploring not only instances of anti-Muslim discrimination, marginalisation or violence but also the conceptual premises underlying Islamophobia as a social phenomenon. Islamophobia has come to be of particular contemporary relevance in recent years following sustained media attention on Islam and Muslim communities following the attacks of 11 September 2001 (9/11) and the London bombings on the 7 July 2005. The term 'Islamophobia' might initially imply either a tangible public fear or identifiable acts of hostility towards Islam or Muslims. However, the term is contested, and scholarly work on Islamophobia has served as a forum for exploring a nuanced debate around what the term actually refers to, how anti-Muslim discrimination might be experienced by Muslims and also what parallels can be drawn with racisms both 'new' and 'old'.

Initially, we do need to consider what 'Islamophobia' might refer to, and how we might initially identify the phenomena as it is articulated and manifested in the public sphere. As part of a far more critical exploration of Islamophobia at the conceptual level, Allen (2010a) argues that a distinct 'Muslim' or 'Islamic' identifier or identification process would appear to be an essential feature (Allen 2010a: 62). Allen's identification of this 'initial identification process' is part of a wider critique of notions of Islamophobia that had been used in the public space, most notably within the seminal Runnymede report *Islamophobia—a challenge for us all* (1997). The report identified Islamophobia as being manifested in three 'closed views' of Islam. The first of these closed views is the perception of Islam is being seen as a 'single monolithic bloc, static and unresponsive to new realities' (Runnymede 1997: 5). The overtones here are twofold. Firstly, Islam is presented as homogeneous rather than diverse. Secondly, it is suggested that Muslim communities are unresponsive to change. If Muslim communities are perceived of as being unresponsive to change, then the implication here is that the scope for resolving any perceived conflicts is minimal. This first interpretation is closely related to a second 'closed' perspective which identifies Islam as separate and 'other', with aims and values being posited in opposition to and resistant of the influence of other cultures (Runnymede 1997: 5). Allen critiques the use of these closed views arguing that they suggest a homogenised notion of Islamophobia which does not effectively allow for the inclusion of the many nuanced and varied ways in which anti-Muslim and anti-Islamic phenomena might occur (Allen 2010a: 55). The implication here is significant, as any anti-Muslim sentiment that falls within the grey area between these binary positions has a licence to gain momentum and form the basis of more indirect forms of Islamophobia (Allen 2010a: 53). This point is of particular relevance here given the implicit parallels that can be drawn with CRT, most notably the conviction that racism has evolved into an evasive phenomenon which exists in many forms, not just in explicit tangible acts of discrimination. The 'shades of grey' forms of Islamophobia might conceptually mirror the more subtle and pervasive forms of racism that CRT has come to focus on as a central tenet of its theoretical apparatus. Crucially, Allen's argument is that the binary conceptualisation of Islamophobia in the Runnymede report could actually function to *facilitate* the more subtle forms of anti-Muslim discrimination with which the concept should be concerned. Thus, whilst identifying 'closed' views of Islam might allow us to identify explicit Islamophobia in the media, they are of little use in identifying how anti-Muslim discrimination might be manifested or experienced in equally important contexts such as in employment, education or service provision (Allen 2010a: 53). Thus, if we are confined to identifying Islamophobia by the reference points in the Runnymede report, much anti-Islamic or anti-Muslim phenomena are likely to fall under the radar.

There are clearly parallels here with the ways in which racism is discussed in CRT. A key tenet of CRT is the notion of racism as becoming less explicit, more nuanced and subtle and thus largely evading identification in the white experience of master-narratives. An interesting explanation around the ways in which this impacts specifically for Muslim communities is offered by Sian (2015). She argues that the racialisation of Muslims occurs in the context of the dismissal of racism and its critique in general society (Sian 2015: 196–197). This conviction is consistent with wider CRT narratives which identify the power of racism in contemporary contexts as coming from the ways in which it evades identification as a result of the wider societal adherence to post-racial logics. Furthermore, we can also identify the Runnymede report as a political piece of apparatus that actually facilitates anti-Muslim and anti-Islamic 'phenomena' whilst purporting to do the exact opposite. Of central relevance here is the work of S. Sayyid, who raises the question of whether Islamophobia is closer to 'anti-Semitism' or 'racism' (Sayyid 2010). He offers a comprehensive discussion which draws a series of comparisons between these phenomena. Constraints do not allow for the replication of this discussion here; however, key comparisons include differential public perceptions between Islamophobia and anti-Semitism. For example, Sayyid argues that anti-Semitism is accepted as an unprovoked phenomenon whereas 'some Muslims are accused of contributing to Islamophobia'. Muslims are differentiated into groups identified as 'good' and 'bad' (Sayyid 2010: 11). This also spills over into differential expectations for Muslims to provide public statements of regret around violent conflicts that may happen across religious lines (Sayyid 2010: 11).

Similarly, Sayyid argues that Islamophobia does not necessarily fit with, what he identifies as, a Eurocentric conception of racism that requires the presence of racists (Sayyid 2010: 12). It is this critical turn that serves as a key step here towards integrating Islamophobia with CRT. Whilst not exclusively the case, racism within a CRT framework certainly includes the acknowledgement of racist outcomes without the necessary presence of active racists. As noted above, a key part of the CRT argument is that racism has become so nuanced that it evades detection in mainstream society. This argument relies on the premise that racist outcomes are not necessarily exclusively the result of the behaviours of active 'racists'. Thus, whilst Islamophobia might not fit with the 'Eurocentric concept of racism' as it is identified by Sayyid, the more nuanced model of racism at the centre of much CRT enquiry might share some fundamental consistencies with Islamophobia. Sayyid argues that racialised bodies have never been exclusively biological, rather they emerged alongside the identification of religion, culture, history and territories which were used to group fabricated distinctions between 'Europeanness' and 'non-Europeanness' (Sayyid 2010: 13). For Sayyid, Islamophobia can arguably be defined as the disciplining of Muslims by reference to an antagonistic 'Western' horizon

(Sayyid 2010: 15). For our purposes here, we can identify that, whilst Islamophobia is nuanced and complex, at its core it implicates the presence of wider anti-Islamic phenomena, which positions Muslims as 'non-European' in European public political settings.

From Islamophobia to CRT

Exploring some of the complexities that have arisen in attempts to conceptualise Islamophobia raises the necessary question as to what a more useful conceptualisation would look like. For example, Allen (2010a) suggests several factors to inform or assist in giving meaning to the phenomenon 'Islamophobia'. Of central relevance for the arguments presented here is the suggestion that Islamophobia is neither consistent nor uniform and in fact the notion of 'Islamophobias' might be a more useful notion rather than a single all-encompassing entity (Allen 2010a: 62). Related to this, Allen argues that Islamophobia apparently overlaps with a series of other related phenomena including 'racism by colour' (Allen 2010a: 62), and would appear to be shaped and determined by national, cultural, geographical and socio-economic conditions (Allen 2010a: 62). Whilst the above acknowledges the many and varied ways in which Islamophobia might occur in nuanced ways, Allen also identifies the presence of a 'Muslim' or 'Islamic' identifier or identification process (explicitly or implicitly, direct or indirect, either expressly acknowledged or not) as appearing to be essential in understanding Islamophobia (Allen 2010a: 63). Allen's suggestions allow for an interpretation of Islamophobia which takes account of differential experience of the phenomena as a result of intersections across religion, 'race' and national identity.

Emergent critical work on Islamophobia is of key importance when considering the ways in which Islam has been positioned in the British public sphere within both mainstream media narratives and the rhetoric of mobilisations such as the British National Party (BNP), the English Defence League (EDL) and Britain First. In a similar vein to Allen, Sayyid (2014) outlines a concept of Islamophobia which takes account of the ways in which Islamophobia can be performed within various contexts. Sayyid's definition is comprised of five strands and includes (1) attacks on Muslim persons or persons assumed to be Muslim; (2) attacks on property considered to be linked to Muslims; (3) organised acts of intimidation (e.g. marches in areas with large Muslim populations); (4) Islamophobia in institutional settings where Muslim individuals receive less favourable treatment than their peers in comparable positions in the same organisation; and (5) sustained and systematic elaboration of comments in the public domain that disparage Muslims and/or Islam (Sayyid 2014: 16). It is interpreted here that the five strands function within a nexus within which these forms or 'types' exert synergetic effects on each other. For example, Islamophobia as organised or mobilised 'acts of intimidation' (Sayyid 2014: 16) in the British context has invariably been fuelled by 'a sustained and systematic elaboration of comments in the public domain that disparage Muslims and/or Islam' (Sayyid 2014: 16). There has certainly been increased media attention on Muslims following the terrorist attacks of 11 September 2001 in New York, the London bombings of 2005 and most recently the murder of British soldier Lee Rigby in Woolwich on 22 May 2013 (BBC 2013a, b). In addition to widespread media attention, there has also been a sustained political focus on Muslims in both American and British contexts. Allen (2010b) identifies that, in the American context, the political response has been primarily centred around international relations. Conversely, the political response within the British context has had a much more 'home grown' focus following the centrality of British-born Muslims in the London bombings (Allen 2010b: 222). The consequence of this is that 'everything Muslim becomes established and embellished, and indeed accepted, as oppositional and threatening to "our" culture, "our" values, "our" institutions and "our" way of life' (Allen 2010b: 222). This has arguably been most clearly demonstrated through the political narratives of the BNP and EDL. Both organisations have openly attempted to construct a dichotomy with notions of 'Britishness' or 'Englishness' being positioned in opposition to notions of the Islamic 'other'.

The more critical notions of Islamophobia explored above have the capacity to serve as an important part of the foundation for applying CRT in understanding the marginalisation of Muslim communities in Britain. As demonstrated above, CRT has traditionally been focused on understanding how 'race' inequality is sustained within particular social-economic, political and national contexts. The more nuanced work on Islamophobia allows us to identify the ways in which British Muslims might experience anti-Muslim discrimination differentially whilst maintaining a sense of coherence in that the root of all Islamophobia has to have an initial 'Islamic' or 'Muslim' identification process. Within this understanding, it is possible to explore the ways in which 'sustained and systematic elaboration of comments in the public domain that disparage Muslims and/or Islam' (Sayyid

2014: 16) might serve to inform the development of master-narratives as understood within CRT. Simultaneously, the emphasis on intersections across different dynamics of identity allows us to explore the ways in which socio-economic position, gender and 'race' might figure in experiences of discrimination which is identifiable as 'anti-Muslim' in the first instance. There is a strong case for advocating the process of counter-storytelling as arguably the most sound methodological tool for accessing the detail of these experiences across Britain's diverse Muslim communities. Given the discussion above, of central interest here are questions around the implications of national identity and 'race' for experiences of anti-Muslim discrimination. For example, how is anti-Muslim discrimination experienced by white Muslim reverts and to what extent do they exist 'on the fringes of whiteness' (Preston and Chadderton 2012)? How does socio-economic position figure in the extent to which these individuals have continued access to white privilege? It is important to acknowledge here that CRT has been applied at both micro and macro levels, and the extent to which the dynamics of these intersections can be qualitatively explored is likely to become more limited where analyses are more macro. For example, when looking at faith schooling at the policy level, it makes more sense to ask a question such as 'what opportunities are there for British Muslims to establish Islamic schools?' Critically reviewing existing policy frameworks and highlighting limitations in those frameworks is likely to result in an analysis that leans more closely towards understanding implications relevant for *any* British Muslim community. Thus, more macro CRT research on Muslims might primarily focus on the 'Muslim' or 'Islamic' initial identification process (e.g. in the analysis of policy or media narratives). However, that is *not* to say that CRT is limited to understanding anti-Muslim discrimination in this way. At the micro level, counter-storytelling (an integral tenet of CRT) can be employed as a means of exploring the intersection of dynamics around national identity, 'race' and socio-economic position. The final section here will explore some of the more macro arguments around Muslims, racialisation and racism as a means of exploring some of their discursive implications for Muslim communities.

Anti-Muslim Racism?

Hussain and Bagguley (2012) have argued that within the UK context, the BNP have focused their attention on Muslims as the 'new enemy' (Hussain and Bagguley 2012) and that the party's propaganda distinguished between non-Muslims as 'good' South Asians and Muslims as 'bad' South Asians (Modood 2005). Even acknowledging that the BNP represents extreme right-wing political voices, the positioning of Muslims as a 'new enemy' raises questions about the extent to which this identification can be equated with racism or racist experience. Meer and Modood (2009) argue that part of the problem with exploring the extent to which Muslims experience racism is bound up with the tendency for the legitimacy of any notion of anti-Muslim racism to be dismissed in the public sphere (Meer and Modood 2009). A comprehensive discussion is provided which offers a series of reasons as to why anti-Muslim discrimination is not viewed with the same legitimacy as anti-Semitism. Part of the explanation for this is directly related to discussions around counter-terror strategies (this will be explored in more detail in Chap. 3). According to Parekh, this has culminated in the 'Muslim question': the conviction in many influential circles within the European Union that Muslims pose a serious cultural and political threat (Parekh 2008: 5). For Meer and Modood, it is anxiety over the 'Muslim question' which informs the hesitancy to name any anti-Muslim sentiment as racism (Meer and Modood 2009: 339). This process is consistent with a wider sidelining of Muslim interests which can be explained as a direct effect of a dominant public perception which sees Muslims as a threat rather than a disadvantaged minority subject to increasingly pernicious discourses of racialisation (Meer and Modood 2009: 354).

However, the reasons for why anti-Muslim sentiment is not accepted as racism are not confined to the complexities of managing the 'Muslim question'. Notions of 'race' are also important factors in explaining why anti-Muslim sentiment is not readily identified as racism. Whereas racial identities are typically thought of as involuntary categories of birth, being a Muslim is about chosen beliefs, and Muslims, therefore, need or ought to have less legal protection than these other kinds of identities (Meer and Modood 2009: 345). This conviction is articulated by Miles and Brown (2003), who draw a clear distinction between Islamophobia and racism. They argue that, unlike racism, Islamophobia constructs the distinctiveness of Islam and its representatives, Muslims, on the basis of belief and practice rather than supposed biological or somatic characteristics (Miles and Brown 2003: 164). However, individuals do not choose to be born into Muslim families and neither do they choose to be born into societies that utilise counter-terror strategies which view Muslims with suspicion (Meer and Modood 2009: 345). As we will explore in Chap. 3, such counter-terror strategies have massive implications for the political marginalisation of British Muslim voices owing to the risk of conflating Muslim political dissidents with Islamic extremists. However, the political marginalisation of British Muslims also happens at a far more subtle level, and this is inherently embedded in conventional notions of 'race' which exclude religious identity as a legitimate facet. As argued by Meer and Modood, 'while curbs on the defamation of conventionally conceived ethnic and racial minorities might be seen as progressive, the mocking of Muslims is seen to constitute healthy intellectual debate' (Meer and Modood 2009: 348). Thus, although we have established that religious identity is no more chosen than prescribed racial categories for those who are born into Muslim families, Muslims as a minority group are not afforded the same protections against anti-Muslim sentiment that other racialised groups are against racism. Thus, failure to acknowledge anti-Muslim discrimination as racialised anti-Muslim racism actually serves as an act of tacit intentionality which ensures that British Muslims are denied the legitimacy afforded in discussions of 'race' inequity.

Whilst the above discussion provides a convincing argument for identifying anti-Muslim discrimination as anti-Muslim racism, critical arguments have been posited which raise questions about applying the notion of racism to religious groups. Hussain and Bagguley (2012) argue that attempting to extend the concept of racism culturally, which may refer to religious belief, runs the risk of inappropriately inflating the concept such that it loses its distinctiveness and empirical referents (Hussain and Bagguley 2012). But this does not rule out the notion of anti-Muslim racism as being political. Whilst the kinds of anti-Muslim sentiment outlined by Meer and Modood may have their roots in notions of cultural racism, anti-Muslim sentiment also has fundamental implications for the political disenfranchisement of British Muslims. Anti-Muslim racism may well have its roots in notions of cultural racism centred around identifying 'good' and 'bad' South Asians as identified by Modood (2005) and Hussain and Bagguley (2012) above, but the racialisation process is farther reaching and impacts across the political struggle between Muslims and the state that are borne out of counter-terror strategies like Prevent. Furthermore, drawing on an intersection between Islamophobia and CRT allows for an effective explanation for how and why anti-Muslim racism impacts beyond South Asian Muslim groups.

Within this wider context, there are specific ways in which anti-Muslim discourses have been manifested in emergent political movements at national levels arguably rooted in assumptions around British Muslims as a homogeneous group. The ways in which political tensions have been most explicitly manifested regarding Muslim communities in the British context can be seen through the rise of the BNP and the EDL. The BNP, in particular, has used quite sophisticated strategies when discussing Islam in the public sphere in a way which perpetuates the notion of Muslims as the 'other' (Allen 2010b: 224). Key examples of this process include using Islamic terms and drawing on very specific or confused interpretations of Islamic teachings, which apparently illustrate that Muslims are incompatible with British society (Allen 2010b: 224). This strategy not only affords the illusion that the BNP have a 'well-informed' (rather than ignorant) understanding of Islam which informs their political cause, but it also serves as a strategy for identifying that the problem of segregation lies with the Muslim community. For the BNP, not wanting to be part of who 'we' are is something that was a requirement in the Islamic faith (Allen 2010b: 224). There is also evidence to suggest that the BNP's focus on anti-Muslim propaganda has entered the public consciousness with some political effect. Allen draws on research conducted by John et al. (2006) which revealed that in parts of England, specifically where the BNP was focusing its resources, around one in four voters had considered voting for them, along with around one in five in certain parts of London (John et al. 2006).

The rise of the English Defence league (EDL) is another example of an explicit political movement which has been centred around positioning Muslim communities in conflict with the notion of Englishness. The political rhetoric manifested in the EDL is centred around the notion of Muslims 'spreading' across 'our country' at the cost of the 'patriotic English' being 'held under siege' (Allen 2010b: 228). Both the political narratives of the BNP and the EDL can be seen to manifest the central idea that Muslims are not part of what is 'British' or 'English' respectively. What is central here is the notion of religious identity as being used as the distinguishing factor to mark out a community as an 'other', distinguishable from what it is to be British or English—a notion which is not being identified explicitly with relation to religions other than Islam. In line with this thinking, Allen identifies that Muslims have indeed been subjected to 'new racism' based specifically on religious identification (Allen 2010b: 230), and that this has been manifested in the Islamophobic political rhetoric articulated by the BNP and the EDL. Furthermore, it is these processes of new racism, as manifested in the political rhetoric of the BNP and

EDL, which serve as the mechanism for the racialisation of Muslims as an 'other' in the British context.

The purpose of this section has been to set out the final premises for identifying Muslim communities in the British context as representing a suitable field of study for the application of CRT. Scholarly work on Islamophobia, such as that offered by Sayyid (2014) and Allen (2010a, b), clearly demonstrates the ways in which Muslim communities have been subjected to discursive processes of anti-Muslim discrimination. These processes are likely to be highly nuanced and intersections across national, religious and ethnic identities along with factors such as social class and migration status are likely to have a significant impact on how discrimination is experienced. However, Muslim communities have also been subjected to processes of *racialisation* whereby they are positioned in conflict with notions of Britishness and Englishness. This process of racialisation operates more by default than with reference to coherent concepts of Islam, Englishness or Britishness. This dynamic of anti-Muslim discrimination starts with an initial identification process of the Islamic or Muslim (Allen 2010a), and is itself a discursive effect of assumptions about Muslims as a homogeneous group. Thus, within this discursive process, religious identity is enough for Muslims to be racialised as other than 'English' or 'British', however incoherently these terms might be articulated in public political discourses. Thus, anti-Muslim *discrimination* equates with anti-Muslim *racism*. If we can accept the idea that British Muslims have been racialised explicitly in particular political contexts and discourses, then we have a clear rationale for applying CRT in the analysis of public policy and political discourses and their implications for Muslim communities at the macro level. The argument here is twofold. Firstly, a quasi-intersectional CRT approach that draws on established work on Islamophobia allows us to explore the nuanced ways in which anti-Muslim racism might be experienced at the micro level. Secondly, public policy and political discourses operate at the macro level based on assumptions about Muslim communities as a homogeneous group. We have explored implications here for processes of racialisation whereby there is an initial identification of the Islamic or Muslim, followed by the discursive positioning of the identified phenomena as 'other to' Britishness or Englishness. As this process is 'anti-Muslim', it logically follows that religion is the key determining factor in who this 'other' refers to. This reasoning also allows for an understanding of how white individuals may experience anti-Muslim racism. Given the above discussion, white Muslims of English or British descent would invariably find themselves as much the racialised 'enemy within' as any minority ethnic Muslim group. However, these experiences are likely to be massively differential for Muslims based on the intersections across religion, national identity, 'race' and social class and migration status. Thus, anti-Muslim racism is political, and in the British context at least, is bound up with public political discourses around national identity and who does not belong.

A MEANINGFUL APPLICATION OF CRT IN THE STUDY OF MUSLIM COMMUNITIES IN BRITAIN

This chapter has aimed to outline the extent to which CRT can be meaningfully applied to the analysis of British Muslims. Care has been taken to establish the premises for such application without making the impulsive slip that analysing British Muslims necessarily means analysing minority ethnic communities. Muslim communities in the UK are far from homogeneous, and therefore it is important that the rationale for applying CRT is not founded on subscribing to the notion of British Muslims as a homogeneous group. At the macro level, the application of CRT has to be rooted in concerns about the wider discursive racialisation of Muslims *as if* they are a homogeneous group. CRT has been applied to the Muslim experience in the UK context previously (Housee 2012). However, in advancing CRT research on British Muslims it is important to engage in and work to resolve critiques which may arise when applying what is essentially a theory of 'race' to the analysis of the experiences of a religious community. This chapter has aimed to set out a rigorous rationale for applying CRT in the analysis of British Muslim communities founded on concerns around Islamophobic discourses around nation and identity. This rationale goes beyond assumptions about the ethnic identities embodied in Britain's Muslim communities. Rather the focus should be on applying CRT at both the macro and micro levels as a means of gaining nuanced understandings of the ways in which discrimination is experienced whilst also acknowledging that public policy and political discourses around British Muslims are likely to operate based on identification through religion with little regard for the nuanced ways in which this intersects with other dynamics of identity. Acknowledging anti-Muslim racism at the macro and micro levels allows us to explore how the following might impact for understanding British Muslims in contemporary social context: interest convergence and public policy, racialisation in public discourse, master-narratives and counter-narratives, whiteness and white privilege, tacit intentionality and more elusive and nuanced forms of racist discrimination.

REFERENCES

Allen, C. (2010a). Islamophobia: From K.I.S.S. to R.I.P. In S. Sayyid & A. Vakil (Eds.), *Thinking Through Islamophobia: Global Perspectives* (pp. 51–64). London: C. Hurst & Co Publishers.

Allen, C. (2010b). Fear and Loathing: The Political Discourse in Relation to Muslims and Islam in the British Contemporary Setting. *Politics and Religion, 4*(2), 221–236.

AMS. (2014). Data from the Association of Muslim Schools UK. Website as of 6 October 2014. Available at: http://ams-uk.org/muslim-schools/

BBC. (2013a). *Woolwich: Michael Adebolajo Charged with Lee Rigby Murder.* Available at: http://www.bbc.co.uk/news/uk-22743438. Accessed 1 June 2013.

BBC. (2013b). Al-Madinah Free School in Derby Labelled 'Dysfunctional' by OFSTED. Available at: http://www.bbc.co.uk/news/uk-england-derbyshire-24548690. 17 October 2013.

Bell, D. (1980). Brown and the Interest-Convergence Dilemma. In D. Bell (Ed.), *Shades of Brown: New Perspectives on School Desegregation* (pp. 90–106). New York: Teachers College Press.

Bell, D. (1990). After We're Gone: Prudent Speculations on America in a Post-racial Epoch. *St Louis Law Journal,* reprinted in R. Delgado & J. Stefancic (eds.) 2000: *Critical Race Theory: The Cutting Edge (second edition)* (pp. 2–8). Philadelphia: Temple University Press.

Bonnett, A. (1997). Constructions of Whiteness in European and American Anti-racism. In P. Werbner & T. Modood (Eds.), *Debating Cultural Hybridity: Multi-cultural Identities and the Politics of Anti-racism* (pp. 173–192). London: Zed Books.

Breen, D. (2016). Critical Race Theory, Policy Rhetoric and Outcomes: The Case of Muslim Schools in Britain. *Race Ethnicity and Education*, published online 8 Nov 2016. Available at: http://www.tandfonline.com/doi/abs/10.1080/13613324.2016.1248828

Crenshaw, K., Gotanda, N., Peller, G., & Thomas, K. (Eds.). (1995). *Critical Race Theory: The Key Writings that Formed the Movement.* New York: Free Press.

Delgado, R. (Ed.). (1995). *Critical Race Theory: The Cutting Edge.* Philadelphia: Temple University Press.

REFERENCES   33

Delgado, R., & Stefancic, J. (2000). *Critical Race Theory: The Cutting Edge (Second Edition)*. Philadelphia: Temple University Press.

Du Bois, W. E. B. (1897). *The Conservation of Races*. Washington, DC: American Negro Academy.

Du Bois, W. E. B. (1903). *The Souls of Black Folk*. Cambridge: University Press John Wilson & Son.

Fanon, F. (1963). *The Wretched of the Earth*. New York: Grove Press.

Garvey, M. (1927). Garvey Recalls History of His Career in United States in Ward Theater Speech, 18 December 1927. In R. A. Hill, B. Bair, E. Johnson, & S. De Sal (Eds.), *1990: The Marcus Garvey and Universal Negro Improvement Association Papers Vol. VII November 1927–August 1940* (pp. 46–63). London: University of California Press.

Gavins, R. (2016). *Buffalo Soldiers. The Cambridge Guide to African American History*. New York: Cambridge University Press.

Gillborn, D. (2005). Education Policy as an Act of White Supremacy: Whiteness, Critical Race Theory and Reform. *Journal of Education Policy, 20*(4), 484–505.

Go, J. (2013). Fanon's Postcolonial Cosmopolitanism. *European Journal of Social Theory, 16*(2), 208–225.

Housee, S. (2012). What's the Point? Anti-racism and Students' Voices Against Islamophobia. *Race Ethnicity and Education, 15*(1), 101–120.

Hussain, Y., & Bagguley, P. (2012). Securitised Citizens: Islamophobia, Racism and the 7/7 Bombings. *The Sociological Review, 60*(4), 715–734.

John, P., Margetts, H., Rowland, D., & Weir, S. (2006). *The BNP: The Roots of its Appeal*, Democratic Audit. Human Rights Centre, University of Essex.

Ladson-Billings, G. (1998). Just What is Critical Race Theory and What's it Doing in a *nice* Field Like Education? *International Journal of Qualitative Studies in Education, 11*(1), 7–24.

Leonardo, Z. (2002). The Souls of White Folk: Critical Pedagogy, Whiteness Studies, and Globalization Discourse. *Race Ethnicity & Education, 5*(1), 29–50.

Lomotey, K., & Staley, J. (1990). *The Education of African Americans in Buffalo Public Schools*. Paper Presented at the Annual Meeting of the American Research Association, Boston.

Meer, N., & Modood, T. (2009). Refutations of Racism in the 'Muslim Question'. *Patterns of Prejudice, 43*(3–4), 335–354.

Miles, R., & Brown, M. (2003). *Racism*. London: Routledge.

Modood, T. (2005). *Multicultural Politics: Racism, Ethnicity and Muslims in Britain*. Edinburgh: Edinburgh University Press.

Parekh, B. (2008). *European Liberalism and 'The Muslim Question'* (ISIM Paper 9). Amsterdam: Amsterdam University Press.

Preston, J., & Chadderton, C. (2012). Rediscovering 'Race Traitor': Towards a Critical Race Theory Informed Public Pedagogy. *Race Ethnicity and Education, 15*(1), 85–100.

Runnymede. (1997). *Islamophobia – A Challenge for Us All*. Runnymede Trust.

Said, E. W. (1978). *Orientalism*. New York: Pantheon Books.

Said, E. W. (1985). Orientalism Reconsidered. *Cultural Critique, 1*, 89–107.

Sayyid, S. (2010). Out of the Devil's Dictionary. In S. Sayyid & A. Vakil (Eds.), *Thinking Through Islamophobia: Global Perspectives* (pp. 5–18). El Paso: Cinco Puntos Press.

Sayyid, S. (2014). A Measure of Islamophobia. *Islamophobia Studies Journal, 2*(1), 10–25.

Sian, K. P. (2015). Spies, Surveillance and Stakeouts: Monitoring Muslim Moves in British State Schools. *Race Ethnicity and Education, 18*(2), 183–201.

Stanley, C. A. (2007). When Counter Narratives Meet Master Narratives in the Journal Editorial-Review Process. *Educational Researcher, 36*(1), 14–24.

Terrill, R. E. (2001). Protest, Prophecy and Prudence in the Rhetoric of Malcolm X. *Rhetoric & Public Affairs, 4*(1), 25–53.

Warmington, P. (2012). A Tradition in Ceaseless Motion': Critical Race Theory and Black British Intellectual Spaces. *Race, Ethnicity and Education, 15*(1), 5–21.

CHAPTER 3

Critical Race Theory, Policy Rhetoric and Outcomes: The Case of Muslim Schools in Britain

This chapter is focused on applying a Critical Race Theory (CRT) analysis on the disparity between (a) educational policy rhetoric around faith schooling generally and British Muslim schools specifically since 1997, and (b) outcomes in terms of numbers of state-funded Muslim schools and the kinds of partnerships with the state that have been manifested through them. One process which is not assumed here is the conflation of religion with 'race'. It is fully acknowledged here that, whilst there are large minority ethnic groups who are Muslim such as British Pakistanis and Bangladeshis, Muslim communities in Britain are also characterised by extensive ethnic diversity (Tinker 2009). It was also acknowledged in Chap. 2 that there are bodies of work (see Allen 2010; Sayyid 2010) which critically challenge the notions of Islamophobia that have been used in public documents such as the Runnymede Trust's *Islamophobia: a challenge for us all* (1997). This chapter will draw on a quasi-intersectional CRT framework that draws on work on Islamophobia to provide an exploration of anti-Muslim sentiment in the public space and the implications of this for the political equity of British Muslims as stakeholders in both education and the state.

As a theory of 'race', CRT is fundamentally concerned with the systematic marginalisation of racialised minorities in contemporary social contexts. As identified in Chap. 2, there are several key tenets of CRT which include Critical Whiteness Studies, master-narrative and counter-narrative, interest convergence and an emphasis on the centrality of 'voice' in qualitative accounts of racism in contemporary contexts. For the purposes

© The Author(s) 2018
D. Breen, *Muslim Schools, Communities and Critical Race Theory*,
DOI 10.1057/978-1-137-44397-7_3

of the enquiry here, we will substantively focus on master-narrative and counter-narrative in the case of state-funded Muslim schools in Britain. One of the central themes in established work on CRT has been on the ways in which policy functions to sustain 'race' inequalities across education (see Gillborn 2005, 2008). To this end, the enquiry here is informed by a critical consideration of public policy and rhetoric around faith schooling since 1997 with a view to comparing narratives around Muslim schools in the political and public spaces with outcomes. A recurring theme in emerging CRT scholarship focused on policy analysis has been the argument that societal structures ensure that 'racial' inequity is sustained at the biting point of tolerable discomfort for marginalised racialised minorities. This article will ultimately argue that there has been a disconnect between public narratives around Muslim schools and real outcomes in the form of numbers. Therefore, access to state-funded Muslim schools remains largely exclusive for the vast majority of British Muslims. These outcomes sit against a backdrop of policy rhetoric which acknowledges the tendency for faith schools to perform strongly in educational league tables.

On the surface, applying a theory of 'race' to look at issues around religion might seem at best restrictive and at worst problematic. The safest option might be to simply focus on one particular ethnic group within the wider religious community of British Muslims. In many ways, this would be completely unproblematic, particularly if the analysis retained a clear set of boundaries around how far arguments might be applicable in terms of clearly identified ethnic groups. However, using CRT in this constrained way raises issues around power, knowledge and the purpose of CRT as an emancipatory framework focused on revealing the fullest extent to which 'racial' inequalities are manifested in contemporary social contexts. Applying CRT in the analysis of only *certain* Muslim communities could arguably contribute to power dynamics around knowledge and the purpose of knowledge which reinforce a 'divide and conquer' effect. There are some important arguments around master-narratives, counter-narratives and the purpose of CRT which will need to be considered in order to fully demonstrate this point, and they will be explored in greater detail later in this chapter. The chapter will now move on to build on some of the arguments presented in Chap. 2 by exploring some of the implications that arise as a result of the systematic racialisation of Muslims in the public sphere. Initially we will look at counter-terror strategies and their implications for political enfranchisement before moving on to explore the role of denominational Islamic schooling for the enfranchisement of British Muslims in terms of polity and the nation-state.

PREVENT: IMPLICATIONS FOR POLITICAL AND EDUCATIONAL EQUITY

One of the mechanisms through which Muslims have been displaced as stakeholders in mainstream political equity is through the residual effects of counter-terror strategies. Kundnani (2009) argues that the logic of the 'Prevent' branch of the counter-terrorist strategy in Britain has been counter-productive and actually serves to perpetuate tensions between British Muslim communities and the state. The Prevent strategy was launched in 2007 as part of the British government's wider counter-terrorism strategy and has been focused on a 'community-led' approach to preventing violent extremism (Kundnani 2009). The rationale for Prevent was to 'win over hearts and minds' of young Muslims in Britain and to lead them away from extremist narratives (Kundnani 2009: 10). At the early stages, the strategy involved the allocation of funding to local authorities for the purpose of targeted capacity building of Muslim communities particularly focused on young people, women and mosques (Kundnani 2009: 10). Central to the Prevent agenda has been the promotion of shared values to challenge extremist ideologies and strengthening the role of faith institutions within those communities. These developments have led to a focus on education standards in general and citizenship education specifically in after-school supplementary provision offered in mosques, *madrassas* and Muslim community organisations (Thomas 2009: 284). However, the 'Muslim-centred' focus within strategies like Prevent functions as something of a self-defeating contradiction, given the evidence that indicates that wider segregation across ethnic and religious lines has been the context within which radicalisation has occurred, at least in the British context (Thomas 2009: 285). Even if we were to ignore this contradiction, Kundnani argues that serious problems arise when deprived communities in need of support consider that their voluntary-sector organisation can only access resources to meet their needs if they are willing to sign up to a counter-terrorism agenda (Kundnani 2009: 10). Furthermore, the allocation of funding within this Muslim-specific approach has the potential to fuel white, working-class resentment, whilst leaving some Muslims feeling that they have been targeted as a result of broad, negative generalisations about their communities (Thomas 2009:

285–6). But there are wider issues here with the ways in which funding has been allocated. Rather than distributing economic resources based on need, funding for 2008–2011 was allocated across cities proportionate to the size of their Muslim communities (Kundnani 2009: 13). Allocating funds in this way reveals a wider discursive set of assumptions about 'risk' relative to the scale of a Muslim presence in a particular space. This approach to distributing resources reveals a subtext to the strategy which equates increased numbers of Muslims with increased risk. The fallout here is discursive, as Islam comes to be associated with risk in public policy, the implication being that it is in the public interest that any increase in Islamic influence in the public space needs to be met with careful monitoring. This point will inform an important part of the master-narrative identified at the end of this chapter. Invariably, this demonstrates one of the ways in which the Prevent strategy has been informed by a myriad of Islamophobic logics, whereby young Muslims are subject to various forms of racialised governmentality (Sian 2015: 197).

There is a more pervasive effect of counter-terror strategies on Muslims as communities in European settings at a time when public political interests are characterised by the 'war on terror'. For example, Fekete argues that the culmination of European security strategies and counter-terrorist policies which have emerged out of public and media narratives around the 'war on terror' represent a structured anti-Muslim racism (Fekete 2004). According to Fekete, these security strategies 'lump together genuine political dissidents and numbers of ordinary Muslims with individuals whom most would regard as terrorists, thus obfuscating rather than clarifying any possible genuine threat' (Fekete 2004: 9). Fekete's concept of anti-Muslim racism goes beyond simply identifying that Muslims experience racialisation as a result of political narratives around the 'war on terror'. Rather, anti-Muslim racism is organised and operates discursively. Fekete argues that intelligence services, police and the media work in conjunction with a political agenda centred around eliciting public consent to surveillance through the evocation of fear, to create a culture of suspicion against Muslims (Fekete 2004: 14). This culminates in Muslims being identified as and policed as a suspect community (Fekete 2004: 10).

There are some interesting implications of the point raised by Fekete, particularly regarding ordinary political dissidents. Counter-terrorism policies and security strategies have resulted in environments whereby the political voices of young Muslims are subject to a dual process of scrutiny and displacement from mainstream democratic discussion. For example, part of the process of identifying radicalisation necessitates an evaluation of an individual's political orientation. Counter-terrorist strategies provide a normative base from which these judgements are made, and therefore British Muslims who are particularly outspoken and oppose the involvement of European nation-states in conflicts in Islamic countries become at risk of being labelled as 'radical'. Conversely, the exact same argument could be articulated by a non-Muslim individual without carrying any risk of being labelled in the same way. It is also important to consider here that, within the UK context, wider public policy documents consistently avoid applying the term 'violent extremism' to any other ethnic, or religious, group (Thomas 2009: 284). The Muslim-centred focus within Prevent in particular results in an agenda which claims even-handedness but allows the continuing development of organisations like the British National Party (Thomas 2009: 286) and the English Defence League. These kinds of public narratives result in Muslim political voices being subjected to a filtration process which has the power to displace particular political interests outside of mainstream democratic discussion. The inability for counter-terrorism strategies to effectively differentiate Muslim political dissidents indicates that these strategies homogenise Muslims based on the kind of 'closed views' of Islam identified by Runnymede in 1997. Inevitably, for Muslims, engaging in political democratic debates becomes weighted with risk and suspicion. In line with Fekete's argument, this constitutes a discursive process whereby the legitimacy of political voices is determined based on an individual's identity as being either Muslim or non-Muslim.

Fundamental British Values

The discussion above is not only relevant to debates about the wider impact of counter-terror strategies on political equity and the differential legitimacy afforded to voices of dissent in democratic politics. The Prevent strategy and its appendages (e.g. the statutory duty for schools to prevent violent extremism) manifest a bridging gap between political equity and education indicating a wider culture of surveillance around Muslim children in schools. This is bound into wider public narratives around the conflating of increased Islamic influence with legitimate threat. This binary reading of the Islamic in the public space completely overlooks one of the key functions of Muslim schools as identified in the voices of stakeholders in Islamic schools in Meer's research (2009). Meer cites Abdullah

Trevathan (head of the Islamia school in Brent) as explicitly stating in an interview that part of the purpose of Muslim schools is to create an emerging British Muslim culture, rather than the conservation of any pre-existing culture (Meer 2009: 383). In this particular instance, the increased presence of the Islamic in the public sphere that necessarily comes with Muslim schools equates with negotiating a space affording educational and civic gains for British Muslims.

However, the UK Government's recent Fundamental British Values (DfE 2015) initiative arguably demonstrates a mechanism for obstructing the objective of creating an emerging British Muslim culture in Muslim schools. The identification of Fundamental 'British' Values has the discursive effect of sustaining the kind of dichotomous positioning of Islam as 'other to' the West discussed in Chap. 2—in this case, Islam is being identified by default as 'other to' that which is 'British'. Furthermore, the Fundamental British Values agenda (FBV) is bound up with the revised Prevent duty guidance (2015), and this invariably cements the purpose of FBV as a strategy for preventing violent extremism through offering a counterpoint to Islamic influence in schools. The relationship between Prevent and FBV assumes that the values identified as British are exclusively so, the inference being that Islamic values do not naturally mirror FBV. Fundamental British values have been identified by the UK government as democracy, the rule of law, individual liberty and mutual respect and tolerance of those with different faiths and beliefs (Prevent 2011). Furthermore, the government has used the identification of 'fundamental British values' as a default measure for identifying, by way of contrast, a definition of extremism. The most recent guidelines around Prevent (2015) state that:

> The government has defined extremism in the Prevent strategy as vocal or active opposition to fundamental British values including democracy, the rule of law, individual liberty and mutual respect and tolerance of different faiths and beliefs.

The identification of the above as fundamentally 'British' has racialised overtones, especially given the arguments considered previously about the positioning of Islam as 'other to' that which is 'British'. However, the institutionalisation of this strategy provides more subtle challenges and problems. The DfE primarily identifies provision around spiritual, moral, social and cultural development (DfES 2005: 12) as the primary mechanism within which the promotion of fundamental British values is assessed through OFSTED inspections. The Academies Act 2010 has served to significantly blur the lines between state-funded and independent schools. Subsequently, the statutory duty is somewhat all encompassing for schools in England and Wales as both independent and maintained schools are required to promote fundamental British values. In particular, the most recently Revised Prevent duty guidance for England and Wales (2015) states that:

> Independent schools set their own curriculum but must comply with the Independent School Standards, which include a specific requirement to promote fundamental British values as part of broader requirements relating to the quality of education and to promoting the spiritual, moral, cultural and cultural development of pupils. These standards also apply to academies (other than 16–19 academies), including free schools, as they are independent schools (DfE 2015: 10).

The applicability of FBV to both independent and state-funded schools ensures a totality of duty to promote FBV for all Muslim schools in England and Wales. Thus, *all* Muslim schools are bound to adhere to a strategy that serves as a further part of the mechanism for sustaining the notion of Islam as distinctive from, and other to, Britishness.

MUSLIM SCHOOLS IN ENGLAND AND WALES

Muslim schools have been present in England and Wales since 1979 (Dooley 1991). It is important to establish here that, whilst many Muslim children receive supplementary Islamic education through the provision of *madrassas* in community mosques, this chapter is concerned with those institutions which are registered as Muslim schools either in the independent or state-maintained sector in England and Wales. Within the frameworks around state-maintained education, particular types of schools are able to identify as having a 'distinctive religious character'. There are two important timeframes to consider here with regard to policy structures and faith schooling. The first state-maintained Muslim schools were established in England and Wales in 1998, and so it logically follows that our starting point should be to explore the frameworks in place at that time. The notion of a 'distinctive religious character' was first introduced under New Labour with the School Standards and Framework Act (UK Government 1998). Under the Act, voluntary-aided schools are permitted to identify themselves as having a 'distinctive religious character' whilst providing denominational Religious Education (RE) in line with their religious character. Arrangements for funding represent an important distinguishing feature of voluntary-aided schools, with costs for individual institutions being met by both the state and a religious organisation affiliated with a given school. The proportion of cost to be covered by each party has changed over time, but in the period between 1998 and 2010 voluntary-aided schools would receive up to 90% of their funding from the state with the outstanding 10% being met by an affiliated religious organisation (DfES 2002) such as a church, mosque or synagogue. Independent schools are able to register a distinctive religious character under the Designation of Schools Having a Religious Character (Independent Schools) (England) Order 2003. The next section will consider the developments around Muslim schools under the frameworks around faith schooling under the Labour government between 1998 and 2010 in further detail. We will then move on to outline how structures around faith schooling changed under the Coalition government of 2010–15.

New Labour: A Sustained Interest in State-Funded Minority Religious Schooling?

Within the last 30 years, there have been a series of changes in the policy frameworks around state provision for faith schooling that have impacted on Muslim schools. The 1993 Education Act first introduced frameworks which would allow independent faith schools to apply for funding directly through central government. Under these frameworks, regulation of the school would also come directly under central government rather than the local education authority. This process would position independent faith schools successful in securing grant-maintained status outside of any local communities of voluntary-aided faith schools. However, it would nevertheless provide an effective mechanism for two Muslim schools, Islamia Primary and Al-Furqan, to successfully be the first to secure state funding in England and Wales (Tinker 2009: 540). These two schools inevitably transitioned into the voluntary-aided sector following the phasing out of grant-maintained status in 1999. It is worth noting here that these initial advances were made under the New Labour government elected in 1997. The sustained interest in faith schooling and the emphasis on encouraging independent minority faith schools to enter the state sector represented a recurring theme within New Labour's wider 'education, education, education' (Coughlan 2007) mandate.

The apparent interest in funding minority religious schools more generally, and Muslim schools specifically, was manifested in a series of parliamentary papers and public documents under New Labour. For example, the 2001 Green Paper *Schools building on success* emphasised that faith schools appear to perform well when compared to non-denominational schools, and subsequently proposed expanding faith schooling within the state sector (DfEE 2001). In 2005, the White Paper *Higher standards, better schools for all* continued this narrative by further encouraging independent schools to join the state sector, with a particular emphasis on encouraging Muslim schools to apply for voluntary-aided status (UK Government 2005). Furthermore, in September 2007 the government, along with representatives of major faith groups, released the document *Faith in the system*. The paper 'unveiled a joint declaration and shared vision of schools with a religious character in 21st century England', stating that the government recognises the aspirations of faith communities to secure more schools to offer education in accordance with the tenets of their faith (DCSF 2007: 4). *Faith in the system* again placed a particular emphasis on encouraging minority religious schools to apply for state funding, stating that there are '15,000 Muslim children and around 11,000 Jewish children, including those from low-income families, whose parents chose to send them to independent schools with a particular religious character and that the availability of places in the maintained sector could therefore provide an important contribution to integration and empowerment of these communities' (DCSF 2007: 18). Under the Labour government the number of voluntary-aided Muslim schools in England and Wales rose steadily and currently stands at 12, a figure which has not changed since 2010 (Breen 2013). New Labour's sustained policy narratives around encouraging the establishment and subsequent expansion of state-funded Muslim schools invariably culminated in real and objective economic gains for British Muslim communities.

ANXIETY FOLLOWING 2010?

The arrival of the Coalition government in 2010 and subsequent Conservative government in 2015 has provided for a confused picture regarding the government's position on faith schools. The political landscape since 2010 has been complex, with a series of developments leaving the future of minority faith schooling open to question. Almost immediately after securing office as Prime Minister, David Cameron declared that 'state multiculturalism has failed' (Helm et al. 2011), a statement that necessarily brings into question the issue of whether or not the state will continue to encourage faith schooling for minority communities. However, the wider implications of the change in government in 2010 for state-funded faith schools generally, and Muslim schools specifically, are far from clear. One key development in education policy came with the Academies Act of 2010 which laid the foundation for the widespread 'conversion' of state schools to academy status, including vast swathes of voluntary-aided schools. The Academies Act also set out the frameworks around 'free schools' which can be established to serve the interests of local communities (UK Parliament 2010). Thus, at least in theory, the frameworks around free schools might provide opportunities for Muslim communities to found Islamic schools and secure state funding for them, even in the light of Cameron's apparent convictions around multiculturalism.

It is worth noting here that David Cameron used the term 'state multiculturalism', implying that it is multiculturalism as an institutionalised strategy, advocated in the Swann Report (1985), that has failed. As an institutional strategy 'state multiculturalism' has been criticised for lacking clear guidelines and national leadership (Parekh 2000), and consequently failing to effectively embody the conceptual premises of 'multiculturalism' as a conceptual tool for challenging 'race' inequality (see Modood 1994, 1998, 2008; Modood and Werbner 1997; Meer and Modood 2009). However, the declaration that multiculturalism has failed represents only one example of the wider revival of assimilationist discourses around education following the events of 11 September 2001, the 2001 riots in the North of England and the London bombings of 7 July 2005 (Sian 2015: 183). Evidence of the revival of assimilationist discourses around education have most recently been revealed with the anxieties around the Trojan Horse letter in Birmingham. Whilst raising some concerns, Ian Kershaw's investigation into the Trojan Horse letter ultimately concluded that there was no evidence to suggest there was 'a systematic plot to take over schools' (Kershaw 2014: 8). The details around Trojan Horse are complex, and there is neither the scale nor scope to explore these in depth here. However, subsequent public debates around Trojan horse did further demonstrate the presence of wider anxieties around the Islamic as representing a threat to British values in the public sphere. Such concerns about increased Islamic influence in the education sector might be more about Muslim schools representing an anathema to assimilation rather than any real 'risks'. The above discussion necessarily raises questions as to what the future might look like for Muslim schooling in the state sector. Short of halting the expansion of state Muslim schools specifically, it would appear that the Academies Act may serve as a strategy for facilitating more Muslim schools, but only on the condition that, in the event of any issues, all responsibility is devolved to individual institutions.

In addition to the developments above, the future of state-funded Muslim schools also comes into question when considering the wider economic conditions that have dominated political debates around public spending following the onset of the recession in 2008. In particular, the Coalition and subsequent Conservative governments both placed economic recovery at the centre with widespread implications for cuts in public spending. Following the general election of 2010, the Coalition government's primary strategy for economic recovery was most notably manifested in a series of 'austerity measures' which have been carried over with the election of a Conservative majority government in 2015. Political and economic conditions since 2010 represent something of a U-turn in levels of state support for the expansion of Muslim schools in the state sector. The question around the extent to which Muslim communities will be able to continue to make gains through quantifiable outcomes is of central relevance. However, recent economic and political events have also impacted on faith schools in far more nuanced ways. The advent of the Academies Act in 2010 has posed existing voluntary-aided schools with the dilemma of weighing up the opportunity cost of retaining their existing status in a competitive and transformative education market against the possible benefits of converting to academy status (Meer and Breen forthcoming). Existing figures demonstrate that this dilemma is impacting on voluntary-aided schools with 33% converting to academy status by 2013 (Bolton 2013: 4). Breaking these figures down across denominations reveals that Church of England (C of E) schools appear to be most active in converting to academy status with 41% of C of E voluntary-aided schools having done so by 2013 compared with 25% of Roman Catholic schools (Bolton 2013: 4). Such transformative trends within the maintained sector are likely to result in new challenges for both existing state-funded Muslim schools and stakeholders in Muslim communities looking to make future gains in denominational schooling.

Numbers of British Muslim Schools

In order to gain an accurate picture of how Muslim schools have been positioned under the Coalition and subsequent Conservative governments, it is important to establish how far Muslim communities have been enfranchised through state funding for Islamic schools to date. Furthermore, it is crucially important to consider the ways in which any gains have been made and the nature of the partnerships that they represent. The discussion in the previous subsection might appear to champion multiculturalism due to ways in which state multiculturalism has informed outcomes in terms of enfranchising Muslim communities through state funding for Islamic schools. It is important to note here that the establishment of state-funded Muslim schools under New Labour did represent a watershed in the educational enfranchisement of British Muslims. Particularly, the establishment of Muslim voluntary-aided schools represents a critical step in bringing Muslim communities into partnerships with the state (Meer 2007: 67–68). However, it is an understanding of both how gains have been made prior to 2010 and the implications for future partnerships with the state after 2010 that position this work firmly within a CRT framework.

The development of voluntary-aided Muslim schools arguably represents the clearest and most tangible example of educational enfranchisement for religious Muslims. Whilst this is significant, in reality, only limited numbers of independent Muslim schools have successfully made the transition into the voluntary-aided sector. As noted above, the central relevance of CRT here is most clearly established through understanding two key factors that need to be considered chronologically in order to avoid confusion. Firstly, the conditions around the initial establishment of state-funded Muslim schools between 1998 and 2010 need to be explored. Secondly, we need to consider what the landscape looks like following the Academies Act of 2010 and the implications of current political conditions for the future of state-funded Islamic schooling. If we focus initially on developments prior to the advent of the Academies Act 2010, we can establish how far Muslim communities were enfranchised under New Labour relative to other religious groups. In 2009, there were approximately 7000 voluntary-aided schools in England with the vast majority being Church of England (C of E) or Roman Catholic (Tinker 2009: 540). Within this number, 53 voluntary-aided schools had a distinctive religious character other than C of E or Roman Catholic (Tinker 2009:

540). Breaking these schools down across religious character reveals that those 53 schools comprised 37 Jewish, two Sikh, one Greek Orthodox, one Seventh Day Adventist (Tinker 2009: 540) and 12 Muslim (Breen 2009: 111). By way of comparison, the vast majority of Muslim schools (approximately 120 at the same point in time) lie within the independent sector (Breen 2013: 42). As noted above, the establishment of state-funded Muslim schools in England and Wales represents a significant step forward in terms of the educational enfranchisement of British Muslims. However, comparing outcomes in this way reveals that, although tangible gains can be identified with the establishment of 12 Muslim schools in the voluntary-aided sector by 2009, ten times this number were residing in the independent sector (Breen 2013: 42). Thus, the vast majority of British Muslims attending Islamic schools were doing so outside of any partnership with the state.

Whilst the above starts to reveal just how few British Muslims have had the benefit of attending a voluntary-aided Muslim school, a crucially important point needs to be acknowledged here. Numbers of Muslim schools within the independent sector have a tendency to fluctuate for two main reasons. Firstly, independent Muslim schools face ongoing financial instability in the struggle to economically sustain themselves (see Breen 2009, 2013, 2014). Within these contexts, the threat of closure is a constant risk, and some schools will be unsuccessful in finding economic sustainability. Secondly, numbers of independent Muslim schools necessarily change as and when any such schools enter the state sector. These two factors have informed the ways in which numbers of independent Muslim schools have been discussed in England and Wales. Consequently, between 2009 and 2013, numbers of independent Muslim schools were estimated at approximately 120 (Meer and Breen forthcoming). Increased access to publicly available data indicates that numbers of Muslim schools in the independent sector appear to be growing with current numbers totalling 158 (AMS data as of October 2014). In the wake of acknowledging the difficulties around identifying exact numbers of independent Muslim schools, it is still clear that the proportion of Muslim schools which have successfully entered the state sector is small. Even based on an approximation, it can still be safely argued that the representation of Muslim schools in the independent sector prior to 2010 was at least tenfold that represented in the state sector.

The trend with Muslim schools outlined above becomes particularly interesting if we compare numbers of Church of England and Roman

Catholic schools across independent and state-maintained sectors. Within the independent sector, there are currently 564 C of E schools (C of E 2013) and 146 Catholic schools (CES 2012), compared with 4800 C of E schools (Chadwick 2012) and 2166 Catholic schools (CES 2012) in the state-maintained sector. Therefore, it is clear that proportional representation across sectors appears to be inverted when comparing state-funded Christian and Muslim provision. Clearly, educational provision for Christian schools is predominantly provided for within the state sector, whereas provision for Muslim schooling is predominantly provided for within the independent sector. It might not be realistic to expect to see Muslim communities having the same proportional access within each sector as that afforded to Christians. Nonetheless, drawing this comparison demonstrates just how small the gains for Muslim schools were between 1998 and 2010. In particular, given the sustained policy rhetoric inviting Muslim schools to enter the state sector under New Labour, it is important to ask why only 12 schools successfully made this transition between 1998 and 2010. The success rate appears to be quite low considering the numbers of Muslim schools that are operating in the independent sector.

The misalignment between New Labour's sustained policy rhetoric around Muslim schools and the outcomes that British Muslims have subsequently acquired reflects a legacy of struggle faced by independent Muslim schools seeking to acquire state funding. Whilst Muslim schools have been active in the pursuit of state funding from as early as 1983 (see Tinker 2009: 540), it is only from 1998 that we see the first state-funded Muslim schools in England and Wales. An explanation for this is offered by Walford, who argues that strict financial and demand-led criteria imposed at the time made it difficult for evangelical Christian schools and Muslim schools to enter the state system (Walford 2003: 165). The challenges faced by independent Muslim schools seeking to enter the state sector have been well documented. As noted earlier in this chapter, the Islamia primary school in Brent was the first independent Muslim school to be awarded state funding through grant-maintained status in January 1998 (Tinker 2009: 540). The school had initially started to explore possibilities around acquiring state funding in 1983 and submitted a formal application in 1986 (Tinker 2009: 540). This application was considered and rejected in 1990 as was a follow-up application in 1993 (Tinker 2009: 540). In 1995, a final application was made which resulted in the school being awarded grant-maintained status in 1998 following a 15-year struggle for state funding (Tinker 2009: 540). Al-Furqan, the second school to successfully attain grant-maintained status, fought a four-year campaign before receiving state funding in September 1998 (Parker-Jenkins et al. 2005: 44). Similarly, Feversham College in Bradford initially applied for state funding in 1994 but did not successfully enter the voluntary-aided sector until six years later in 2000 (Tinker 2009: 540). In the case of Islamia and Al-Furqan, the struggle for state funding began well before New Labour came to power and ended under that government. However, Feversham College endured a lengthy struggle similar to that of Al-Furqan, much of which took place under New Labour. Whilst this is only one documented case, it is important in demonstrating that acquiring state funding for Muslim schools was still characterised by struggle after the change of government in 1997. This point is further demonstrated in the low numbers of Muslim schools that successfully qualified for voluntary-aided status prior to 2010. Thus, New Labour's rhetoric around inviting independent Muslim schools to enter into partnerships with the state may have served as a smokescreen to obscure an unseen tacit intentionality focused on offering only marginal gains. From this position, New Labour appears to be progressive, able to commend themselves on offering the first state-funded Muslim schools, whilst ensuring that the criteria for doing so effectively prevents widespread enfranchisement for British Muslims.

Issues Around Faith Schooling and Muslim Schools Post-2010

The disparity between policy rhetoric and outcomes in terms of numbers of state-funded Muslim schools under New Labour played out in the form of marginal gains in the state sector for British Muslims. However, the arrival of the Coalition government in 2010, and the subsequent Conservative government of 2015, represents something of a game changer in terms of how policy plays out for stakeholders in Islamic schooling. As demonstrated above, the landscape of state-funded Islamic schooling between 1998 and 2010 was largely characterised by slow-paced and hard-fought gains being secured through the voluntary-aided system (Meer and Breen forthcoming). Demand for Muslim schools also appears to be on the increase with numbers of independent Muslim schools seemingly rising. As noted above, numbers of independent Muslim schools around 2009–2013 were estimated at approximately 120 (Meer and Breen forthcoming). More recent figures place numbers of independent Muslim schools at 158 (AMS data as of October 2014). As noted above, there are some difficulties with establishing exact numbers of independent Muslim schools due to the impact of financial instability being manifested through fluctuating numbers. Owing to the difficulties in establishing exact numbers in recent years, it would be problematic to claim objectively that numbers of independent Muslim schools have risen by 38 since 2009. However, the number standing at 158 as of 2014 certainly demonstrates that Islamic schooling is in demand. Furthermore, we can identify that it is likely that some growth has taken place in the independent sector, even if negating factors make it difficult to quantify progress in precise terms.

Alongside the apparent growth of Muslim schools in the independent sector, numbers of state-funded Muslim schools have increased since 2010 and at a relatively faster rate compared with the 1998–2010 era. Rather than favouring the voluntary-aided sector, gains in terms of state-funded Muslim schools are now being made most notably following the shift in policy manifested in the Academies Act 2010 (UK Government 2014). In addition to championing academies, the Academies Act (2010) set out the framework for free schools as a mechanism for 'communities and faith groups' (UK Government 2014) to develop schools to cater to local needs. Whilst the number of voluntary-aided Muslim schools has remained at 12 since 2009, in subsequent years, the number of state-funded Muslim schools in England and Wales has risen to 21 (AMS data as of October 2014). The most substantive gains since 2010 have been made through the new and emergent frameworks around free schools. Currently, the landscape of state-funded Muslim schooling comprises 12 voluntary-aided schools, eight free schools and one academy (AMS data as of October 2014). Although the number of voluntary-aided Muslim schools has remained at 12 since 2009, it is important to point out that the single Muslim academy was previously operational in the voluntary-aided sector. This means that at some point following the Academies Act (2010), one voluntary-aided Muslim school made the transition to academy status leaving 11 Muslim schools in the voluntary-aided sector. Given that the number currently stands at 12, this suggests that one independent Muslim school has successfully entered voluntary-aided sector since 2010. It is also worth identifying a further point of clarity here, in that many independent Muslim schools use the term 'academy' in their name. However, as independent schools, these institutions are entirely privately funded and are not 'academies' in terms of the criteria and frameworks set out for state-maintained schools under the Academies Act 2010. Nevertheless, the tendency for independent Muslim schools to refer to themselves as 'academies' may have distorted public perceptions of how far Muslim communities have become educationally enfranchised since 2010.

GAINS MADE IN THE POST-2010 ERA

As noted above the most notable gains that have been made post-2010 in terms of state-funded Muslim schools have taken place through the frameworks around free schools. Whilst it seems that objective economic enfranchisement has been on the rise for Muslim communities seeking state funding for their faith schools, deconstructing the structures around free schools reveals something of a counter-narrative in the CRT sense. An overall increase in the number of state-funded Muslim free schools since 2010 might appear to demonstrate the suitability of the Academies Act as a strategy facilitating a sustained commitment to increasing educational equity for British Muslims. However, the dynamics of the relationship between local stakeholders and the state is fundamentally different to that which has been manifested in the voluntary-aided Muslim schools established between 1998 and 2010. Voluntary-aided schools operate within local authority control. In the pre-2010 era, this had meant that state-funded denominational faith schools within a given local authority effectively constituted a network of institutions working in direct relation to local government. Whilst resources invariably impact on real-life experiences, within this dynamic it is at least possible for the local authority to work in conjunction with schools to meet the needs of local communities. The Academies Act (2010) represents an important watershed in the erosion of the role of government in the maintained sector. Free schools operate outside of local authority control and as such are answerable only to central government as do academies. Trends discussed above demonstrate that voluntary-aided schools are slowly but surely converting to academy status, and so the role of local government in educational provision is steadily changing. Whilst these developments are presented in ways which highlight the 'freedoms' afforded by stepping out of local government control, in reality any liberation is afforded at the cost of massively increased individual accountability for schools. The 2010 Act arguably represents the manifestation of uber-neoliberal principles around education and the shifting of accountability for its provision away from local government. However, of crucial importance here, the nature of the relationship between schools and central government is fundamentally different to that manifested in a system under local education authorities. In the post-2010 era, all schools that convert or operate under academy or free school status do so in partnership with central government. From a purely logistical standpoint, this system cannot possibly offer the same level of presence and support that is possible in the partnerships manifested in voluntary-aided schools.

A clear example of this can be seen with the ways in which media narratives have been constructed around the Al-Madinah free school in Derby, UK. Since the advent of the Academies Act (2010) and the Coalition's commitment to advocating academies and 'free schools', there has been some increase in the number of Muslim schools in the state-maintained sector. In addition to the 12 voluntary-aided Muslim schools, there are now eight Muslim free schools and one Muslim academy (AMS 2014). Since 2010 then, the total number of state-funded Muslim schools has risen from 12 to 21, with the predominant gains being made through the mechanism of 'free schooling'. This is consistent with the rhetoric around 'free schools' as mechanisms for communities to establish schools which suit their local needs from the ground up. However, whilst this has yielded gains for Muslim communities, this has taken place against a sustained backdrop of public concern around Muslim free schools in the media. This is demonstrated in the case of Al-Madinah, which has seen sustained negative media attention as a result of concern from OFSTED, the Education Funding Agency (EFA) and the Department for Education (DfE). The Al-Madinah School in Derby opened in September 2012 as the first Muslim free school to offer provision at nursery, primary and secondary levels. The school was investigated for 'financial irregularities' in August 2013, and an OFSTED report which followed raised further concerns about the school (BBC 2013). Much media speculation has been generated around the nature of the concerns raised by OFSTED, with references being made to girls being made to wear compulsory *hijabs* (headscarves) and segregated classes (BBC 2013). Whether these concerns are or are not realised or evidenced in the public space remains to be seen.

However, there are two important points which can be raised when considering the case of Al- Madinah. The first of these is concerned with the contextual points of reference which have been used in media discussions. The problems which have been raised have been consistently attributed to the school's faith character, rather than its position as a free school operating within new and emergent educational structures. At least one other free school has also faced closure in the 'Discovery' school in Crawley (Adams 2013), whilst funding was pulled from the 'One in a Million' free school in Bradford nine days before it was due to open (Beckett 2012). This evidence demonstrates that there have been systemic problems with the structures around free schools. However, when Al-Madinah is discussed in the media, problems have been primarily attributed to the school's faith status, rather than the wider systemic problems around free schools. A second point which can be raised with regard to the case of Al-Madinah is that the very occurrence of concerns around the functioning of the school demonstrates a clear necessity for greater dialogue between communities and the state. Communities may be free to found schools which serve local needs, but under the structures around free schools, they are also positioned as ultimately accountable should problems occur. Given that Muslim schools have largely been excluded from the state-maintained sector, prior experience and expertise around providing mainstream faith schooling is not likely to be present within communities looking to establish Islamic free schools. In many senses, the structures around free schooling seem to be too 'free'. Responsibility for any issues of concern is instantly attributed to the school rather than the absence of support and guidance from the state. Thus, whilst Muslim communities might be making objective gains, the structures around free schools leave these communities vulnerable to public criticism and Islamophobic media narratives where the mechanisms around *free schooling* reveal themselves to be inadequate. Thus, such mechanisms are inadequate for furthering the expansion of mainstream, state-funded Islamic schooling in a way which politically enfranchises British Muslims through joint-enterprise partnerships with the state. We may have more state-funded Muslim schools, but the nature of these emergent partnerships is such that accountability is not shared where these structures fail. But there is a more serious issue here. The uber-neoliberal foundations which underpin free schools represent the epitome of passivity to Islamophobic discourses which demarcate the boundaries of possibilities for expanding mainstream British Islamic schools for Muslim communities. It is through this passivity, a political act in itself, that the state has acted to position itself in opposition to the interests of British Muslims.

In Conclusion: Identifying Master-Narratives Around British Muslims and Implications for State-Funded Islamic Schooling in Britain

The preceding discussion allows us to identify a series of components to the master-narratives around British Muslims, which have implications for the mobilisation of community interests through denominational Islamic schooling. Firstly, there is substantive evidence above which suggests that Islam has been constructed as 'other to' Britishness and Englishness in the public space. It is argued here that the master-narrative begins with this perspective, and consequently the first component of the master-narrative that can be identified based on the evidence above is the notion that Islam can only ever exist in tension with Britishness or Englishness. This point is far too big to be substantively addressed in this monograph. However, it is important to acknowledge that the positioning of Islam as inevitably problematic in the European/British public space is a crucial component of the master-narrative. Closely related to this, British Muslim communities exist in a political climate within which counter-terror strategies function against a backdrop comprised of media-led narratives around the 'war on terror'. The second component of the master-narrative that can be identified within this context is inherently bound in with the anxieties around Islam in the public space that have been manifested in strategies around counter-terror discussed earlier in this chapter. It is deduced here that one of the discursive by-products of the ways that wider anxieties around threats to national security have played out has been through the implicit policing of Islam within the public space. Thus, the second component of master-narrative that can be identified here is the discursive implication that substantive Islamic influence or mobilisation in the public space should be met with suspicion and concern and therefore needs to be policed, restricted or closely monitored. This positioning of Islam within a wider political climate characterised by anxiety also has significant implications for the political equity available to British Muslims as stakeholders in the state. Whilst master-narratives reinforce the notion of Britain as being a political democracy which advocates freedom of speech, (a principle that, crucially, was at the centre of media debates following the *Charlie Hebdo* attacks in Paris), in reality, the political voices of Muslims are constrained. Counter-terror strategies work in conjunction with media narratives around the 'war on terror' to ensure that being Muslim and speaking out against the state carries with it the risk of being labelled as a threat to national security.

This informs the third component of the master-narrative that can be reasonably identified here: the notion that British Muslims have access to an equitable stake within democratic politics in contemporary Britain. This is clearly an issue which requires sustained attention in new and emergent research on British Muslims and political equity. For our purposes here, critical engagement with this component of the master-narrative is broadly confined to the conceptual discussion offered in Chaps. 2 and 3 of this monograph. However, in the light of those discussions, it can reasonably be established that public political climates around national security impact on Muslims and stifle public political engagement in ways that do not (currently) apply for other ethnic or religious groups. The fourth component is related to the second and third, but is more specifically focused on education. The wider climate of anxiety has permeated education through particular manifestations of the Prevent strategy which has culminated in a culture of surveillance around Muslim children in education. These effects are discursive, in that Muslim interests come to be positioned at the margins of educational provision. One of the ways that this has been manifested is through the misalignment between policy rhetoric and outcomes in terms of both numbers of Muslim schools and the nature of the partnerships they embody with the state. As evidenced in this chapter, policy rhetoric evidently reinforces a fourth component of the master-narrative which asserts that the state has consistently afforded ample opportunities for British Muslims to be politically enfranchised through state-funded denominational Islamic schooling. The critical analysis presented in this chapter has conceptually demonstrated the ways in which this has failed, but research insights will allow us to consider why outcomes appear to be misaligned with policy rhetoric. Finally, drawing on critical discussions around Islamophobia in Chap. 2, it is argued that there is a fifth and double-edged component to the master-narrative which assumes that Muslim schools are likely to be monocultural and, related to this, that the purpose of denominational Islamic schooling for Muslim communities is to satisfy broadly homogeneous 'needs'.

The remainder of the monograph will set out to contest these components of the master-narrative through meeting two primary aims. Firstly, the complexities around *need* and how this is mobilised through denominational Muslim schools will be explored. Secondly, insights gained from exploring *need* and how this is met by independent and state-funded Muslim schools will be used to develop a counter-narrative to contest components two (Islamic mobilisations should be viewed with suspicion and monitored), four (there have been ample opportunities to meet community needs through facilitating state-funded denominational Muslim schools through policy) and five (that Muslim schools are likely to be monocultural with broadly homogeneous 'needs') of the master-narrative identified here. Whilst the foundations for the counter-narrative have been established in this chapter, insights from first-hand research will be used to outline the highly complex and nuanced manifestations of *need* that are embodied in Muslim schools. The counter-narrative presented in subsequent chapters will demonstrate that past and existing frameworks around state funding for denominational schools offer only very particular models of schooling. It is important to recognise that increasing the numbers of state-funded Muslim schools at all represents an important step in increasing the educational enfranchisement, and by proxy the political equity, of British Muslims. However, existing models of state provision for denominational schooling may not facilitate substantive educational enfranchisement given that the vast majority of British Muslims who are stakeholders in Islamic education are currently committing to investing in the independent sector.

The process of contesting these points in the master-narrative will incrementally inform the concluding argument of the monograph. At the centre of the argument is conviction that Muslim schools represent important opportunities for the state to acknowledge and redress the wider political and educational inequity experienced by British Muslims through actively entering into partnerships with Muslim communities. Progress in the 1998–2010 period was slow enough to raise questions about how far New Labour actually was interested in increasing numbers of state-funded Muslim schools. However, for those that were successful, the resulting voluntary-aided schools represented more of a partnership between local government and communities than those currently offered through free schooling. The voluntary-aided sector allows (at least in principle) for schools to seek support and guidance where needed as part of a localised network of institutions—this is not the case for new Muslim free schools (the requirements for qualifying for voluntary-aided status and some of the sacrifices that this sometimes, but not always, requires for Muslim schools will be explored in subsequent chapters). Whilst numbers of Muslim free schools have increased in the post-2010 era, state involvement in these partnerships is minimal. Thus, at the concluding stages, the counter-narrative presented in this monograph will also consider the power dynamics around responsibility and accountability manifested in the new and emergent mechanisms around free schools and the implications that this might have for Muslim communities within wider political climates characterised by anxieties around Islam in the public space.

REFERENCES

Adams, R. (2013). Government Shuts Free School Amid Claims Taxpayers' Money Was Wasted. *The Guardian*. Available at: http://www.theguardian.com/education/2013/dec/13/government-shuts-free-school-discovery-west-sussex

AMS. (2014). Data from the Association of Muslim Schools UK. Website as of 6 October 2014. Available at: http://ams-uk.org/muslim-schools/

BBC. (2013). Al-Madinah Free School in Derby Labelled 'Dysfunctional' by OFSTED. Available at: http://www.bbc.co.uk/news/uk-england-derbyshire-24548690. 17 October 2013.

Beckett, A. (2012). Bradford Free School Fiasco: The Hard Lessons Learned. *The Guardian*. Available at: http://www.theguardian.com/education/2012/sep/10/bradford-free-school-fiasco-lessons

Bolton, P. (2013). *Converter Academies: Statistics*, 12 June 2013, House of Commons Library.

Breen, D. (2009). A Qualitative Narrative of the Transition from Independent to Voluntary-Aided Status: A Problem for the Concept of the Muslim School. In A. A. Veinguer, G. Deitz, D. Jozsa, & T. Knauth (Eds.), *Islam in Education in European Countries – Pedagogical Concepts and Empirical Findings* (pp. 95–112). Münster: Waxmann.

Breen, D. (2013). State-Funded Muslim Schools: Stakeholders and Legitimacy in the UK Context. In J. Miller, K. O'Grady, & U. McKenna (Eds.), *Religion in Education: Innovation in International Research* (pp. 41–57). London: Routledge.

Breen, D. (2014). British Muslim Schools: Institutional Isomorphism and the Transition from Independent to Voluntary-Aided Status. In R. Race & V. Lander (Eds.), *Advancing Race and Ethnicity in Education* (pp. 32–46). Hampshire: Palgrave Macmillan.

CES. (2012). *Collecting Data on Catholic Schools and Colleges*. Catholic Education Service. Available at: http://www.catholiceducation.org.uk/news/ces-blog/item/1000075-collecting-data-on-catholic-schools-and-colleges. Accessed 24 May 2013.

Chadwick, P. (2012). *The Church School of the Future Review*. Church of England Archbishop's Council – Education Division.

Coughlan, S. (2007, May 14). Education, Education, Education. *BBC News*. Available at: http://news.bbc.co.uk/1/hi/education/6564933.stm

DCSF. (2007). *Faith in the System: The Role of Schools with a Religious Character in English Education and Society.* London: Department of Children Schools and Families.

DfE. (2015). *The Prevent Duty: Departmental Advice for Schools and Childcare Providers.* London: Department for Education.

DfEE. (2001). *Schools Building on Success: Raising Standards, Promoting Diversity, Achieving Results.* Norwich: Her Majesty's Stationary Office.

DfES. (2002). *Regulatory Reform (Voluntary-aided Schools Liabilities and Funding) (England) Order 2002.* London: Department for Education and Skills.

DfES. (2005). *Registration of Independent Schools: A Guide for Proprietors on the Statutory Requirements for Registration,* Independent and Education Boarding Team.

Dooley, P. (1991). *Muslim Private Schools.* In G. Walford (Ed.), *Tradition, Change and Diversity.* London: Chapman.

Fekete, L. (2004). Anti-Muslim Racism and the European Security State. *Race & Class, 46*(3), 3–29.

Gillborn, D. (2005). Education Policy as an Act of White Supremacy: Whiteness, Critical Race Theory and Reform. *Journal of Education Policy, 20*(4), 484–505.

Gillborn, D. (2008). *Racism and Education: Coincidence or Conspiracy?* London: Routledge.

Helm, T., Taylor, M., & Davis, R. (2011, February 5). David Cameron Sparks Fury from Critics Who Say Attack on Multiculturalism Has Boosted English Defence League. *The Guardian.* Available at: http://www.guardian.co.uk/politics/2011/feb/05/david-cameron-speech-criticised-edl. Accessed 21 July 2014.

Kershaw, I. (2014). *Investigation Report: Trojan Horse Letter – Report of Ian Kershaw of Northern Education for Birmingham City Council in Respect of Issues Arising as a Result of Concerns Raised in a Letter Dated 27 November 2013, Known as the Trojan Horse Letter.*

Kundnani, A. (2009). *Spooked – How Not to Prevent Violent Extremism.* London: Institute of Race Relations.

Meer, N. (2007). Muslim Schools in Britain: Challenging Mobilisations or Logical Developments? *Asia Pacific Journal of Education, 27*(1), 55–71.

Meer, N. (2009). Identity Articulations, Mobilization, and Autonomy in the Movement for Muslim Schools in Britain. *Race Ethnicity and Education, 12*(3), 379–399.

Meer, N., & Breen, D. (forthcoming). Muslim Schools in Britain: Between Mobilisation and Incorporation. In M. Abu Bakar (Ed.), *Living the Faith Engaging the Mind: Rethinking Madrasah Education in the Modern World.*

Meer, N., & Modood, T. (2009). Refutations of Racism in the 'Muslim Question'. *Patterns of Prejudice, 43*(3–4), 335–354.

Modood, T. (1994). Political Blackness and British Asians. *Sociology, 28*(4), 859–876.

Modood, T. (1998). Anti-essentialism, Multiculturalism and the 'Recognition' of Religious Groups. *The Journal of Political Philosophy, 6*(4), 378–399.

Modood, T. (2008). A Basis for and Two Obstacles in the Way of a Multiculturalist Coalition. *The British Journal of Sociology, 59*(1), 47–52.

Modood, T., & Werbner, P. (1997). *The Politics of Multiculturalism in the New Europe: Racism, Identity and Community.* Hampshire: Palgrave Macmillan.

Parekh, B. C. (2000). *The Future of Multi-ethnic Britain: Report of the Commission on the Future of Multi-ethnic Britain.* London: Profile Books.

Parker-Jenkins, M., Hartas, D., & Irving, B. A. (2005). *In Good Faith, Schools, Religion and Public Funding.* Hampshire: Ashgate Publishing.

Runnymede. (1997). *Islamophobia – A Challenge for Us All.* Runnymede Trust.

Sayyid, S. (2010). Out of the Devil's Dictionary. In S. Sayyid & A. Vakil (Eds.), *Thinking Through Islamophobia: Global Perspectives* (pp. 5–18). El Paso: Cinco Puntos Press.

Sian, K. P. (2015). Spies, Surveillance and Stakeouts: Monitoring Muslim Moves in British State Schools. *Race Ethnicity and Education, 18*(2), 183–201.

Swann, M. (1985). *Education for All: The Report of the Inquiry into the Education of Pupils of Children from Ethnic Minority Groups.* London: HMSO.

Thomas, P. (2009). Between Two Stools? The Government's 'Preventing Violent Extremism' Agenda. *The Political Quarterly, 80*(2), 282–291.

Tinker, C. (2009). Rights, Social Cohesion and Identity: Arguments for and Against State Funded Muslim Schools in Britain. *Race, Ethnicity and Education, 12*(4), 539–553.

UK Government. (2005). *The Schools White Paper: Higher Standards, Better Schools for All.* London: Her Majesty's Stationary Office.

UK Government. (2014). *Types of School: Free Schools,* UK Government Website. Available at: https://www.gov.uk/types-of-school/free-schools. Accessed 3 Jan 2015.

UK Parliament. (1998). *School Standards and Framework Act.* London: Her Majesty's Stationary Office.

UK Parliament. (2010). *The Academies Act.* London: HMSO.

Walford, G. (2003). Muslim Schools in Britain. In G. Walford (Ed.), *British Private Schools: Research on Policy and Practice* (pp. 158–176). London: Woburn Press.

CHAPTER 4

Applying CRT in Research on Muslim Schools

One of the key purposes of Critical Race Theory (CRT) is to offer critical narratives which expose the tacit nature of racism and marginalisation. This is achieved through an emphasis on 'counter-narratives', which are central to developments in CRT. For the purposes of this monograph, it is important to draw a distinction between counter-narratives and counter-storytelling. Drawing on the work of Stanley (2007), counter-narratives within CRT are understood here to embody 'perspectives that run opposite or counter to the presumed order of control' (Stanley 2007: 14). These 'counter-narratives' challenge and deconstruct 'master-narratives' and offer alternatives to dominant discourses (Stanley 2007: 14). One of the purposes of this monograph is to explore how far policies around the state funding of minority faith schools actually offer feasible and satisfactory strategies for Muslim communities to mobilise state-funded schools. Within the New Labour political rhetoric, and more recently the emergence of 'Free Schools', the 'master-narrative' seemingly indicates that accessible strategies are openly available to Muslim communities looking to develop state-funded religious schools. The comparative numbers of independent Muslim schools at approximately 158 (AMS 2014) and state-funded Muslim schools at 21 (AMS 2014) indicate that processes are at work which result in Muslim schools primarily residing in the independent sector. This monograph draws on highly qualitative insights to explore what these processes of exclusion might be as a means of offering a counter-narrative to those master-narratives embodied in policies around the accessibility of state funding for Muslim schools.

© The Author(s) 2018
D. Breen, *Muslim Schools, Communities and Critical Race Theory*,
DOI 10.1057/978-1-137-44397-7_4

Counter-narratives do not merely describe a methodological preference amongst academics with an interest in CRT; there is also an epistemological purpose to counter-narratives which is inherently tied into the convictions which underlie CRT. As argued by Gillborn, a powerful and dangerous dynamic of whiteness is that many (possibly the majority) white people have no awareness of whiteness as a construction, let alone their own role in sustaining and playing out inequities at the heart of whiteness (Gillborn 2005: 490). It is this lack of awareness which serves to cloud the tacit processes of marginalisation which are manifested in phenomena such as interest convergence. Given the complexity of the relationship between white people and whiteness, passivity, in and of itself, can be seen to be a political act (Preston and Chadderton 2012: 92). Preston and Chadderton posit this argument from the position of viewing whiteness as property, and argue that protecting whiteness requires the daily tacit choices by whites in accepting white privilege (Preston and Chadderton 2012: 92). The purpose of counter-narratives then serves to challenge such passivity and exposes tacit processes of racism and marginalisation which otherwise lie hidden. Within the understanding as explored above, counter-narratives might be informed by reviewing both macro and micro processes as a means of offering an informed alternative to master-narratives.

Counter-narratives should be distinguished from the process of 'counter-storytelling' whereby participants offer insights into tacit experiences of exclusion or racist experiences. The research that informs this monograph is centred around the voices of participants within the context of ethnographic research. It is important to clarify here that, for the purposes of this monograph, a CRT framework has been applied to the research as a means of exploring themes which arose that could not be addressed in full in the doctoral research. Therefore, the methodology in the initial research design was formulated without a CRT framework. However, this chapter will demonstrate the suitability of the research methodology and methods employed to a CRT analysis. A consideration of existing literature on CRT methodology will inform the argument that the interviews in the research embody instances of 'counter-storytelling', whereby participants offer highly qualitative insights into the lived experiences of stakeholders in British Muslim schools. Each of these instances of 'counter-storytelling' represents one piece of the wider counter-narrative which is constructed throughout the monograph. This chapter will also draw on existing work to argue that ethnographic research and grounded theory analysis represent a strategy for synthesising long-established methodological traditions in educational research with emergent theoretical developments in CRT. For example, ethnography can be utilised with a grounded theory analysis to construct 'counter-stories' centred around participant voice. However, the wider counter-narrative is also informed by a critical macro analysis of education policies which appear to be targeted at alleviating the experiences of British Muslims (see Chap. 3). Within the analysis of Muslim schools, policy rhetoric demonstrates a sustained focus on encouraging independent Muslim schools to apply for state funding. However, as demonstrated in Chap. 3, the number of schools which have been successful in this regard is limited. Thus, the intention of this monograph is to explore the reasons why so few schools have secured state funding through existing initiatives by drawing on the lived realities of stakeholders in both independent and state-funded Muslim schools. The highly qualitative research is centred around facilitating the 'voices' of participants and allowing opportunities for developing 'counter-stories' within the wider objective of providing a counter-narrative to challenge the master-narrative or discourse embodied in recent and emergent policy rhetoric around state-funded Muslim schools. The chapter concludes by arguing the merits of a symbiotic research strategy whereby ethnography and grounded theory are positioned within the wider CRT rationale of developing and providing counter-narratives.

CRITICAL RACE THEORY: AND METHOD

Before we can establish how particular research strategies might lend themselves to the development of counter-narratives, it is important to identify a coherent sense of purpose in CRT research. Solorzano and Yosso (2002) argue that CRT:

> advances a strategy to foreground and account for the role of racism in education and works towards the elimination of racism as part of a larger goal of opposing or eliminating other forms of subordination based on gender, class, sexual orientation and national origin (Solorzano and Yosso 2002: 25).

The discussion in Chaps. 2 and 3 has rigorously explored the scope for applying CRT in the analysis of British Muslim communities, and intersections of religious and national identity as well as political marginalisation were identified as key factors in anti-Muslim racism. Over Chaps. 2 and 3, it was demonstrated how conditions around the marginalisation of Muslims in the British context draw parallels with the new, more nuanced and less tangible forms of racism at the centre of the CRT tradition. In line with this, it logically follows that religion is undeniably an increasingly relevant factor in the intersections of racialised discrimination in contemporary social settings. Thus, it is argued here that the definition offered by Solorzano and Yosso can be expanded to acknowledge the ways in which 'race' and religion intersect for religious minorities particularly in European political democracies. The following subsections will discuss the centrality of 'voice' in CRT before moving on to discuss counter-storytelling. This section will then conclude by presenting the rationale for considering the interviews conducted for this research as examples of 'voice' suitable for a CRT analysis.

Voice and Counter-Storytelling in CRT

Voice has long been and continues to be identified as a central tenet to CRT (see Ladson-Billings and Tate 1995; Delgado and Stefancic 2000; Chapman 2007; Malagon et al. 2009). The rationale for positioning voice at the centre of CRT is inherently interconnected with the ways in which master-narratives function in the wider social contexts within which marginalised minorities live their lives as social beings. As argued in Chap. 2, a crucial objective of CRT is to provide 'counter-narratives' to challenge the narratives in dominant discourses (Stanley 2007: 14). The process of constructing counter-narratives can be multidimensional, with analysis at both macro and micro levels coming together to inform the new narrative. Whilst counter-narratives can be constructed at the macro level through processes such as secondary analysis (see Gillborn 2009) or policy analysis (see Bell on *Brown vs the Board of Education* 1980), at the micro-level 'voice' can and should be used to inform 'counter-stories' as part of this process. Whilst 'counter-narratives' should not be conflated with 'counter-storytelling', the two are not mutually exclusive. Solorzano and Yosso (2002) define the counter-story as a method of telling stories of those people whose experiences are not often told such as those at the margins of society (Solorzano and Yosso 2002: 32). But the purpose behind counter-storytelling also inevitably results in the counter-story being used as a tool for 'exposing, analysing, and challenging the majoritarian stories of racial privilege' (Solorzano and Yosso 2002: 32). Within this line of thinking, it is understood here that counter-storytelling refers to the process of capturing the voices of individuals and their experiences of racism and marginalisation. Within this understanding, counter-stories would represent a significant contribution to counter-narratives which might also be informed by wider macro CRT analyses of policy and public discourses around 'race' and 'race' inequality.

Whose Voice?

The emphasis on the centrality of voice in CRT methodology is inevitably bound up with how power relations across 'race' are manifested in the wider public space. For Ladson-Billings and Tate (1995: 58):

> The 'voice' component of Critical Race Theory provides a way to communicate the experience and realities of the oppressed, a first step on the road to justice. As we attempt to make linkages between Critical Race Theory and education, we contend that the voice of people of color is required for a complete analysis of the education system.

It is the failure to accommodate the voices of racialised minorities in debates around education that serves as the principal rationale for the centrality of voice in CRT methodology. But the issue here is not just about bringing in voices that have previously been displaced. A much deeper problem is raised around the priority of interests that are sustained by default where the voices of racialised minorities are absent. Considering the implications of absent voices exposes some of the dangers of accepting notions of neutrality. For Solorzano and Yosso (2002), CRT 'challenges traditional claims that educational institutions make toward objectivity, meritocracy, colorblindness, race neutrality and equal opportunity' (Solorzano and Yosso 2002: 26). From this perspective, a CRT methodology in education should challenge white privilege whilst rejecting notions of neutral or objective researchers (Solorzano and Yosso 2002: 26). The sense of purpose here is rooted in concerns about the ideological function implied by a normative or passive acceptance of neutrality. If the voices of racialised minorities are largely ignored or absent in wider discourses around education, then passively accepting 'neutral' notions of objectivity, meritocracy or 'colourblindness' actually equates with ideologically reinforcing white interests. This argument is effectively captured by Malagon et al. (2009) in their synthesis of the work of early CRT scholars. They argue that the state of 'race' relations in a post–civil-rights USA has been maintained by a colour-blind ideology that hid and protected white privilege, while masking racism within the rhetoric of 'meritocracy' and 'fairness' (Malagon et al. 2009: 255). Within this logic the key strategy for countering or rejecting notions of neutrality and objectivity is manifested in the positioning of 'voice' at the centre of CRT methodology.

Clearly, for the purposes of this monograph the voices of Muslim stakeholders in denominational Islamic schooling are at the centre of informing the development of the counter-narrative. Part of that counter-narrative is concerned with clarifying the relatively limited degree to which Muslim communities have been educationally enfranchised in the state-maintained denominational sector. However, part of the counter-narrative is concerned with drawing on participant voice as a means of identifying highly nuanced needs of particular Muslim communities. As demonstrated in Chap. 3, wider master-narratives have been characterised by anxieties around increased Islamic influence in the public space. Existing master-narratives around Muslim schools are characterised by something of a double-edged sword. On the one hand, any evidence of the increasing presence of the Islamic in the public space is met with macro level Islamophobic responses from far-right organisations which equate Islam with a threat to national identity. On the other hand, as this happens at the macro level, any anxieties are founded on notions of increased Islamic influence in public institutions or increased numbers of Islamic public institutions themselves, rather than any meaningful exploration of the quality or character of this influence. It therefore becomes an imperative objective for the remainder of this monograph to explore the very particular and nuanced ways in which the schools in the study sought to fulfil the needs of Muslims. The very essence of the micro-level dimension of the counter-narrative constructed throughout this book is founded upon exploring the vastly diverse characteristics of the schools in the study and their immediate stakeholders.

The Research Design

The main original research consisted of a comparative case study of an independent Muslim primary school (referred to as Medina Primary) and a voluntary-aided Muslim primary school (referred to as Hiqmah School). The comparative case study comprised several integrated ethnographic research methods. In addition, in-depth retrospective interviews were conducted with a head teacher (referred to as Nasira throughout) who had overseen two further Muslim primary schools through the transition from independent to voluntary-aided status. These historical narratives were not based on the life course of the head teacher, but rather focused on the history of two schools. Subsequent chapters offer an in-depth analysis of findings from the interviews, and for the purpose of the monograph 'Al-Falah' and 'Al-Iman' are employed as pseudonyms throughout. The prefix 'Al' is used to easily distinguish the schools where Nasira was head teacher from the two schools where detailed ethnographic data was collected (i.e. Medina Primary and Hiqmah School).

Yin (2003) argues that case studies are the preferred strategy when 'how' or 'why' questions are being posed, when the investigator has little control over events and when the focus is on a contemporary phenomenon within a real-life context (Yin 2003: 1). Numbers of Muslim schools in England are increasing, with small numbers each year entering the state system. Muslim schools that are granted state funding have usually been in the independent sector for several years (see Walford 2003), and so the fact that Muslim schools are slowly moving into the state sector draws attention to the long-term plans of Muslim schools in the independent sector by default. Do they want to continue as independent schools or do they wish to enter the state system? What is the rationale behind either objective?

Muslim schooling in England more generally then is a developing contemporary phenomenon. The effect of state funding on the character of Muslim schools is a new contemporary phenomenon, as state-funded Muslim schools simply did not exist prior to 1998 (Walford 2003: 164). The schools in which the research was conducted represent 'real-life' contexts within which children experience their education, and members of staff experience their occupational lives. With reference to Yin, a case-study approach was employed as the most effective research strategy for addressing the focus of the research. Burgess identifies that the 'case' is open to definition in case-study research (Burgess 2000: 45). Based on this interpretation of case study, the research comprises three cases: the case of Medina primary (informed by ethnographic research), the case of Hiqmah School (informed by ethnographic research) and the case of Nasira and her experiences at Al-Falah and Al-Iman (ethnographic research informed primarily through interviews and a limited amount of observation on site at Al-Falah and Al-Iman). Defining the case in this way facilitates the comparative dimension to the research and clarifies the distinction of employing the case-study approach as a *research strategy*, drawing on ethnographic or highly qualitative *research methods*. Yin argues that case studies are often mistaken for ethnographies, or participant observation (Yin 2003: 12). However, the employment of ethnographic methods does not imply a case study, nor does the case-study approach assume ethnography, or indeed any other data-collection method (Yin 2003: 12–13). Rather, the case-study approach is best considered a research strategy, having grown from the aims and objectives of the research (Yin 2003: 12). Several integrated research methods were used to provide ethnographic accounts from an inside perspective of each school. Observation, semi-structured interviews and documentary analysis were the primary data collection methods employed in the cases of Medina Primary and Hiqmah school. The case study of Nasira was informed primarily by interviews, although some observation was conducted in both Al-Falah and Al-Iman. The original focus for the doctoral research was on the influence of state funding or fee-paying status on provision in the Muslim schools studied. The application of a CRT framework to the research for the purposes of this monograph necessitates a re-visioning of the focus that retains authenticity to the data collected and its analysis. Drawing on the areas covered in Chaps. 1, 2 and 3, the focus of this monograph requires a three-part primary research question:

In what ways did the schools in the study cater to the needs of Muslim stakeholders?
In what ways do frameworks around state funding for denominational faith schools impact on autonomy for Muslim schools?
What are the implications of the above for constructing a counter-narrative around Muslim schools, what happens in them and the extent to which they have autonomy over their provision?

The Rationale for Ethnography

The focus on provision *within* Muslim schools served as the rationale for using ethnographic research methods. However, there are also emergent methodological arguments within CRT which advocate the use of ethnography in CRT research. In practice, applying Hammersley and Atkinson's (1995) definition of ethnography allowed for insights into everyday life *inside* the schools. Their definition of ethnography states:

> In its most characteristic form, it involves the ethnographer participating, overtly or covertly, in people's daily lives for an extended period of time, watching what happens, listening to what is said, asking questions (1995: 1).

This interpretation of ethnography necessitates drawing on a series of qualitative research methods to inform a written narrative with a view to effectively situating the experiences, thoughts and feelings of participants in a given environmental setting. Within the context of CRT research, it has been argued that ethnography has a particular place given some of the issues around epistemology and ontology that surround CRT. The currency that master-narratives yield ultimately raises questions around epistemology and how particular ontologies normatively and discursively reproduce racialised inequalities. For example, Duncan (2005) argues that CRT requires a focus on the interplay of different ontologies that reproduce differing received realities if we are to expose the processes that give oppression and inequality their appearance of normalcy and naturalness (Duncan 2005: 101). Duncan draws on Carspecken's (1996) ontological categories, or states of existence, to illustrate his argument. These states of existence are identified as follows: *subjective ontological categories* that refer to existing states of mind and feelings to which only one actor has access; *objective ontological categories* that refer to existing objects, conditions and events to which all people have access; and *normative–evaluative ontological categories* that refer to existing agreements on the rightness, goodness and appropriateness of certain states of mind and objects (Carspecken 1996 cited in Duncan 2005: 101). Duncan argues that many discourses serve a narrative function in that they offer an understanding of the world which is presented as an exhaustive account, thus obscuring the particularity of its particular perspective and discounting alternative points of view (Duncan 2005: 101). As such they exist within *normative–evaluative ontological categories* (Duncan 2005: 101), and so it would logically follow that master-narratives would also be positioned within this category.

The solution to normative–evaluative ontologies that has been adopted by CRT scholars has been to offer counter-narrative or counter-story (Duncan 2005: 101). These would of course sit within *subjective ontological categories*, which is where the substantiveness of the epistemological base underpinning much CRT research has been critiqued. Duncan identifies that CRT has been criticised for an over-reliance on evidence that derive from *subjective ontological categories* (Duncan 2005: 106). This critique opens up the methodological rationale for employing ethnography in CRT research. Duncan argues that Critical Race Ethnography 'follows the lead indicated by proponents of CRT to take the words of people of colour seriously and, instead of stopping there, to allow these voices to inform how we approach our examination of the material conditions that are basic to and inextricably a part of lived experience' (Duncan 2005: 106). From this position, a Critical Race ethnography seeks to engage the multiple ontological categories that give meaning to lived experience (Duncan 2005: 106). Engaging with multiple ontological categories has implications for the research process as it necessitates 'gathering data from different sources, for example, sociolinguistic, interview, observational, statistical, documentary and so forth, to provide stronger warrants for or even more plausible alternatives to the claims that result from our inquiries' (Duncan 2005: 106). Clearly, from this perspective, participant voice should be situated within an understanding of the research environment informed by multiple research methods. Thus, utilising ethnography in CRT research provides a rigorous strategy for constructing counternarratives based on epistemological foundations that go beyond evidence derived from *subjective ontological categories.*

The Insider/Outsider Debate: Preparation, Ethics, Practice

It is important to take into consideration issues of positionality when undertaking any research. It is important to acknowledge here that the researcher identifies as a white Irish British-born male. One of the key issues raised in research on 'race' and ethnicity is the extent to which the researcher's 'racial' identity impacts on the research process. One of the complexities that was faced in this particular piece of research has been discussed at length in Chap. 3: the extent of ethnic diversity within Islam and the extent to which this will inevitably result in nuanced experiences of Islamophobia or racialised discrimination. A broad range of dynamics across identity is likely to intersect, a process that confuses the compartmentalised thinking around what has been called 'insider/outsider' issues in research. Conversely, it can be demonstrated that ethnicity and religion sometimes have a complex relationship which has important implications for racialised discrimination.

Ethnic Diversity and British Muslims

Although the relationship between ethnicity and Islam is one characterised by ethnic diversity, the single largest group of Muslims in England and Wales (67.6%) fall into the ethnic category of 'Asian or Asian British' (MCB 2014: 24), referring to those of Bangladeshi, Indian, Pakistani,

THE INSIDER/OUTSIDER DEBATE: PREPARATION, ETHICS, PRACTICE 71

Chinese and 'other Asian' descent (ONS 2011). As 'Asian or Asian British' constitutes the single largest group of Muslims in England and Wales, the ways in which my own positionality as a white non-Muslim male could affect the research became a primary concern when preparing for fieldwork. In practice, the problem of making assumptions about ethnicity was realised at the earliest stages of negotiating access to Medina Primary. A meeting was arranged with the head to discuss the possibility of researching the school. Through prior contact I was aware that the head teacher of Medina Primary had reverted to Islam and was of a white ethnic background. This initially seemed to be significant for considering the feasibility of the research in terms of insider/outsider debates. Although initially, at the categorical level, I am an outsider as a non-Muslim, in terms of my own identity as a white male, I shared his ethnicity. However, when discussing which data collection methods would be appropriate, the conversation gave insights into perceptions of ethnicity at Medina Primary and the ways in which gender might affect the research. I explained to the head that a breakdown of the school's intake by ethnicity would be important, and the head's response reflected fatigue with the question. His response was that 'to ask a Muslim about their ethnic background is a bit of an insult, we're trying to move away from all that'.

Considering ethnicity as a contextual point of reference in the early stages of the research raised a series of complex issues and anxieties. These anxieties were amplified when considering interrelationships between ethnicity and gender. Kalwant Bhopal (2000) argues that her shared ethnicity and gender with participants was of great methodological importance for her own research on South Asian women in east London communities. She claims that she negotiated access to situations which simply would not have been accessible to an outsider. Bhopal elaborates, arguing that common 'race' assists the researcher and the researched in placing each other within the social structure, and so this can have a positive bearing on the relationship between the interviewer and the interviewee (Bhopal 2000: 73). According to Bhopal, commonality between the researcher and the researched makes it easier for each party to identify with each other, thus assisting the establishment of a rapport (Bhopal 2000: 73).

Bhopal uses her research experience to argue that shared ethnicity between the researcher and the researched is beneficial. However, examples of research conducted by white male researchers who do not share ethnicity or gender with participants *do* exist and offer insights into the lives of the researched. A good example is Mairtin Mac an Ghaill's *Young*

Gifted and Black (1988) which focused on South Asian and Black female sixth-formers' experiences of school life through retrospective interviews (Mac an Ghaill 1988: 15). His work provided accounts of institutionalised racism within the school, racist teachers, bullying and the social grouping of students in relation to their ethnicity, and retrospective accounts of the allocation of bright Black males to low streams (Mac an Ghaill 1988). Through these insights, Mac an Ghaill's work has contributed to a socio-logical understanding of the position of minority ethnic female students in education. Thus, although there is logic to Bhopal's argument that her ethnic and gender identity assisted her negotiation of access to South Asian women, this is not to say that, for example, white male researchers cannot research minority ethnic communities. The wider academic argu-ment is simply that researchers who do not share their gender and ethnic identity with their respondents will produce different kinds of research to those who do. But in the case of this monograph, there are some quite big questions that need to be acknowledged. Revisiting this research now with a CRT framework raises two key questions that have important overtones with regard to power. The first question to ask has to be 'is it appropriate for me, as a white male who does not identify as Muslim, to facilitate 'voices' of Muslims with regard to the marginalisation of Islamic interests in education?' Secondly, and more painfully, 'is writing a monograph on these issues an act of white supremacy in itself?' With these questions in mind, there is one key way that my positionality can work *to* further a CRT cause and that is to use my own 'whiteness' to decode the *master*-narratives around Muslim schools. From this position, the voices of participants are only ever being used to challenge the discursive effects of master-narratives on British Muslims, however subtle and nuanced those effects might be.

Gender in the Context of Research in Muslim Schools

In addition to my positionality in relation to ethnicity and religion, it is also important to take into consideration gender. Primary schools typically have a higher percentage of female staff than male staff, and all the schools in the study reflected this. My research revealed that gender represented a more consistent point of reference than ethnicity for my positionality as a researcher. High-profile and widespread debate in the first decade of the twenty-first century, particularly concerning the wearing of the *hijab* (headscarf) and *niqab* (veil covering the face) by Muslim women (see Ali 2005; Bigger 2006; Freedman 2004; Hirschmann 1998; Laborde 2005), increased my self-consciousness as a male researcher. Some of my initial concerns were quickly realised. In the first interview with the head of Medina Primary, it became apparent that there were two possible restrictions in terms of gender and the research process. Firstly, a high turnover of female staff in the school had resulted in several teachers having only joined the school a month before the research began. As a result, the head felt that they might be uncomfortable with my presence in the class (although three new teachers did volunteer to be interviewed). The main implication was that I might have only limited access to conduct observation.

The second main concern was that some female staff members might not be comfortable either with being interviewed by me or (solely because they wore the *niqab*) with my presence in their classrooms during observation. The head explained that there were two female class teachers who wore the *niqab*, but that the women only covered their faces when in the presence of men and not when teaching children. My presence as a male in the classroom then would alter the environment as the teacher would have to cover her face. As the only two men in the school were the head and a supplementary specialist in Qur'an and Arabic, my concerns were that it would be unusual for the teachers to be teaching for any length of time whilst wearing the *niqab*. The two potential implications of this were that my presence in the classroom during observation would result in children being taught in a way that they are not familiar with for long periods of time (i.e. not being able to see their teacher's face), and consequently observation notes would not represent typical classroom interaction.

Conducting Research Among Muslim Women: Reality in the Field

Despite early concerns about how issues related to gender might impact on female participants, in practice these anxieties were not realised in any substantive way in the field. For example, when carrying out research at Medina Primary, one of the most forthcoming female participants, the year 2 teacher, wore the *niqab*. She made it clear early on that observation could be conducted in her class whenever other teachers were not available for interviews or observation. In contrast to the concerns developed whilst preparing for the research and in negotiating access, it was not necessarily the case that my presence as a male would alter the teaching environment. For example, the male specialist teacher in Qur'an and Arabic taught supplementary lessons in all of the classes in the school which implies that pupils are familiar with some female teachers wearing the *niqab* during Arabic lessons. On several occasions, our schedules were synchronised so that observation was conducted whilst the *Qur'an* teacher was present. This effectively reduced the extent to which my gender was affecting the teaching environment. Observation was also conducted in the year 2 class on several occasions without the *Qur'an* teacher being present. Also, the classroom itself was located near the school entrance where male parents would periodically enter the school. The year 2 teacher's consequent awareness of the ongoing possibility of men being near her classroom arguably reduced the impact of my own presence.

The above discussion illustrates how preconceptions can develop when preparing for research in apparently 'sensitive' situations. The reality of the research experience highlights the extent to which the pursuit of ethical practice resulted in developing negative preconceptions which turned out to be partially unfounded. Although the emphasis above is on the experiences of conducting observation with only one teacher who wore the *niqab*, in total I interviewed four women (three teachers and one teaching assistant) who wore the *niqab* in the independent school. As the research progressed, the male to female ratio of participants demonstrates that gender was less of an issue than I had anticipated when preparing for the research. As the research progressed and data collection started at the voluntary-aided Hiqmah School, I openly asked the head if there were any issues that I should be aware of as a non-Muslim man researching among Muslim women. She explained:

> It depends upon individuals and how they have understood Islam, and for Muslim members of staff, how they have chosen to practice it. I would normally say not to shake hands for example. Though there are some Muslim women who don't have any problems with that, and distance, in terms of not sitting too close. But other than those two, the rest I think is very much of a personal thing... Some ladies would like to be able to cover their faces whilst they're having a conversation. Some don't like to be interviewed, or have conversations with a male on their own... I know that there are some females who don't like to have eye to eye contact and so those are very much personal choices.

The above illustrates just how individualised the appropriate etiquette can be. The specific advice to avoid close proximity can be taken as a universal given when interviewing women as a male researcher. The individualised nature of the remaining etiquettes outlined above illustrates the extent to which making assumptions about how to engage with Muslim women can be problematic in the research context. A professional etiquette of respect for the female individual best described my approach as a non-Muslim male conducting research with a high proportion of my participants being Muslim women.

Moving from Methodology to Method

The above discussion outlines both the complexities of revisiting the research through the prism of a new theoretical framework. Care has been taken to provide as much transparency as possible around this process and the three-part primary research question has been revisioned in a way that remains true to the authenticity of the data collected and its analysis. Whilst this revisioning of the research within a new framework raises intellectual challenges this chapter has aimed to build on the case for using CRT in the analysis of Muslim communities in Britain. In addition to these intellectual challenges, experiences at the earliest stages of the research also necessitated a consideration of the researcher's positionality relative to participants. Revisiting these discussions for the purpose of the monograph raises further questions about the appropriateness of a white, male researcher facilitating 'voice' on behalf of Muslim, mainly female participants. It is argued here this specific dynamic further necessitates the purpose of the CRT framework. Facilitating 'voice' for Muslim participants *has* to serve the purpose of informing a counter-narrative that challenges master-narratives around Muslim schools in Britain. My role as a white male in this dynamic *has* to be to decode master-narratives with a view to exposing the racialised discursive power dynamics that are manifested within them. The coming chapter will move the discussion on to outline the methods and approaches to data analysis that were used and will further explore the suitability of these approaches in CRT research.

References

Ali, S. (2005). Why Here, Why Now? Young Muslim Women Wearing Hijab. *The Muslim World, 95,* 515–530.

AMS. (2014). Data from the Association of Muslim Schools UK. Website as of 6 October 2014. Available at: http://ams-uk.org/muslim-schools/

Bell, D. (1980). Brown and the Interest-Convergence Dilemma. In D. Bell (Ed.), *Shades of Brown: New Perspectives on School Desegregation* (pp. 90–106). New York: Teachers College Press.

Bhopal, K. (2000). Gender, 'Race' and Power in the Research Process: South Asian Women in East London. In C. Truman, D. M. Mertens, & B. Humphries (Eds.), *Research and Inequality* (pp. 67–79). London: UCL Press.

Bigger, S. (2006). Muslim Women's Views on Dress Code and the Hijaab: Some Issues for Education. *Journal of Beliefs and Values, 27*(2), 215–226.

Burgess, R. G. (2000). Some Issues and Problems in Cross-Cultural Case Study Research. In C. J. Pole & R. G. Burgess (Eds.), *Studies in Qualitative Methodology Vol.6: Cross-Cultural Case Study* (pp. 43–52). New York: Elsevier Science.

Carspecken, P. F. (1996). *Critical Ethnography in Educational Research: A Theoretical and Practical Guide*. New York: Routledge.

Chapman, T. K. (2007). Interrogating Classroom Relationships and Events: Using Portraiture and Critical Race Theory in Education Research. *Educational Researcher, 36*(3), 156–162.

Delgado, R., & Stefancic, J. (2000). *Critical Race Theory: The Cutting Edge (Second Edition)*. Philadelphia: Temple University Press.

Duncan, G. A. (2005). Critical Race Ethnography in Education: Narrative, Inequality and the Problem of Epistemology. *Race Ethnicity and Education, 8*(1), 93–114.

Freedman, J. (2004). Secularism as a Barrier to Integration? The French Dilemma. *International Migration, 42*(3), 5–25.

Gillborn, D. (2005). Education Policy as an Act of White Supremacy: Whiteness, Critical Race Theory and Reform. *Journal of Education Policy, 20*(4), 484–505.

Gillborn, D. (2009). Education: The Numbers Game and the Construction of White Racial Victimhood. In K. P. Sveinsson (Ed.), *Who Cares About the White Working Class?* (pp. 15–22). London: Runnymede.

Hammersley, M., & Atkinson, P. (1995). *Ethnography: Principles in Practice* (2nd ed.). London: Routledge.

Hirschmann, N. J. (1998). Western Feminism, Eastern Veiling, and the Question of Free Agency. *Constellations, 5*(3), 345–368.

Laborde, C. (2005). Secular Philosophy and Muslim Headscarves in Schools. *The Journal of Political Philosophy, 13*(3), 305–329.

Ladson-Billings, G., & Tate, W. F. (1995). Towards a Critical Race Theory of education. *Teacher's College Record, 97*(1), 47–68.

Mac an Ghaill, M. (1988). *Young, Gifted and Black*. Oxford: Alden Press.

Malagon, M. C., Huber, L. P., & Velez, V. N. (2009). Our Experiences, Our Methods: Using Grounded Theory to Inform a Critical Race Theory Methodology. *Seattle Journal for Social Justice, 8*(1), 252–272.

MCB. (2014). *British Muslims in Numbers: A Demographic, Sociology-Economic and Health Profile of Muslims in Britain Drawing on the 2011 Census.* The Muslim Council of Britain's Research and Documentation Committee, London, Muslim Council or Britain.

ONS. (2011). *Ethnicity and National Identity in England and Wales: 2011.* London: Office for National Statistics.

Preston, J., & Chadderton, C. (2012). Rediscovering 'Race Traitor': Towards a Critical Race Theory Informed Public Pedagogy. *Race Ethnicity and Education, 15*(1), 85–100.

Solorzano, D. T., & Yosso, T. (2002). Critical Race Methodology: Counter-Storytelling as an Analytical Framework for Education Research. *Qualitative Inquiry, 8*(1), 23–44.

Stanley, C. A. (2007). When Counter Narratives Meet Master Narratives in the Journal Editorial-Review Process. *Educational Researcher, 36*(1), 14–24.

Walford, G. (2003). Muslim Schools in Britain. In G. Walford (Ed.), *British Private Schools: Research on Policy and Practice* (pp. 158–176). London: Woburn Press.

Yin, R. K. (2003). *Applications of Case Study Research* (2nd ed.). Thousand Oaks: SAGE.

CHAPTER 5

Researching Muslim Schools in Practice

Having discussed the theoretical considerations prior to the research process, I must outline the rationale for the research methods employed. As explained above, the emphasis on observing everyday life inside Muslim schools provided the rationale for an ethnographic approach in each school. The main methods employed at Medina Primary and Hiqmah School were qualitative interviews and observation. The empirical research findings were also supplemented by documentary analysis of school mission statements, curriculum materials and promotional materials designed for parents. This approach collectively provided an ethnographic case study of Medina Primary and Hiqmah School respectively. Retrospective interviews were conducted exclusively with Nasira on-site at both Al-Falah and Al-Iman and were the primary source of data informing the narratives of those schools. However, and as acknowledged in Chap. 4, my observations whilst on-site at the schools did to some degree inform the research findings. It is important to note here that the research conducted with Nasira may only *loosely* resemble ethnography. However, it is equally necessary to acknowledge that observations of the environments at Al-Falah and Al-Iman do inform writings around the contributions from Nasira in this monograph.

ETHNOGRAPHIC INTERVIEWS

Ethnographic interviews were conducted with members of staff at Medina Primary, Hiqmah School and with Nasira. There were two reasons for deciding against interviewing pupils. Firstly, teachers and other members

© The Author(s) 2018
D. Breen, *Muslim Schools, Communities and Critical Race Theory*,
DOI 10.1057/978-1-137-44397-7_5

of staff in Muslim schools contribute to provision on a day-to-day professional basis, and so their insights will be of primary importance in understanding such provision within the context of a voluntary-aided/ independent school. Secondly, one of the schools made it clear early on in the research that organising interviews with children would require an extra workload for staff. Formal letters explaining the purpose of my presence at the school would have to be sent out with an option for parents to reply if they wished their children to be excluded from the research. Involving children directly in interviews would necessarily result in parents becoming active stakeholders in the research. Complications could arise, say, if a parent declared their child should not be interviewed, nor take any part in the research. This could result in confusing implications for conducting observation in classes. In the event that the process of contacting parents did not provoke any complications, administrative staff at the school would still have to identify which children to interview. In schools with intakes of over 200 each, administering this process could indeed be time consuming. Thus, in the interests of symmetry in the research, children were not interviewed at either Medina Primary or Hiqmah School.

As discussed in Chap. 4, theoretical considerations prior to the research resulted in the development of some preconceptions which were not realised in the field. These theoretical considerations and preconceptions can be reduced to one central inference: that the research would be 'sensitive' in its nature. In consequence, from the beginning of the research process, careful consideration was given to appropriate approaches to interviews. Given the nature of the political and media attention concerning faith schools generally during the research period, and on Muslims in particular following the terrorist attacks in New York on 11 September 2001 and the London bombings on 7 July 2005, an approach to interviews was employed which demonstrated awareness of the current climate. Fontana and Frey offer a useful review of different types of interviews (2005). They argue that whereas attitudes to interviewing in the past have centred on ideas of the interview as a neutral tool, more recent trends in qualitative methodology suggest that the interview is historically, politically and contextually bound. According to Fontana and Frey, it has been argued convincingly that the interview is not merely an exchange that consists of asking questions and giving answers, but it is a collaborative effort involving two or more people called 'the interview' (Fontana and Frey 2005: 696). They refer to Scheurich's (1995) assertion that the interviewer is a person, historically and contextually located, carrying unavoidable conscious and unconscious motives, desires, feelings and biases (Scheurich 1995: 241). Fontana and Frey argue that within this approach of *empathetic interviewing*, neutrality is not possible, and therefore taking a stance is unavoidable. They argue that those who adopt the newer, more empathetic approaches take an ethical stance in favour of the individual or group being studied, and so the interviewer becomes an advocate and partner in the study, hoping to be able to use the results to advocate social policies and ameliorate the conditions of the interviewee (Fontana and Frey 2005: 696).

The arguments in support of empathetic interviewing appear to be more realistic than those which describe the interviewer as a cool abstracted individual who collects objective, positivistic data (Fontana and Frey 2005: 705). This is because Fontana and Frey take into consideration the fact that the researcher is human, and they also legitimise unavoidable occurrences (Fontana and Frey 2005: 705). For example, the perception of the interview as a neutral tool rules out the possibility of the interviewer laughing with a respondent or sharing his/her own thoughts on a particular issue, or changing the topic of conversation drastically. Saeeda Shah (2004) pragmatically argues that objectivity, implying neutrality and detachment, is not necessarily desirable on the part of the interviewer and interviewee (Shah 2004: 552). Shah's argument was of particular relevance for the research, as she concludes that 'there are possibilities of misunderstanding, error and bias in every interview situation, which increase with additional variants such as culture' (Shah 2004: 552). For my study, the concept of empathetic interviewing was useful because it takes into consideration the human interaction and thus legitimises the agency of both the researcher and the interviewee.

The interviews were more unstructured than structured in nature, particularly during early stages of the research. Fontana and Frey use an example of Malinowski's approach to research as a means of drawing the distinction between structured and unstructured interviews. According to a diary entry, Malinowski documented becoming annoyed when some of his 'participants' laughed at his questions, and secondly documented talking to villagers about war. Fontana and Frey state that Malinowski committed what structured interviewers would see as two capital offences, firstly he answered questions asked by respondents and secondly, he let his emotions influence him, and thus deviated from the 'ideal' of a cool, distant and rational interviewer (Fontana and Frey 2005: 705). They continue by arguing that Malinowski's example captures the difference between structured and unstructured interviewing, as the former aims at capturing precise data of a codable nature so as to explain behaviour within pre-established categories, whereas the latter attempts to understand the complex behaviour of members of society without imposing any *a priori* categorisation that may limit the field of enquiry (Fontana and Frey 2005: 706). For this reason, I conducted largely semi-structured interviews. Owing to the lack of empirical qualitative research on Muslim schools in England and Wales, the areas of interest which emerged from my data during analysis could not have been predicted. As a result, there were no *a priori* categories which could be employed with any justification. Therefore overly structured interviews would have curbed the data collection process.

Having discussed the theoretical background and rationale behind the approach to interviewing that was employed, it is important that I explain the actual procedure. Prompt sheets were devised for each of the interviews and, after the initial stages of research gained momentum, these were informed by prior findings. For example, typically when interviewing a teacher, I would refer to a particular session of observation in her class (see the discussion of Agar below). Pole and Lampard argue that many researchers deploy a combination of structured and unstructured approaches during the same interview, as some questions may require a short, standardised or numerical response, whereas others may require an expansive response from the interviewee (2000: 128). Examples of this arose repeatedly during the research process. During interviews, there were numerous examples of the interview fluctuating from structured to unstructured and vice versa. For example, on one occasion when I asked Nasira how many children at Al-Falah were representative of the local Pakistani Muslim community, the answer given was a numerical estimate, but a discussion of South Asian communities, the history of migration, and differentiation between religious and ethnic groups followed. Consistently with Pole and Lampard (2000: 128), fluctuation between a structured and unstructured approach in the interviews was employed, giving scope for interviewees to introduce topics through two-way *empathetic* interviews.

The ways in which prompt sheets for the interviews were devised developed over time. Prompt sheets became more focused as relevant concepts emerged. The first prompt sheet for the interview with the head of Medina Primary arose from issues, conflicts and limitations in existing literature concerning faith schooling, which had become apparent through background reading. A methodical approach was employed whereby interviews conducted during the early stages of data collection were predominantly unstructured until concepts began to emerge. As the process developed, emerging concepts laid the foundations for further interview prompt sheets. Subsequently, there was a trend for interviews to be more structured and focused as the data collection process developed. It is worth noting here that the trend for interviews to become more focused over time suited the format which the research eventually took. Whilst the ethnography was conducted over nine weeks at Medina Primary, the research at Hiqmah School was conducted over a seven-week period. Early research experiences at Medina were invaluable in tightening up interviews and collecting data over a shorter period of time at Hiqmah.

As explained by Pole and Lampard, interviews which do not make use of a rigid schedule of questions, and in which there is a capacity for the interviewer to explore issues as they arise, are often seen as providing inside accounts of social phenomena with the interviewer and interviewee having a close relationship based on a conversation (2000: 131). My research experience prior to the doctoral research indicated that the tightening up of interviews developed simultaneously along with familiarity and subsequent rapport with participants. An ethnography of a Catholic primary school was carried out as the original research for my MSc dissertation and later informed a peer-reviewed journal publication (see Breen 2009). Consistent with Burgess (1988), earlier interviews during both my MSc and doctoral research were concerned with asking numerous questions and largely consisted of the teacher talking to me as an 'informant' (Burgess 1988: 138). For Burgess, prompts for interviews which occurred later on were more concerned with challenging a respondent on certain recurring issues. During the research at Medina and Hiqmah, it was the later interviews which were more likely to take the form of two-way conversations. During this time, prompt sheets became more focused, as lists of searching questions gave way to pointers concerning issues which laid the foundation for informed two-way conversations.

As demonstrated above, a conversational approach to interviews was employed in conducting largely empathetic, semi-structured interviews. In referring to interviews as 'conversations', Burgess (1988) promotes a naturalistic approach to research, arguing that in educational research, it is important to develop the conversational style with participants, or 'informants' as a means of gaining access to information (Burgess 1988: 138). Referring to interviews as conversations implies the kind of two-way

84   5 RESEARCHING MUSLIM SCHOOLS IN PRACTICE

relationship between the researcher and the informant discussed by Fontana and Frey (2005). Consistent with Burgess, a conversational style was employed with the intention that it would encourage participants to volunteer information (Burgess 1988: 138). Although I had been anxious that my gender would lead to problems in the field (see the discussions concerning gender in Chap. 4), I considered that the conversational style was a necessary facet of developing rapport with female interviewees.

PARTICIPANT OBSERVATION

In addition to interviews, access was negotiated to conduct participant observation at both Medina Primary and Hiqmah School. Observation took place during classes at both schools in the comparative case study and also assemblies and prayers at Medina. Observation was of central importance in establishing the 'real-life context' to which Yin (2003) refers, and it contextualised each 'case' of Muslim schooling. This process is demonstrated in the example given above whereby observation notes informed prompt sheets prior to interviewing class teachers. Another example was my observation of prayers prior to my discussing with a teacher the process by which children learn to practise Islam. Qualitative interviews collect data which is entirely comprised of the spoken word, or 'talk' (Agar 1996: 161), whereas the use of observation helped to broaden the spectrum of data collection to include non-verbal interaction, the layout of classrooms, group behaviour, collective worship and visual trends. A good example of this was the issue of whether or not the *hijab* (headscarf for girls) was compulsory in each school. The level of observance was immediately obvious to me when I entered classrooms. However, on the basis of interviews with teachers, without conducting observation, the level of observance would have been harder to establish.

Fieldnotes were taken as the primary means of collecting data from observation. Throughout the research process, I also kept an audio diary in which I recorded accounts of the day's events. As audio diary entries were recorded accounting events retrospectively, their primary purpose was to inform the overall development of the research. Fieldnotes taken in the class provided the most concrete record of the observation conducted. Scholars express mixed views on the usefulness of fieldnotes in data collection. For example, Hammersley and Atkinson (1995) state that fieldnotes represent relatively concrete descriptions of social processes in their contexts (1995: 175). They proceed to argue that sound academic practice is necessary if fieldnotes are to be of any use, arguing that poor note-taking in recording observation is like using an expensive camera with poor-quality film (Hammersley and Atkinson 1995: 175). Agar (1996) has a more critical perspective on fieldnotes. Through stressing the importance of the relationship between observation and interviews, he argues that fieldnotes should only ever be used as a means to an end, either in contextualising a previous interview or setting the agenda for the next (Agar 1996: 161). The central theme of Agar's argument is that that when employing observation and interviews, they interact with each other simultaneously or sequentially in ethnographic research (Agar 1996: 158). Thus interviews provide a context for observational research, yet they also provide an arena within which to discuss what has been observed (Agar 1996: 161). He accepts that observation is critical for understanding and providing accounts of events, but that if observation is conducted before any interviews have taken place, then the researcher has yet to establish what the relevant concepts are and thus has no idea of what to record (Agar 1996: 161).

Chronologically the earliest stages of the research took place at Medina Primary. Following an initial interview with the head clarifying the terms of access, the first stages of data collection were sessions of observation in the classroom. This experience highlighted the nature of the relationship between interviews and observation in practice. The interview with the head had raised some areas of interest which informed the focus of early observation sessions. As the interview was conducted prior to any other fieldwork, the topics raised were simply 'working topics' (e.g. the use of Arabic in the classroom) which developed or changed over time, constantly informed by developments in the data collection. Although Agar's argument focuses on a critique of fieldnotes it can also be applied just as easily to semi-structured interviews. Prompt sheets or interview schedules which are devised before the data collection has begun cannot possibly predict what the relevant concepts are going to be. This particular limitation which Agar has associated with observation is relevant to the early stages of data collection in ethnographic research in general and thus does not stand as a criticism of observation alone or the use of fieldnotes in data analysis.

Agar develops his criticism of fieldnotes, through arguing that in observational research, notes have to be made, and therefore time has to be taken to write. This inevitably draws the attention of the researcher from observing what is happening, to writing what has just happened. While the researcher is writing notes to record observations, his or her concentration is elsewhere (Agar 1996: 161). Agar infers from this that fieldnotes can only ever offer 'patchy' data (Agar 1996: 161). His criticisms are interesting because he is less critical of the concept of observation itself but is more concerned with inherent problems in *accessing* what has been observed so that it can be tapped, accurately, as data later on.

Agar's solution to this problem with fieldnotes is that 'talk' (i.e. qualitative interviews) should be central to research (Agar 1996: 161). There is an inherent problem with this assumption which derives from the argument that all research is flawed. Any social science research inherently involves a researcher or researchers, and as such is human dependent. For example, even statistical tests are chosen on quantitative data sets based on theoretical assumptions and currently accepted models of best practice. Similarly, researchers are reliant on the responses of humans in social science research. Agar regards 'tape-recorded' accounts of interviews as solid, reliable sources of data. However, if we are to accept that all research is dependent on humans, it is unclear how relying on the researcher's memory for the construction of fieldnotes is any less accurate than relying on the memory of the interviewee. As an empirical social scientist one is dependent on memory when using the medium of interviews or observation for data collection. As a result it is not useful to play one approach off against the other as a means of establishing which approach is more reliable. The strength in Agar's argument lies in the emphasis placed on a relationship between interviews and observation in the ethnographic context, rather than the need to establish one method as more effective than another. The practicalities of the research environment should inform the researcher as to what data collection methods are appropriate in a given instance.

As discussed above, prior to the fieldwork, there were some anxieties related to the potential problems for a male researcher specifically in relation to Muslim women. Although they were displaced throughout the research process, at the earliest stages of observation at both schools some fears proved to have some basis. As demonstrated in the discussion above, my presence would prompt female teachers and teaching assistants who wore the *niqab* to cover their faces in classes. My intention was, as far as possible, to avoid altering the educational environment, but this was only possible to a point. At both Medina Primary and Hiqmah School the assistant head and deputy head respectively adopted the role of organising access to interviews and observation. The shortness of notice given, both to the teachers and myself, sometimes resulted in my conducting observation in classes as the only male present with either a teacher or teaching assistants who wore the *niqab*. It is also worth noting that there was a higher staff turnover at Medina Primary compared with Hiqmah School, and this meant that there were some newer staff members who wore the *niqab* who were less keen on being observed whilst teaching. This scenario led me to interviewed veiled women who were new to the school with a focus on discussing their classes, rather than observing in the field. The above demonstrates the ethical complexities of conducting observation but also illustrates how certain data collection methods may be more appropriate at certain times owing to the practicalities of the research environment.

Using Grounded Theory for Data Analysis

There has been an emphasis throughout this chapter on developing the rationale behind methods not only from a practical methodological perspective but also in terms of epistemology. An ethnographic approach to data collection implies a 'grounded theory' (Glaser and Strauss 1967; Strauss and Corbin 1997; Corbin and Strauss 2008) approach to data analysis whereby concepts emerge during data analysis. Data collected from empathetic interviews and observation allowed for a 'grounded theory' approach to data analysis. This in turn allowed for the depth and scope necessary to discuss emerging concepts.

However, it is also important to identify the applicability of grounded theory analysis to Critical Race Theory given the repositioning of the research within a CRT framework in this monograph. Recent methodological debates in CRT have identified emergent frustrations with traditional modes of qualitative data collection and analysis. Part of this argument is inevitably bound up in the wider ways in which data collection and analysis processes facilitate the positioning of findings within existing bodies of knowledge. This point is most clearly articulated by Malagon et al. (2009), who argue that CRT necessitates the adoption of research methodologies that are critically sensitive in their abilities to situate lived experience within a broader socio-political frame—both in the final research product and throughout the entire research process (Malagon et al. 2009: 253). Counter-storytelling is clearly focused on facilitating participant 'voice' with a view to informing the development of wider counter-narratives. Grounded theory arguably provides a framework within which counter-stories can be positioned within wider socio-political frameworks. Malagon et al. acknowledge that grounded theory was not developed as a methodology for collecting knowledge and building theory from the lived experiences of 'People of Color' (Malagon et al. 2009: 259). Yet there remains a strong rationale to argue that 'when used in partnership with a critical race framework, the researcher can utilize grounded methodology to interpret the perspectives and voices of the narratives that remain unacknowledged, invalidated, and distorted in social science research' (Malagon et al. 2009: 259). Parallels can also be drawn between the centrality of voice in CRT and the ability for grounded theory to facilitate new or novel contributions to knowledge roots in the data itself. Furthermore, grounded theory allows for a sense of continuity from the point of identifying participants based on their ability to provide new insights and positioning those insights within a wider socio-political narrative. Indeed, Malagon et al. argue that this component of grounded theory is attractive to the CRT researcher as sampling can be approached with a view to theory construction, instead of population representativeness (Malagon et al. 2009: 261).

It is important at this stage to clarify the interpretation and approach to grounded theory that was used in the data analysis process. Corbin and Strauss (2008) describe grounded theory analysis as involving coding, the process of taking raw data and raising it to the conceptual level (Corbin and Strauss 2008: 66). This involves interacting with the data using techniques such as asking questions about the data, making comparisons between the data, and in doing so, deriving concepts to stand for those data and then developing those concepts in terms of their properties and dimensions (Corbin and Strauss 2008: 66). For Corbin and Strauss, being an analyst means using common sense and making choices about when and what bits of data to ask questions about (Corbin and Strauss 2008: 71). Analysts have to follow their instincts about what seems important in data and continue from there. Corbin and Strauss argue that there is no right or wrong in this approach to data analysis, nor is there a set of rules or procedures that must be followed. Analysis is largely intuitive and requires trusting the self to make the right decisions (Corbin and Strauss 2008: 71).

Corbin and Strauss' conviction that analysis is intuitive and requires the researcher to trust themselves in making the right decisions was the underlying reason why NVivo was not used for data analysis. The benefits and limitations of using Computer-Assisted Qualitative Data Analysis Software

(CAQDAS) such as NVivo are increasingly being discussed in methodological debate. For example, fervent critics have argued that CAQDAS programmes can assist the analyst in organising documents, categorising them and facilitating searches within documents. However, the process of interpreting and building results from categories and developing the relationships between them has to come from the researcher (Carvajal 2002: 9), and so computers and CAQDAS programmes do not and cannot *analyse* data (Roberts and Wilson 2002: 21, Carvajal 2002: 9, Kelle 1995: 3). Roberts and Wilson (2002) go as far to argue that CAQDAS and qualitative research have developed from opposing philosophical standpoints. They argue that there are fundamental differences between the philosophies which on the one hand underpin information and communication technology (ICT) and on the other the philosophical thinking behind qualitative research (Roberts and Wilson 2002: 5). From this perspective, computing technology assumes a positivistic approach to the natural world composed of objects that humans can study, understand and manipulate (Roberts and Wilson 2002: 5). Within sociology generally, this positivistic orientation encompasses the idea, copied from the natural sciences, that social phenomena can be counted, measured or otherwise quantified and that there is a particular process that allows 'true understanding to be arrived at' (Roberts and Wilson 2002: 5).

The highly qualitative focus of the research served as the rationale for adopting an entirely manual approach to coding the data. It was also felt that an entirely manual approach would better facilitate an integrated approach to data collection and analysis, whereby analysis occurs throughout the data collection process. Corbin and Strauss describe the process of coding as extracting concepts from raw data and developing them in terms of their properties and dimensions (Corbin and Strauss 2008: 159). The emergent concepts can range from lower level to higher level, with higher-level concepts representing themes which tell us what a group of lower-level concepts are indicating (Corbin and Strauss 2008: 160). Coding involves the researcher scrutinising data in an attempt to understand what is being expressed in the raw data. The researcher then delineates a conceptual name to describe that understanding. Coding in this way requires putting aside preconceived notions about what the researcher expects to find and letting the data and interpretation of it guide analysis (Corbin and Strauss 2008: 160). Concepts can then be linked together into a theoretical whole, whereby theory denotes a set of well-developed themes and concepts that are systematically interrelated through statements

90   5 RESEARCHING MUSLIM SCHOOLS IN PRACTICE

of relationship to form a theoretical framework that explains some phenomenon (Corbin and Strauss 2008: 55). The cohesiveness of the theory occurs through the use of an overarching explanatory concept. That overarching concept, taken together with the other concepts, explains the what, how, when, where and why of something (Corbin and Strauss 2008: 55).

During the data analysis, themes initially began to reveal themselves when transcribing interviews. Although ideas, leads and indeed restrictions had informed and shaped the data collection process in the field, it was through transcribing interviews that themes began to emerge in fully coherent ways. At the earliest stages of coding, numerous themes appeared, spread across the data. These emergent themes, and later on fully developed lower-level concepts, served to inform the data collection in a reciprocal relationship where interview schedules evolved over time. As the coding of interviews continued, consistencies with emergent themes were found in the observation data. Some of these early themes developed dramatically as more of the data were coded. Other themes which appeared at the early stages of coding ceased to develop much. An integral part of this process early on was the ongoing comparison of existing and emergent themes with a view to identifying substantive lower-level concepts. This constant comparative method, where there is a simultaneous engagement of data collection and analysis, is one of several characteristics of grounded theory that lends itself effectively to CRT methodology (Malagon et al. 2009: 261). Over time relationships between like themes strengthened, and it became clear that in some instances, groups of coded data were pointing towards a common lower-level concept. Accordingly, these codes were collapsed once a common theme took shape between them.

Conclusion

The rationale for the key data collection methods employed and the approach to data analysis has been discussed. A conversational approach to interviews helped the development of rapport with the interviewees, which in turn helped to facilitate participant 'voice'. A largely empathetic approach to interviews was employed as a means of moving beyond the methodological assumption that the interview is a neutral tool. Participant observation contributed to the process of developing emerging concepts and prompt sheets for interviews and also offered insights into issues and themes which would otherwise have remained un-contextualised. Fieldnotes provided accurate accounts of data in their own right and were fully integrated with developments arising from interviews. The central aim of this chapter has been to communicate methodological transparency in the research process as a means of contextualising research findings in the chapters which follow. The above discussion has considered the theoretical assumptions underlying the methods employed in the research and in doing so has illustrated the rationale for ethnography, more specifically largely *empathetic* interviews and observation, in relation to methodological and epistemological implications.

One final point to note revolves around the repositioning of the research findings within a CRT framework. The contributions and insights from participants that are discussed in subsequent chapters emerged out of the data. Ideally the data collection would have been approached through a CRT lens at the time of data collection. However, the fact that this was not the case does not limit the extent to which CRT can be applied here. As Malagon et al. argue:

> a prior theoretical framework like CRT is necessary to emancipatory theory building. A CRT framework may influence what is observed, how discussion topics arise, and so forth, but the emerging theory is driven by the data, not by a theoretical framework. Accordingly, as anti-racist, social justice scholars, we use the synergy between CRT and grounded theory in our research as we connect everyday life experiences of People of Color to systemic processes of oppression. (Malagon et al. 2009: 263)s

The data-driven character of grounded theory research indicates that the concepts that emerged in the data analysis should be substantial enough to offer insights that can be discussed within a CRT framework. This argument, coupled with reflections following the research and the socio-political framing of narratives afforded within CRT, ultimately led to the decision to revisit the research findings from a Critical Race Theory perspective. It is important again to clearly acknowledge the reframing of the research and the implications that this has for the format of the discussion in chapters that follow. This monograph draws in insights from a piece of grounded theory doctoral research to inform a CRT discussion around Muslim schools. For the remainder of the monograph, these discussions are arranged around four key issues relevant for constructing counter-narratives rather than the initial lower-level and higher-level concepts themselves. The original thesis with full details of the higher- and lower-level concepts can be accessed through the University of Warwick library here http://wrap.warwick.ac.uk/35176/

REFERENCES

Agar, M. H. (1996). *The Professional Stranger: An Informal Introduction to Ethnography* (2nd ed.). London: Academic Press Limited.

Breen, D. (2009). A Qualitative Narrative of the Transition from Independent to Voluntary-Aided Status: A Problem for the Concept of the Muslim School. In A. A. Veinguer, G. Deitz, D. Jozsa, & T. Knauth (Eds.), *Islam in Education in European Countries – Pedagogical Concepts and Empirical Findings* (pp. 95–112). Münster: Waxmann.

Burgess, R. G. (1988). Conversations with a Purpose: The Ethnographic Interview in Educational Research. In R. G. Burgess (Ed.), *Studies in Qualitative Methodology: Conducting Qualitative Research* (Vol. 1, pp. 137–156). London: JAI Press.

Carvajal, D. (2002). The Artisan's Tools: Critical Issues When Teaching and Learning CAQDAS. *Forum Qualitative Sozialforschung/Forum: Qualitative Social Research*, *3*(2), article 14, [47 paragraphs], http://nbn-resolving.de/urn:nbn:de:0114-fqs0202147. Accessed 1 Aug 2010

Corbin, J., & Strauss, A. (2008). *Basics of Qualitative Research* (3rd ed.). Thousand Oaks: SAGE.

Fontana, A., & Frey, J. H. (2005). The Interview: From Neutral Stance to Political Involvement. In N. K. Denzin & Y. S. Lincoln (Eds.), *The SAGE Handbook of Qualitative Research* (pp. 695–727). Thousand Oaks: SAGE.

Glaser, B. G., & Strauss, A. L. (1967). *The Discovery of Grounded Theory.* Chicago: Aldine Publishing.

Hammersley, M., & Atkinson, P. (1995). *Ethnography: Principles in Practice* (2nd ed.). London: Routledge.

Kelle, U. (1995). Introduction: An Overview of Computer-Aided Methods in Qualitative Research. In U. Kelle (Ed.), *Computer-Aided Qualitative Data Analysis: Theory, Methods and Practice* (pp. 1–17). London: SAGE.

Malagon, M. C., Huber, L. P., & Velez, V. N. (2009). Our Experiences, Our Methods: Using Grounded Theory to Inform a Critical Race Theory Methodology. *Seattle Journal for Social Justice*, *8*(1), 252–272.

Pole, C., & Lampard, R. (2000). *Practical Social Investigation: Qualitative and Quantitative Methods in Social Research.* London: Prentice Hall.

Roberts, K. A., & Wilson, R. W. (2002). ICT and the Research Process: Issues Around the Compatibility of Technology with Qualitative Data Analysis. *Forum Qualitative Sozialforschung/Forum: Qualitative Social Research, 3*(2), article 23, [52 paragraphs], http://nbnresolving.de/urn:nbn:de:0114fqs0202234. Accessed 1 Aug 2010.

Scheurich, J. J. (1995). A Postmodernist Critique of Research Interviewing. *Qualitative Studies in Education, 8,* 239–252.

Shah, S. (2004). The Researcher/Interviewer in Intercultural Context: A Social Intruder! *British Education Research Journal, 30*(4), 549–575.

Strauss, A., & Corbin, J. (1997). *Grounded Theory in Practice.* London: SAGE.

Yin, R. K. (2003). *Applications of Case Study Research* (2nd ed.). Thousand Oaks: SAGE.

CHAPTER 6

Muslim Schools as Mobilisations of Interests: How Islamic Schools Come into Being

As noted in Chap. 4, the primary purpose of this monograph is to address the three-part research question:

1. In what ways did the schools in the study cater to the needs of Muslim stakeholders?
2. In what ways do frameworks around state funding for denominational faith schools impact on autonomy for Muslim schools?
3. What are the implications of the above for constructing a counter-narrative around Muslim schools, what happens in them and the extent to which they have autonomy over their provision?

This chapter serves to start the process of addressing the above primarily through offering insights into how Islamic interests come to be mobilised in the form of Muslim schools. This chapter explores the ways in which each of the Muslim schools in this study came into being. Exploring these processes serves as a strategy for identifying the initial purpose behind provision in each case. All of the schools in the study were founded as independent schools, and consequently this chapter is primarily concerned with the identification of need and provision where Muslim interests come to be mobilised through independent Islamic schools. Exploring the independent education sector as a site for mobilisation of Islamic interests allows us to gain insights into the ways in which Muslim schools cater to the needs of Muslim stakeholders. The chapter draws on first-hand research insights to lay the foundation stone for the process of

© The Author(s) 2018
D. Breen, *Muslim Schools, Communities and Critical Race Theory,*
DOI 10.1057/978-1-137-44397-7_6

95

addressing the research question 'in what ways did the schools cater to the needs of Muslim stakeholders?' This in turn represents the first step in taking the counter-narrative in its conceptual state as it is presented at the end of Chap. 3 and further developing it, drawing on first-hand, highly qualitative research findings centred around participant voice.

THE INDEPENDENT SECTOR: A SITE FOR ISLAMIC SCHOOLING

This chapter is the first of three chapters which detail insights from the research that informs this monograph. Each chapter will focus on one key issue as part of the wider counter-narrative constructed throughout this monograph. These key issues are as follows: *Muslim schools as mobilisations of interests: how Islamic schools come into being; community, connectivity and nuanced needs; and manifesting educational and Islamic interests in independent and state-funded contexts*. This chapter will focus on Muslim schools as representing mobilisations of community interests and will also detail the origin stories of each of the four schools that took part in the research process. Whilst the structure of the research was detailed in Chaps. 4 and 5, it is important to establish that each of the four schools where data was collected started life in the independent sector. Under part 10 of the Education Act 2002, all independent schools in the English education system have to register with the Department for Education and Skills (DfES, now the Department for Education, DfE) before the school begins operation (DfES 2005: 1). According to the DfE, an independent school is defined as 'any school which provides full-time education for five or more pupils of compulsory school age or one or more such pupils with an EHC (Education, Health and Care) plan or statement of special educational needs or who is "looked after by a local authority" and is not a school maintained by a Local Authority or a non-maintained special school' (DfE 2016: 5). Registering with the DfE binds independent schools to fulfil certain criteria related to several aspects of the school's provision. Registration requires the school to submit documents illustrating how content focused on developing children's linguistic, mathematical, scientific, technological, human and social and aesthetic and creative skills will be integrated into the school curriculum (DfES 2005: 11–12).

These regulations are not intended to be prescriptive concerning the curriculum, and they do not require the school to follow the national curriculum. However, the school should give experience in the relevant areas (DfES 2005: 11). It is compulsory for all independent schools as defined above to be registered with the DfE. Illustrating the requirements of independent schools within the policy framework reveals that although less constrained than voluntary-aided schools, independent Muslim schools in the English education system are still required to fulfil certain criteria. Moreover, the shifts in policy frameworks around maintained faith schools since 2010 have also resulted in the advocation of denominational free schools, a model which has borrowed heavily from the independent sector. This may seem like a fairly liberal solution for independent Muslim schools which might be looking for state funding without having to subscribe to the level of regulation required in the voluntary-aided sector. However, the implications of this new mechanism for faith schools and some of the risks that might be faced by Muslim communities looking to utilise them have been outlined in detail in Chap. 3. One element of regulation which is required for all independent schools is participation in compulsory inspections by either OFSTED or the Independent Schools Inspectorate. The extent to which independent schools fulfil relevant criteria is monitored with compulsory inspections taking place at least once every six years (DfES 2005: 24). These inspections cost a given school between £200 (at £40 per pupil for a school with five pupils) and the maximum charge of £10,000. Whilst there are Muslim schools within the independent sector, these institutions can typically expect to face economic instability for a number of reasons which are discussed later in this chapter and throughout subsequent chapters. As it will become clear, for some Muslim schools the prospect of consistently providing the economic resources required to facilitate compulsory inspections is likely to be particularly challenging.

However, the regulation of independent schools also extends to elements of provision around spiritual, moral, social and cultural development (DfES 2005: 12). The primary mechanisms for meeting these requirements are identified as personal, social and health education (PSHE) and religious education (DfES 2005: 12). Furthermore, as alluded to above, the Academies Act 2010 has served to significantly blur the lines between state-funded and independent schools. This can be demonstrated when looking at the recent statutory duty for independent and maintained schools to promote 'fundamental British values', which is assessed through OFSTED inspections (the implications of this statutory duty for Muslim schools are at the centre of other emerging work by this author, and as such we will not go into detail here). Specifically, the *Revised Prevent Duty Guidance: for England and Wales* (2015) states that:

> independent schools set their own curriculum but must comply with the Independent School Standards, which include a specific requirement to promote fundamental British values as part of broader requirements relating to the quality of education and to promoting the spiritual, moral, cultural and cultural development of pupils. These standards also apply to academies (other than 16–19 academies), including free schools, as they are independent schools (DfE 2015: 10).

The above extract clearly communicates the identification of academies and free schools as 'independent schools' in emergent statutory guidance. For private, fee-paying independent schools that receive no state funding, it is clear that owing to registration requirements, the economic implications of compulsory inspections and the regulation of critical aspects of denominational faith provision including the duty to promote 'fundamental British values', independent Muslim schools are not as free to act as they may initially appear to be. As evidenced in Chap. 3, current figures indicate that the conversion of local authority schools to academy status is steadily progressing. Moreover, the now-withdrawn proposal by the former Conservative education secretary Nicky Morgan for all schools to become academies by 2022 (Adams 2016) ultimately exposed the extent to which the government would be willing to support the removal of local authorities from compulsory education altogether. Evidence would suggest that we are moving towards a system whereby the central mechanisms for the regulation and assessment of schools employ a universal 'one size fits all' approach. Within this line of thinking, it is not beyond the realm of possibility to envisage all schools being referred to as 'independent', with a proportion of those schools identified as academies and free schools which receive state funding. It is important to acknowledge that the first-hand data informing this monograph was collected before the advent of the Academies Act 2010, and so at the time of the research the distinction between 'state-funded' and 'independent' schools was much more clearly demarcated than it has been in recent years. In line with this, and to avoid confusion, for the remainder of this monograph the term 'independent school' will refer to schools which are registered as an independent school, and which are free to have a denominational religious character, but which do not receive any state funding. The term 'state-funded school' will refer to schools which do receive funding from the state such as voluntary-aided schools, academies and free schools which are free to have a denominational religious character. Given that each school that took part in the research was founded as an independent Muslim school, this chapter will now move on to explore their origin stories. Initially the two schools within which detailed ethnographic research was conducted will be introduced, namely Medina Primary and Hiqmah School. The chapter will then move on to introduce 'Nasira' and discuss her role at Al-Falah and Al-Iman.

Introducing Medina Primary: Positioning the School Within the Independent Sector

Medina Primary is a comparatively small Muslim school in England's independent education sector. Traditionally independent schools are fee-paying schools and reviewing the level of fees a given independent school charges gives an insight into elements of the school such as size, boarding/non-boarding, reputation, prestige and so on. An example of one of the schools at the high end of the fee-paying spectrum is an independent Catholic school which was originally to be the comparator school for Medina Primary in the earliest stages of the research design. This particular two-tier Catholic school (with primary- and secondary-level provision) had annual fees of over £25,000 in 2005, whereas parents at Medina Primary pay comparatively little at £1250–£1400 per year. Medina Primary then is on the lower end of the fee-paying spectrum within the context of the independent education sector in England and Wales. The comparatively low fees at Medina Primary reflect certain characteristics of the school to an extent. The school is based in a main building with two mobile units located behind the playground. The main building houses the Masjid (prayer room), reception area, the secretary's office, the children's cloakroom area, two classrooms on one corridor for foundation 1 and foundation 2 (nursery) and two classrooms on a parallel corridor for years 1 and 2. Classrooms for years 3 and 4 are in a mobile unit located behind the main school building, and years 5 and 6 are based in a mobile unit to the side of the main school building. Although a small-sized building, Medina Primary is a one-form entry school admitting around 30 pupils to year 1 each year and catering for around 230 pupils in total (the exact figure is constantly fluctuating and increasing as families on the waiting list fill empty spaces). However, classrooms are not crowded. A large proportion of pupils can be accounted for in the foundation 1 and foundation 2 classes, each of which consists of two groups, one attending in the morning and one in the afternoon. With an internal policy of having an absolute upper limit of 30 pupils in any one class, the foundation 2 cohort is halved each year as the classes, consisting of both the morning and afternoon groups, enter year 1. Foundation classes alone then can account for up to 120 of the school's pupils at any one time. Class sizes of year groups 2 and upwards were typically between 20 and 25 pupils, reflecting a balanced approach to the school's dilemma of aiming to provide a particular quality of Islamic education whilst also having oversubscribed waiting lists. Although particular cities will not be referred to by name, it remains important that prevalent characteristics of the surroundings of each school are outlined here, although the intake and profile of teachers will be discussed in more detail later. Medina's surroundings are characterised with an ethnically and religiously diverse community. Residents living in immediate proximity to the school mainly consisted of white and South Asian families. The South Asian community neighbouring Medina Primary consisted of first-, second- and third-generation families of mainly Gujarati descent. Moving from the school and towards the city centre reveals a predominantly South Asian community, including a large Muslim majority, but also including significant numbers of Hindus and Sikhs.

Introducing Hiqmah School: Location, Community and Intake

Hiqmah School represented something of a success story as a Muslim school which had been founded in the independent sector and had secured state funding initially as a grant-maintained, and later a voluntary-aided, school. Similar to Medina Primary, Hiqmah bordered a large Muslim community in a district located outside a large city centre. The characteristics of the school's surroundings were revealed when travelling from the city centre to the school. Two prominent Muslim communities neighboured each other, the first of which is a Somali community located just prior to entering the district that the school is located in. Distinctive features include a Somali day centre, general grocery shops and small local businesses such as Internet cafes and small-scale supermarkets typically occupying properties in a seemingly utilitarian manner. This was an area of small, local businesses rather than of housing. On gaining closer proximity to the school, the surroundings change dramatically to a more residential area occupied by a large South Asian community. Small local businesses are still present, although primarily in the form of small-scale supermarkets. The majority of residents visible in the streets and local facilities were Muslim women, typically dressed in traditional Islamic dress of modest colours, with many wearing the *hijab* (headscarf) and some wearing the *niqab* (veil). In contrast to the community bordering Medina Primary, the community immediately neighbouring Hiqmah School was largely of Pakistani descent, with a trend for second-generation British Pakistanis to marry first-time migrants. Therefore, the predominantly second- and third-generation migrant population living around Medina Primary, themselves descended from second-generation migrants from India to Uganda (Singh 2003: 42), was in contrast with the culturally regenerative aspect of Hiqmah School's surrounding community. The school itself is located just beyond the limits of the Pakistani community. The very immediate surroundings of Hiqmah School are characterised by social clubs, car repair industries, family cafes and public houses, all of which appear to be devoid of influence from the nearby Muslim community. However, on turning onto the road where the school is located, it is clear that the immediate setting is a mixed residential area in which white non-Muslim families constitute an approximate majority of at least three-quarters. The remaining families are South Asian, the vast majority of which are represented by the presence of traditionally dressed and occasionally veiled Muslim women.

Medina Primary and Hiqmah School: Origins

Medina Primary had originally started in a small village in 1997. The head teacher (at the time and also currently) had previously been closely involved with a Muslim school which made the transition from the independent to the state-funded sector, before moving on to undertake a role with the Association of Muslim Schools UK (AMS). The head also had occupied the position of governor of a nearby independent Muslim school and, upon resigning from that position, took the initiative to set up a new school (together with his wife, who became the deputy head) which would 'cater for a need' (deputy head). The new school was located on the site of an independent Islamic education organisation located in a rural village setting. The original site consisted of a mobile unit containing a small classroom and part of a staff room, access to a library and a neighbouring mobile unit as a mosque catering for the whole site, which doubled as the school hall. Medina Primary was opened in September 1998 with four students, completing the academic year with an intake of 22. Growth in the school's intake was gradual, with 29 students starting the following academic year. This slow, gradual growth allowed the school to cope with adapting to functioning in restricted space over time. Support from the Islamic education organisation also helped with financial limitations faced by the school. In addition to providing facilities for the school, the Islamic organisation also absorbed numerous financial overheads in times of difficulty. Over time, Medina Primary was given access to further facilities on-site. For example, an unused office was given to the school and served as a staff room, allowing for expansion inside the mobile unit to include three classrooms. At its inception, Medina Primary was a fee-paying school with fees starting at £1250 per year, which remained the annual cost for six years. The head teacher and deputy head met the cost personally for the first academic year's budget, taking on the responsibility for paying for resources and staff salaries with the complete cost for the first year being between £2000 and £3000. The bulk of the year's expenses went towards the salary of the school's first qualified teacher, currently assistant head at Medina. The head and deputy head were also proactive in maximising the school's status as a charity by contacting local schools which donated numerous spare and used resources such as desks and paper, further reducing financial costs for the year. During the early years at the first site, parents also played a significant role in co-ordinating both large and small fund-raising events for the school in order to meet annual costs.

The active role of parents in fund-raisers for the school reflects a wider family-based environment which had been sustained over time at Medina Primary. For example, the two children of the head and deputy head were frequently present during the period of time when data was being collected. This gave the school a sense of 'family atmosphere', which was commented on by staff in interviews. The daughter, as the older sibling, would help out in the office at least two days a week, whilst the son, approaching his GCSE exams at the time of the research, was sometimes present after school hours. Having the head and deputy head and their children at the core of the school may have contributed to the strong sense of family atmosphere referred to in interviews, which interviewees attributed largely to the school's independent status. In interviews with the head, there was a clear emphasis on the unity between the staff and a sense of purpose with the constant common goal being the continuity of the school. The head felt that this was part of the struggle as a comparatively small school in the independent sector but, more significantly to him, as a

Muslim school in the faith sector. Evidence of the commitment to this 'struggle' can be seen when considering that the head had taken a salary in the year prior to the research of £6000 as the lowest-paid member of staff. It is noteworthy that, unlike Al-Iman, at the time of the research Medina did not appear to be on the verge of financial collapse. The concept of the struggle refers to the aim of offering a standard of provision of resources to rival state schools of a similar size, rather than simply struggling to keep the school open each year. An underlying theme in interviews with the head was that state funding would relieve this struggle to an extent; however, in doing so Medina Primary would lose elements of its character which made it a distinctly Islamic school.

Predating the founding of Medina Primary by some years, Hiqmah School originated as a small study group in October 1989. The intention at its inception was not that the study group would become a school. Rather, consistent with the origins of Medina Primary, the aim was simply for the head to provide education for her daughter in an Islamic environment. The motivation for developing the study group grew from the head's conviction that nothing was available in terms of bringing together both the national curriculum and Islamic education. The head (both at the point that the school was founded and at the time of the research) had previously taken the initiative to teach her daughter at home, but, on hearing that subsequently this would mean the head giving up her teaching job, colleagues suggested that their children might also become part of the study group. Initially, one room was rented to cater for four to five children, with that figure growing to ten by the end of the first year. Following this initial growth, members of the local Muslim community expressed great interest in developing the study group to cater for their own children. In order to cater for the new interest, the study group moved firstly into a three-room property, before settling into a larger building in September 1992 as an established primary school with approximately 100 pupils and subsequently adopted its current name as Hiqmah School. A recurring concern among staff was that the head would only be active in the school until her daughter's education at primary level was complete. This apprehension affected parents and the surrounding community who also shared the concern about the future of their children's school. As a school within the independent sector, financial constraints also posed questions about the feasibility of continually serving the surrounding community. According to the head, 'as an independent school, because, we had to make a lot of sacrifices, so, it wasn't sustainable in the long term'. This offers the first affirmation of the economic positioning of independent Muslim schools in the independent sector as discussed above.

The head's conviction that the school was 'not sustainable' at that stage embodies a sense of economic fragility that necessarily accompanies the initiative to offer educational provision with a distinctive Islamic character in the independent sector. This necessary evil represents an ever-present obstacle that must be successfully negotiated in order for independent Muslim schools to survive. The struggle faced by Hiqmah School when in the independent sector, along with demand in the Muslim community, led governors and the head to look into alternative options for ensuring the longevity of the school. The head recalled:

> We then began to look at alternatives and options that were available. And we explored the voluntary-aided option, other options that were available as well which was grant-maintained, and decided to go down the grant-maintained route to become a more sustainable school. Because, of course, sacrifices are fine but there are only so many people who, you know, not everybody could make the same sacrifices whereas if we were able to become a mainstream school we, teachers would be paid well and we'd become a more sustainable school.

The above statement clearly implies that, whilst the head and some others at Hiqmah may have been willing to continue to support the school without expecting any substantive financial remuneration for their role, there is also an awareness that this level of commitment was exceptional and as a result could not be expected of all staff in the long term. Having considered the option of state funding, there was a consensus among staff and parents that this would be a realistic option provided the process required no major changes to the curriculum. On presenting the possible options for moving into the state sector, parents initially voted in favour of applying for grant-maintained rather than voluntary-aided status. On reviewing the application process, the head and managerial staff held the conviction that Hiqmah School could feasibly become a grant-maintained school with 'virtually no change at all' (head, Hiqmah School). The transition would not affect teaching staff as all members already held the necessary teaching qualifications to enter the state sector, and on analysis the head and managerial staff concluded that the curriculum that was being delivered already met the needs of the national curriculum, and thus Hiqmah School 'was the same as any other school other than the ethos being slightly different' (head, Hiqmah School).

THE INDEPENDENT SECTOR: A SITE FOR ISLAMIC SCHOOLING   105

The head and staff decided to submit the application for a 'one-form entry School' (taking on a single class of approximately 30 pupils at the beginning of each academic year) with the view that being a relatively small school would make it easier to maintain the ethos that had developed whilst in the independent sector (see Chap. 8 for a detailed definition of 'ethos'). The head stated that:

> we always wanted to ensure that there was a mix of teachers, at least there were 50 per cent, around 40 to 50 per cent of the teachers were Muslim in order to be able to maintain the ethos of the school. And recruitment might become an issue if it became more than a one-form entry school.

It was felt then that being a one-form entry school would help with the sustainability of the school in terms of staff, along with having implications for retaining the character of Islamic provision at Hiqmah. The school opened the autumn term of September 1998 as a grant-maintained Muslim school and operated under that funding system for one year before converting to its current status as a voluntary-aided Muslim school.

Introducing 'Nasira', Al-Falah and Al-Iman

As detailed in Chaps. 4 and 5, 'Nasira' was a key participant in the research process and as a head teacher had led successful bids for state funding at two independent Muslim schools. These schools are identified throughout the monograph as 'Al-Falah' and 'Al-Iman'. Al-Falah had been an independent Muslim primary school for between 10 and 12 years before making the transition into the state sector for the beginning of the academic year 2004–2005, and at the time of the research, the school was in its fourth academic year as a voluntary-aided school. Al-Falah had started out with eight children from three families in a small room in a mosque, before growing steadily and moving location several times. Growth had been slow and gradual over a period of five to six years as word of the school spread between parents and prospective families. After growing to around 120 pupils, the school's intake stabilised mainly due to limitations on space, before moving to a different building to accommodate the children more effectively. Moving to a larger school building allowed the school to grow again from around 120 to approximately 240 pupils, Al-Falah's largest intake as an independent Muslim primary school. On entering the state system as a voluntary-aided school, the intake dramatically grew in size again over a three-year period to around 420 pupils, with 60 new pupils joining each year as a two-form entry school, which subsequently grew from the bottom up. Following the move into the state sector, the school was able to have a new premises built as Al-Falah's third and current home.

As a trained teacher who had worked in the state sector over several years before moving on to teacher training, Nasira had extensive experience of the state education system prior to joining Al-Falah, which was her first Muslim school. The school itself had initiated the process of applying for voluntary-aided status and had called upon Nasira to offer guidance in the light of her expertise in the state sector. The rationale behind inviting Nasira to assist in the application was for the school to draw on her experiences as a means of 'bridging the gap'. This would aid the journey towards completing the application process for voluntary-aided status and developing a rapport based on trust with the local authority given Nasira's knowledge of the system. Nasira joined Al-Falah with a view to staying for six months and stayed for five years, quickly becoming head teacher and spending two years leading up to the transition and three years following the successful application for voluntary-aided status.

Nasira's personal background also formed part of the rationale for her involvement with Muslim schools starting with Al-Falah. The experience of seeing the school through the transition into the state sector, along with her personal experiences, gave her insights into the rationale behind Muslim schools. Reflecting on her own experience of growing up as a Muslim, Nasira explained:

> If you look back a generation or two, my generation, for us, we learnt about our faith but, you practised in the home, and you practised when you went to the Mosque in the evening or supplementary school. You lived a sort of a twin role. You were children in a school, and you behaved in a particular way; you went home and you behaved in a different way.

Reflecting on her own particular background, Nasira suggested that the approach demonstrated above fitted the context of the time and had positive implications because children did learn about their faith. However, she pointed out that the Muslim schools which have been established since her childhood not only teach Muslim children about their faith but allow children to practise their faith in an educational context without compromising either their faith or their education. In Nasira's view, the capacity

THE INDEPENDENT SECTOR: A SITE FOR ISLAMIC SCHOOLING 107

to practise one's faith in the current educational climate further strengthened the rationale behind Muslim schools. Nasira explained:

> Unless you're able to practise things, unless you're able to do it and you're doing it all the time then it becomes almost second-hand and further back... So coming back into it, what we want to do is to be able to take our children full circle back to where they live it. Living something teaches you much more than you ever learn about, you also understand the application, but it's not about knowing about faith – it's about practising faith in everything that you do all day.

Nasira's personal background along with her experiences prior to and during the process of Al-Falah's transition to voluntary-aided status gives a rationale for her own personal convictions surrounding Muslim schools. She maintained that this rationale was consistent with that behind Muslim schools in England and Wales in general.

Having served as the head at Al-Falah for approximately five years, Nasira moved on to take up the role of head at Al-Iman. Al-Iman was a primary school in the process of making the transition from independent to voluntary-aided during the time that the research was conducted. The school's history echoed many of the characteristics to that at Al-Falah. For example, Al-Iman had been in the independent sector for around 12 years before Nasira arrived. The school had started life in a mosque, next to the current school building, with a small number of parents from around six families who felt the state system was unsuitable for them. Nasira became involved with Al-Iman in July of 2007 following contact with the trustees. At that point, the trustees had been working for a year towards gaining voluntary-aided status. In addition to heading Al-Falah through the transition to voluntary-aided status, Nasira had also played an instrumental role as a trustee of another school which had acquired state funding and she had 'led all the negotiations and discussions with the council, though I didn't head that school personally'. Her experience in liaising with the council was an influential factor in Al-Iman's pursuit of Nasira's expertise. Knowing that Nasira had already seen Al-Falah through the transition to voluntary-aided status, they invited her to stay at the school for a six-week period to assist and offer guidance with the application process. For Al-Iman, economic conditions were such that the future of the school was dependent on securing state funding through voluntary-aided status. Drawing on her experience, Nasira expressed the concern that many

Muslim schools face a finite existence in the independent sector, often surviving in conditions that were challenging. Reflecting on her first impressions at Al-Iman she stated:

> [The school] had not a single penny. Muslim schools, typically, if you go into any of the 120 [at the time of the research] that don't have state funding their conditions are pretty dire. They live hand to mouth. What they don't realise necessarily is that for a third party the first impression counts, and if the person can't even imagine it being a state school, they can't get beyond that to what you're teaching, what the children are learning, what the school has to offer, what the staff are like, because they cannot even see it.

The school building itself had changed dramatically in the year-long period over which the interviews were carried out. At the time of my last visit work that had been completed included the installation of laminate floors, what was previously a hatch for the school office had become a large, open office space neighbouring a medical room with a sink and bed, and classrooms previously void of evidence of the presence of children were home to colourful displays of pupils' work. Nasira's conviction was that, even though developments had been made swiftly over a short period of time, 'this now looks the best it can in the building as a state school'. Prior to the final inspection in the application process, to take place two weeks following my last visit, Al-Iman had been informed that the school would indeed be awarded state funding. However, their assessment in the inspection would determine whether they received it for the academic year 2008–2009, or for 2009–2010. On anticipating the school's inspection, Nasira explained that acquiring state funding had become a necessity for the school owing to the time and money which had been invested in meeting the necessary criteria required of applicants. Although she had been assured that the school would be given more time if it failed the assessment in the final inspection, Nasira expressed concerns about the future of the school:

> That amount of work required to take something from here, almost at the starter, to a state school standard in the period of time, no matter how much time you've got unless you resource it funding, people, knowledge, experience, it ain't going anywhere. Time itself is not a solution, it's what you do with that time that makes a difference.

Her emphasis on using time efficiently demonstrated Nasira's commitment to completing the transition as a step towards sustainability. As with

Al-Falah, Nasira argued that acquiring state funding was a necessary step in ensuring a future for Al-Iman. An extended deadline simply meant an extension of the amount of time struggling to survive in the independent sector. The final inspection was ultimately successful with Al-Iman opening its doors as a voluntary-aided school in September 2008.

MUSLIM SCHOOLS AS A RESPONSE TO 'NEED'

One of the key issues that was raised by participants throughout the research was the question over the ways in which state funding might impact on provision for Muslim schools. For example, there were distinctive aspects of the environment at Medina Primary which staff felt were clearly inherently related to the school's position in the independent, rather than state-funded, sector. On first entering the school, the environment immediately gave the impression that particular objectives were manifested within the environment at Medina Primary. Discussing the purpose of Medina as a school specifically, and the staff's perceptions of the purpose of Muslim schools as a whole, represented a recurring theme throughout the research. In our first interview, the assistant head referred to the school's mission statement to outline the specific objectives at Medina. The central objective for her was to develop the 'Islamic personality' of the child. As a central individual in curriculum development at Medina Primary, the assistant head used examples of approaches in the classroom to illustrate one of the ways that the school aimed to develop the Islamic personality of the child. She explained that a holistic approach to education was employed so that children 'understand that being a Muslim is not just a spiritual act', but that it is a 'whole way of life so that everything you do is ultimately linked to pleasing the Lord' (see also Hussain 2004: 379). This approach demonstrates that the key objective in developing the Islamic personality of the child was to instil in pupils the notion that everything has a purpose in an Islamic way of life. The assistant head explained how this would work in the classroom:

> Whether you're doing maths, or you're doing science, ultimately there's a purpose behind it... I taught in the state system. I've done the same thing, where you pretend to be a tree and you're growing up; we do exactly the same thing but here, the language used during that lesson was there for another reason, [for] the objective of creating that understanding that Allah is the creator, and things only grow by the command of Allah.

The Qur'an teacher (who also specialised in teaching Arabic) at Medina Primary supported this view that developing the Islamic personality was the central objective of the school. He explained that one of the key focuses of faith schools, and Medina Primary specifically, was to offer 'a focused education about manners and behaviour which should give you a method of dealing with people...whoever and wherever you meet them in the future'. This is consistent with the assistant head's concept of developing the Islamic personality of children through instilling in them the notion that Islam is a way of life and that everything done within that context serves a purpose.

The objective of a Muslim school, as articulated at Medina Primary, was to develop the Islamic identity of the child through instilling in them the concept of Islam as a lived way of life (see Hussain 2004: 322). In keeping with this perspective, among teaching staff there was an emphasis on the role of the school offering provision for necessary everyday practices whilst providing a 'safe environment' (year 3 teacher). The conviction here was that the school's position in the independent sector had implications for maintaining the Islamic environment of the school.

The influence of parents on the environment of the school was also considered an important factor at Medina. Attitudes towards this were reflected in the admissions policy. There was an overall emphasis on striving for a balance in admitting the children of parents who reinforced the values promoted by the school in their home life. Coming to decisions in the admissions process necessarily required careful attention. Although the principal aim was to admit parents who reflected the values promoted at Medina Primary in their home lives, the managerial staff were also careful to avoid an over-exclusive policy. The assistant head explained that 'a lot of interviewing' took place with prospective parents, as the key aim for Medina was to provide a service for the community. Although the school emphasised the importance of prospective parents reflecting the values at the school in their home lives, the assistant head explained that there was a mix of parents ranging from active practising Muslims to those who practised less. With parents fitting the latter profile, the intention was to:

> have a positive impact on those families. ...we've had parents coming in and saying 'it's made a radical difference to us because my child is coming home and talking about what they've learnt and displaying love for Allah and creation.'

MUSLIM SCHOOLS AS A RESPONSE TO 'NEED'   111

This illustrates a perception among the management staff that values promoted in the home represented an important factor in the total development of the Muslim child as a pupil at Medina Primary. Although continuity and mutual reinforcement between the school and the home represented a preferred model, approaches to admissions were not exclusive to parents who fit the mould. When there was less continuity or mutual reinforcement, the school emphasised the importance of having a positive influence. Within this understanding, provision at Medina can be seen to be inherently bound up with meeting specific and variable 'need' among parents as stakeholders in the school.

The emphasis on offering provision in response to 'need' was echoed in the narrative around provision at Hiqmah School. In line with the account at Medina Primary, at Hiqmah parents also represented an important point of reference and influence on provision at the school. This was particularly important in informing the character of the school from its earliest stages of inception as the purpose behind the growth of the school whilst in the independent sector had been to meet the needs of parents. There was a recurring emphasis at Hiqmah on part of the need identified by parents being around preparing children for life outside of the school. Staff interpretations of parental need initially identified the Islamic, rather than educational, provision offered by the school as being of central importance for parents. The head of teaching and learning explained that for parents 'education is very important obviously, but I think overriding that is the, we call it the feel, it's the manners, the Islamic element of it, the basic teachings of Islam, the religion, so the child will know the basics'. The year 4 teacher elaborated further explaining:

> From a parent's point of view people are different, there are lots of Muslim children in the state schools, but the kind of parents we have they want their religion, the Islamic tradition to be a very important part of their children's life. That's why they've chosen the child to be in this school... I think it's a school by choice for parents, and there is a long list.

Whilst there was a collective emphasis among staff that parents initially chose the school due to the Islamic provision, educational provision was also identified as a key priority in preparing children for life after Hiqmah School. The head described the aims, mission and vision statement of the school, explaining that children should be educated 'in a well rounded way' informed by the national curriculum. This would prepare children for life outside of the school, where they would need to be prepared for a society characterised by cultural and religious diversity whilst also developing the skills necessary to 'go on to university'. Thus, the purpose at Hiqmah was organised around the identification of a need for providing an Islamic environment within which Muslim children could achieve educational success.

MUSLIM SCHOOLS AS MOBILISATIONS OF COMMUNITY INTERESTS

The narratives presented in this chapter clearly demonstrate that each of the Muslim schools that took part in the research was founded as a response to the identification of 'need' within local communities. Common to the origin stories of each school is the initial intention to provide an Islamic environment within which Muslim children could be educated in line with the traditions of the faith. However, as we will see in the coming chapters, the ways in which each school has catered to community 'need' have been manifested in highly specialised ways. Whilst there is evidence to suggest here that all of the schools in the study were concerned with providing an Islamic educational environment, the ways in which this was manifested in each case was fundamentally intertwined with the specific characteristics of the Muslim communities connected with each school. Having established their origin stories, Chap. 7 will explore some of the more nuanced ways in which each school catered to local community 'need'.

REFERENCES

Adams, R. (2016). Government Drops Plan to Make All Schools in England Academies. *The Guardian*, 6 May 2016. Available at: https://www.theguardian.com/education/2016/may/06/government-backs-down-over-plan-tomake-all-schools-academies. Last accessed 20 June 2017.

DfE. (2015). *The Prevent Duty: Departmental Advice for Schools and Childcare Providers*. London: Department for Education.

DfE. (2016). *Registration of Independent Schools: Departmental Advice for Proprietors and Prospective Proprietors of Independent Schools in England*. London: Department for Education.

DfES. (2005). *Registration of Independent Schools: A Guide for Proprietors on the Statutory Requirements for Registration*, Independent and Education Boarding Team.

Hussain, A. (2004). Islamic Education: Why is There a Need for it? *Journal of Beliefs and Values, 25*(3), 317–323.

Singh, G. (2003). Multiculturalism in Contemporary Britain: Reflections on the "Leicester Model". *International Journal on Multicultural Societies (IJMS), 5*(1), 40–54.

CHAPTER 7

Community, Connectivity and Nuanced Needs

This chapter will build on themes around community and connectivity between Muslim schools and their relevant stakeholders. In line with a Critical Race Theory (CRT) methodological tradition (see Chaps. 4 and 5), this chapter and Chap. 8 will focus on the voices of participants as a strategy for presenting informed insights into the realities of Muslim schooling in independent and state-funded contexts. The purpose here is to set out the characteristics of the schools studied with a view to contributing informed insights into the broader counter-narrative objectives of the monograph. The substantive CRT analysis will then take place in Chap. 9, where insights from the research findings will inform a systematic interrogation of the master-narratives identified at the end of Chap. 3. Exploring the profile of the primary stakeholder groups identified here as staff, intake and surrounding communities provides rich and detailed data that highlights the fundamental problems around homogenising Muslim groups. This process also necessarily reveals parallels with the more critical notions of Islamophobia which emphasises the complexities of anti-Muslim discrimination. Whilst instances of Islamophobia are not necessarily at the centre of participant voices here, the data does provide an important contribution to understanding the complex intersections across nationality, ethnicity, language, gender and generation in the constitution of Muslim identities among primary stakeholders in the schools studied. This further substantiates the argument that the needs of Muslim communities in Britain, in terms of denominational Islamic schooling, cannot be uniformly met by the 'one size fits all' policy responses to facilitating

© The Author(s) 2018

D. Breen, *Muslim Schools, Communities and Critical Race Theory*,

DOI 10.1057/978-1-137-44397-7_7

115

needs around state funding in place at the time of the research. This chapter focuses on stakeholder groups across all four of the schools in the study. However, it is important to acknowledge that three of those schools have ultimately become state funded. Consequently, where the term 'state-funded' is used in reference to schools in the research, it refers to denominational schooling through grant-maintained and voluntary-aided status, as it was within these frameworks that Hiqmah School, Al-Falah and Al-Iman operated. Policy frameworks around state funding for denominational faith schooling post 2010 and their implications will be discussed in detail later in this monograph. There is some contrast in voices of stakeholders at the state-funded schools in the study. For example, participants at Hiqmah School invariably reinforce the narrative that, in spite of the initial decision to pursue grant-maintained status, the inevitable transition to being voluntary aided suited the needs of stakeholders. However, the narratives from Al-Falah and Al-Iman demonstrate that transitions to voluntary-aided status have been more challenging for those schools. Similarly, the caution in voices at Medina Primary also suggests that state funding has been avoided as a way of minimising compromise in terms of the staff vision for the school. This chapter details the nuanced character and needs of stakeholders in the schools studied. The foundations are laid here for the wider argument sustained for the rest of the monograph that Muslim communities need *both* a more nuanced and flexible strategy for providing sustainable denominational Islamic schools alongside *more* state investment in the way of shared responsibility and support. The chapter will discuss stakeholders at Medina Primary, Al-Falah and Al-Iman initially, before moving on to discuss the very specific case of Hiqmah School which has operated as an independent, grant-maintained and voluntary-aided school.

INTRODUCING THE PRIMARY STAKEHOLDERS: FAMILIES AND INTAKE AT MEDINA PRIMARY

The intake at Medina Primary, although initially demonstrating slow manageable growth, has changed dramatically over the lifespan of the school. When based on-site with the Islamic education organisation, children were accepted into the school without families having to demonstrate an active interest in the Islamic dimension to the school's provision. The small size of the school, in terms of intake rather than available space, led

INTRODUCING THE PRIMARY STAKEHOLDERS: FAMILIES AND INTAKE... 117

to a particular approach to recruitment. In the deputy head's words, the strategy was: 'we're a small school, we desperately need your children, please come'. In discussing the nature of the intake in the school's infancy, the deputy head explained:

> I don't think it was entirely healthy for the school because, in many ways, sometimes I felt we were used as a babysitting service, because the PhD students coming in from Saudi and Kuwait felt more comfortable with an Islamic environment than perhaps a state school. So we had children coming in from [a nearby town] but parents didn't quite take [Medina Primary] as seriously as they should have, because the children used to go to [a supplementary Islamic] school. Children from Saudi need to keep abreast of their curriculum so that when they go back they will go into the class that the age dictates, otherwise they'll put them right back regardless of their age...so that always took precedence over [Medina Primary]. I felt, we were just there as a babysitting service... That wasn't very good for the teachers or for the school as a whole because I felt we weren't taken seriously enough.

On leaving the village site, Medina Primary had an intake of 84 children comprising six classes with one teacher to each class. On arrival at the new site, located in the city, the initial intake was 200 children with eight teachers, although several teachers left shortly and were subsequently replaced by more-qualified staff. The transition to a larger building had been eased by the new location of the school as the city site provided convenient access for prospective parents and teachers. Whilst at the village site, a school-owned minibus had been employed to transport children to and from the school. Although some parents with access to minibuses continue to offer a service for children at Medina Primary, improved access to the city site reduced the financial burden of the school maintaining its own minibus. Although the school itself doubled its intake of children following the move to the city site, the fees remained close to the £1250 of the opening year. The deputy head explained the necessity to keep fees low stating:

> We are a community school, a service. A lot of parents struggle to pay the fees. They can pay to a limit, we're now at £1,400. If it goes beyond that we're going to start losing students because they can't afford it.

The decision to keep fees relatively low is inevitably tied to the school's status as an independent Muslim school catering for families with average incomes.

One of the most immediately striking characteristics at Medina Primary was the extent to which ethnic diversity was manifested in the school's intake. Although reluctant to discuss ethnicity, the head described the intake as being 'predominantly from a Gujarati background, but not by very much'. The small majority of children from Gujarati families were of either Indian or Indian-Ugandan descent, and approximately half of the school's intake overall was of South Asian origin. The remaining intake at the school embodied a broad range of backgrounds including significant numbers of children of Somali, African-Caribbean, French and dual-heritage families. A projection from the school was that for families, English was the most common first language spoken at home, French was the second main language, Gujarati the third most common and Arabic the fourth. Because the majority of local Gujarati adults were predominantly second- or third-generation members of a settled migrant community, English was typically the language most used at home alongside Gujarati. The profile of the community explains the projection of Gujarati as only the third most commonly spoken language, even though Gujaratis constituted the largest single ethnic group at Medina Primary. Other languages spoken by families at the school included Bengali, Italian, Punjabi, Somali, Tamil and Urdu. A year 3 teacher explained how this diversity impacted on approaches to teaching. In the earliest years, children were taught 'the main aspects of Islam' (year 3 teacher, Medina Primary) so that content was universally relevant. However, children would occasionally contribute in classes in a way which facilitated discussions of parents' differing approaches to practice. These discussions would provide an opportunity for children to learn from each other's experiences. The extent of ethnic and cultural diversity at Medina clearly represented a heterogeneous range of influences. This point will be developed further in Chap. 9, where a CRT analysis will be more explicitly employed to refine a counter-narrative which will contest assumptions about the homogeneity of British Muslim communities.

In addition to the ethnic diversity at Medina Primary, the intake was also diverse in terms of distances between family residences and the school. Whilst the majority of Gujarati children reflected the nearby community, the school did not necessarily serve families in close proximity to the school. Consistent with the profile of intake at Al-Falah prior to entering the voluntary-aided sector, Medina Primary attracted families who lived outside the city. Some families travelled considerable distances. For example, many parents brought their children each day from a town on the outskirts of the county. This particular town had a sizeable Bengali community, and some families had moved from the town to the city primarily to make it easier for their children to attend the school. Interestingly, whilst the intake reflected the ethnic diversity within the Muslim community in the surrounding city, and further afield, the head made it clear that, in his view, ethnic differentiation was an anathema to the school's purpose in terms of offering Islamic provision. In his own words, his conviction was that all of the staff and intake were Muslims in the first instance, and with reference to discussing ethnic groups 'we're trying to get away from all that' (head, Medina Primary). Whilst the head's position on discussing ethnicity was insightful, it was also impossible to ignore the evident ethnic diversity among the intake at Medina Primary. In relation to themes concerning ethnic segregation and 'ghettoisation' in the faith schools debate, Medina Primary's intake clearly demonstrates the extent to which a faith school can be both distinctly Islamic whilst being both ethnically and culturally diverse. Taken together, the head's convictions about ethnicity, the diverse intake of the school, and the extent to which it represented the antithesis of an ethnically 'ghettoised faith school' demonstrated an interesting interplay which has substantive implications for our counter-narrative. These substantiated insights allow us to apply the kind of critical reasoning that has informed academic analysis in CRT, in particular the interrogation and negating of master-narratives. The research findings presented here stand in stark contrast to anxieties manifested in master-narratives which discursively affirm and reaffirm concerns about Muslim schools being monocultural in the wider public consciousness. The evidence presented here suggests, at the very least, that this is not necessarily the case. These insights will be located within (albeit limited) existing research conducted within Muslim schools in Britain in Chap. 9.

FAMILIES AND INTAKE AT AL-FALAH AND AL-IMAN

Whilst there are a series of similarities between Al-Falah and Al-Iman, there were also distinctive differences—one of the key examples being the families and intake at the schools. During the early stages of life at Al-Falah, the school's intake was predominantly of South Asian descent. However, in the years following the transition to voluntary-aided status, the intake of the school had changed in terms of the representation of ethnic backgrounds. Although the local Muslim population had been mainly South Asian, the number of Somali pupils at Al-Falah grew steadily over a period of two to three years with around one-third of the intake being of Somali descent at the time Nasira moved to Al-Iman. The South Asian groups represented at Al-Falah comprised a majority from Pakistani families, with smaller numbers of Gujarati and Bengali families. At the time of the research, Somali families represented the second largest ethnic group in the school after children with a Pakistani background. Reflecting on the Somali families at Al-Falah, Nasira stated that there was an enthusiasm for their children to have an Islamic education which was demonstrated by the 'huge distances' that Somali families would travel to get to the school. There were approximately 24 languages spoken overall among children at Al-Falah as either first or second languages, indicating diversity beyond South Asian and Somali communities.

At the time of the research, the majority of the intake at Al-Iman, approximately two-thirds, were Somali. This trend had been a recent development in the school's history, as it had been founded by a largely revert community. According to Nasira, this community had been ethnically 'very mixed', but financial restrictions over a 12-year period of maintaining the school and the mosque saw the founding community diminish. Changes over time included an increase in the Somali presence in the wider mixed community, which had recently invested a limited amount of funds into Al-Iman on the premise that the school would soon be voluntary aided. The remaining third of the school's intake was described by Nasira as follows:

> So here we're two thirds Somali, we have some African-Caribbean, lots of mixed marriages, Algerians, there's quite a mix, and in the families you've got some Irish families, you've got some White families, lots of revert families, got some Chinese families, from all over, the grouping is very different [to Al-Falah] here.

In addition to the tuition fees the only financial support that Al-Iman received from the community came from the local mosque (which, as in the case of Hiqmah School, shared its name with Al-Iman). However, the mosque itself was struggling financially and as such could not make significant contributions. By way of contrast, the community surrounding Al-Falah had been relatively affluent 'in terms of a migrant community' (Nasira). Conversely, the community surrounding Al-Iman was predominantly young, consisting of first-generation migrants comprising asylum seekers and refugees. At the time of the research, this community's principal concern was to raise the necessary funds to develop the mosque, with the school being a secondary priority. According to Nasira, 'elders' in the community were as young as 30–35 years of age, and as a result the responsibilities of community leadership were new to them.

One of the key distinctions between Al-Falah and Al-Iman at the time of the research was the former's status as a voluntary-aided school and the latter's aspiration to achieve the same status (which would be ultimately successful—see Chap. 6). As noted above, the ethnic groups represented in the intake at Al-Falah and their proportional presence changed in the period after the school secured state funding. In addition to these changes, the characteristics of families at the school also changed over time—more directly in relation to the removal of fees when acquiring voluntary-aided status. Nasira explained that when in the independent sector both the faith-based nature of the school and its often-delicate financial situation had resulted in a dependency on two particular characteristics in parents. They needed to be either committed to the faith, or able to pay fees, or both if they were to obtain an Islamic education for their children. In exchange the school would attain the financial targets required to continue functioning. Although some parents would be in receipt of state welfare support, they would still demonstrate an economic commitment to providing an Islamic education for their children through the payment of fees. Nasira reflected on the limited resources at Al-Falah in its early days in the independent sector:

> I used to say they used to pay money to send children to my prison, because that's what I used to compare it to because of the lack of resources and the tiny rooms! But they valued something they got there that they couldn't get anywhere else.

On entering the state sector, the profile of the parents changed. Initially waiting lists increased dramatically, peaking at around 1000 at one point. The new increase in parental interest was necessary for the sustainability of a school in the state sector, as Nasira explained that a school needed to be at least one-form entry, admitting one new class of around 30 per year. Whereas in the independent sector it had been possible to have a smaller intake, to be sustainable in the state sector it would be necessary to have a total intake of at least 200–210 children.

Retaining a larger intake of pupils would become a cyclical process as one of the immediately obvious effects of the removal of tuition fees was that the financial commitment of parents to providing Islamic education for their children was no longer necessary. The primary implication of this was that many families who could not afford to pay tuition fees would now have access to the school. A secondary implication was that the removal of the requirement for personal economic investment resulted in interest being shown by families who might not have otherwise considered Islamic education for their children. One outcome of the above was that some parents did not have the same enthusiasm for their faith as families who invested economically in Al-Falah whilst it was in the independent sector. The removal of fees brought with it the prospect of amassing lengthy waiting lists, and as a result the transition to the state sector necessitated changes to the admissions criteria. Whereas previously in the independent sector, intake was based primarily on parental enthusiasm and willingness to commit financially, on joining the voluntary-aided sector numerous filters came into effect, reducing the numbers of prospective families. In Nasira's experience, the admissions criteria typically came to prioritise siblings and pupils within a certain locality, with those living closest to the school taking priority. The obligations and complex systems in place in the voluntary-aided sector, had a dramatic effect on the nature of the intake at Al-Falah immediately following the transition from independent to voluntary-aided status. The dramatic change in the characteristics of intake at Al-Falah, as experienced by Nasira, suggests that the profile of a school's intake has a central role in distinguishing the character of the school itself. In the case of schools making the transition from the independent to voluntary-aided sector, the infrastructure around admissions processes is fundamentally and necessarily changed. Furthermore, the contrast in the ethnic groups represented in the intake at Al-Falah and Al-Iman also demonstrates the highly nuanced range of needs that each school was responsible for catering to. The intersections of ethnicity, socio-economic position and religious enthusiasm interplay in complex ways that make effective provision dependent upon highly nuanced understandings of variable community needs. The argument here goes beyond simply identifying and describing the extent to which the schools studied are ethnically diverse. Considering evidence from Medina and Al-Falah and Al-Iman, thus far it is clear that the local needs of Muslims are both complex and variable. This point lays the foundation for exploring the extent to which frameworks around state funding for Muslim schools can effectively facilitate the kinds of diverse need identified above. The connection between nuanced needs and the ability for policy to deliver on

THE ROLE OF STAFF IN PROVISION: PROFILES OF STAFF AND IMPLICATIONS...   123

those needs will be addressed through the substantive CRT analysis provided in Chap. 9. Before this is possible, it is necessary to consider the role of staff in provision at Medina Primary, Al-Falah and Al-Iman before exploring Hiqmah's transition into the state sector.

THE ROLE OF STAFF IN PROVISION: PROFILES OF STAFF AND IMPLICATIONS FOR THE SCHOOL ENVIRONMENT

Profile of the Staff at Medina Primary

The presence of cultural and ethnic diversity at Medina was also manifested in the profile of the staff. A small majority were of South Asian descent, and the assistant head (curriculum), class teachers for years 1, 2, 3 (part-time) and 4; the deputy head (co-founder of the school and married to the head); two nursery teachers; the secretary and a number of teaching assistants were included in this group. Among the staff of South Asian descent, there was evidence of diversity in relation to nationality and familiarity with certain languages. For example, the secretary was French and spoke English as a second language, whilst the year 4 teacher would frequently use common short Punjabi phrases in conversation with all members of staff. The secretary, year 4 teacher and year 6 teacher were all first-time migrants from France, northern India and north Africa respectively. There were also a number of white reverts among the staff. These staff included at least two teaching assistants (who both sported regional British west-country accents), a part-time year 3 teacher of white descent and the head (both of whom had northern British accents). The above demonstrates that the very specific profile of the staff had implications for local, national and global influences on the general environment of the school.

Following the move from the more rural Islamic organisation to Medina's current site, the number of staff increased. Interviewing for recruitment for the newer, larger premises had begun over the summer period to allow for a smooth transition at the start of the academic year. This process continued in line with the departure of several staff members and afforded the opportunity to employ more-qualified teaching staff. The profile of the staff at Medina Primary more accurately represented diversity in the wider Muslim community not necessarily reflected in the school's more local surroundings. All of the staff were female with the exception of the head teacher and another male teacher specialising in Qur'an and Arabic. Of the female members of teaching staff, three wore the *niqab*, while a larger number of the female teaching assistants also wore the *niqab*. The remaining female staff members, such as the assistant head (curriculum), deputy head and secretary did not wear the *niqab*, although all female staff members wore the *hijab*. There was some variety in dress among staff. For example, whilst the majority of teaching assistants who wore the *niqab* also dressed entirely in black, there were also teaching assistants who wore pink or blue *hijabs* whilst also wearing the *niqab*. The head teacher and Qur'an teacher also dressed in distinctive ways, with the head wearing modest colours (e.g. white or grey) and a small cap, and the Qur'an teacher ordinarily dressing in white and wearing a turban with two tails. Both the head and Qur'an teacher wore clothing resembling a *shalwar kameez*.

During interviews with the head, it was repeatedly asserted that the emphasis during any recruitment at Medina was primarily on appointing teachers who could demonstrate the ability to work well with children, and who also had an interest in contributing to the Islamic environment of the school. At the time of data collection, the educational level of the teaching staff for years 1 and upwards (nine staff including the assistant head [curriculum]) was of at least university graduate level and above with five having either Qualified Teacher Status (QTS) or a Post-Graduate Certificate in Education (PGCE). The only teaching staff not qualified at university level were four members in charge of the nursery and foundation level 2, although they collectively held the required qualifications for childcare at early years level (CACHE diploma level 3, BTEC national diploma, Childcare Diploma, and Montessori Early Childhood Qualification level 3). As an independent school Medina Primary is afforded the flexibility to employ non-qualified staff with the rationale that desirable criteria or qualities among staff go beyond simply possessing QTS. By way of contrast, making the transition to voluntary-aided status would have fundamentally affected the school owing to the requirement for all teaching staff to carry QTS. This prerequisite would mean that Medina would stand to lose a number of valued staff who were considered to be making positive contributions whilst in the independent sector.

The head explained that interest from prospective teachers had changed, with more-qualified teachers approaching the school over time. However, the financial limitations faced by Medina Primary as an independent school necessarily affected teacher's salaries with the result that 'you get very dedicated people' (head, Medina Primary). Although recruitment of teaching staff was not restricted to qualified teachers, the head argued that

THE ROLE OF STAFF IN PROVISION: PROFILES OF STAFF AND IMPLICATIONS... 125

quality of teaching was of the highest priority in both qualified and non-qualified staff. The head clarified the approach to recruitment:

> Obviously we want the best and see that we can have very, very good non-qualified teachers, but we also have very, very good qualified teachers, and that boosts your credibility. So although I'm not averse to employing some-body who's not qualified, and would be quite happy to employ someone who's not qualified as long as they're a good teacher, having the qualifica-tion does help obviously. And so the salaries had to go up and things like that so that's a rather long winded way of saying that the fees have crept up.

Whilst there was an emphasis on appointing 'good teachers' rather than simply those with the relevant teaching qualifications, emphasis was placed on the value of experience gained in studying at university level. Experience of the university system was seen as valuable for administrative responsi-bilities around teaching. Skills such as lesson planning and general work-load management were seen to be more developed in university graduates than in teachers with no higher qualifications whatsoever. Thus, although specific teaching qualifications such as QTS or PGCE training were not seen to reflect teaching ability in prospective teachers, there was a prefer-ence, borne of experience with teachers of varying qualifications over time, for a university background in members of the teaching staff.

It is important to recognise here that the loss of relative autonomy to appoint staff would not necessarily impact for independent schools like Medina who may be pursuing state funding in the post-2010 era. Making the transition to free school or academy status would not necessarily require the school to appoint qualified teaching staff as a prerequisite for that fund-ing. However, at the time of the research, voluntary-aided status was the only viable option for state funding for denominational Muslim schools, and the transition into the state sector would have required a purge of those teachers at Medina without NQT or QTS status. There are two important points here. The first is that, in order to negate the requirement for QTS among teaching staff, Medina Primary's only option at the time of the research was to remain in the independent sector. The comparative auton-omy in making appointments to posts also allowed the school to prioritise candidates who would be able to lead children by example in their faith as part of their contribution to the school's distinctive Islamic character. Pursuing this approach to provision would only be possible in the indepen-dent sector; however, that brings with it financial constraints. As identified above, salaries for teaching staff were at a level which ensured that 'you get very dedicated people'. Whilst this may seem like a simple example, it demonstrates the hidden outcomes of the frameworks that were in place around state funding for Muslim schools at the time of the research. CRT has traditionally focused on drawing attention to the outcomes of policy where this results in the marginalisation of racialised minorities. In this case, the requirement for QTS under voluntary-aided status may appear to represent a neutral standard required for satisfactory educational provision. However, Medina represents an example where the approach to appointing staff at the school effectively meant disqualification from eligibility for state funding. Rather than prioritising formal teaching qualifications, the emphasis at Medina was on appointing individuals who were skilled in the ability to teach, whilst also being capable of contributing to the school's existing character. The prerequisites for voluntary-aided status simply displaced any possibility for the model of schooling embodied at Medina Primary to be realised in a financially stable way in the state sector. Thus, it was only possible to realise the kind of need manifested at Medina within the financially unstable conditions of the independent sector. This also has financial implications for families looking to attend the school through the necessity for tuition fees. Whilst the shift away from the requirement of formal teaching qualifications in free schools and academies may appear to alleviate this process, this is offset by further risks which impact on Muslim schools in specific ways. These issues will be discussed in full in Chap. 9.

As stated above, the ability for staff to lead children by example was considered to be more important than formal teaching qualifications at Medina Primary. This was a conscious initiative that was strategised through the appointment of an all-Muslim staff. The principle behind this strategy was the conviction that children would be exposed to Muslim role models in a continuous process. The head argued that part of the reason for establishing a Muslim school was to have role models among the staff:

> I couldn't imagine employing non-Muslims here, with best will in the world and with no disrespect to anybody, but they have to be an example. So when it comes to prayer time and general *adab*, behaviour, we've got to practise our faith. That to me is the crucial issue.

Whilst Medina Primary's position in the independent sector made this approach feasible, financial constraints also had a knock-on effect for stability. In relation to stability among staff, the head explained:

THE ROLE OF STAFF IN PROVISION: PROFILES OF STAFF AND IMPLICATIONS... 127

That's one of the things you would get in the state sector cos you've got decent salaries, then you're likely to have more stability. We look at it the other way and say what we lack in stability we get in commitment, because people are committed to work here, they come in at a lower salary.

Holding a particular level of autonomy over employing staff has obvious implications for employing role models with whom children will be in contact in their everyday lives.

Employing Staff in the Voluntary-Aided Sector: Non-Muslim Staff at Al-Falah

Within the context of life at Al-Falah, there was a comparable emphasis on the responsibility for staff to lead children by example. The main point of contrast with Medina Primary was the school's status as voluntary aided at the time of the research. Al-Falah represented a Muslim school that had undergone the transition to being voluntary aided and following that process had started to appoint non-Muslim staff. In the early stages of life for Al-Falah in the independent sector, the use of Arabic was one of the more identifiable ways in which the staff led children by example. The use of Arabic phrases such as *masha'Allah* ('well done', when someone has acted appropriately) and *insh'Allah* ('God willing') represented a consistent practice at Al-Falah from the school's inception. The perspective articulated at Medina Primary indicates that leading children by example necessitates an all-Muslim staff. However, Nasira insisted that being led by example was a key element of Al-Falah's Islamic provision and a responsibility which all teachers, Muslim and non-Muslim, shared. She explained that non-Muslim staff members were encouraged to use Arabic phrases as a means of leading children by example. In referring to non-Muslim staff members' use of Arabic, Nasira recalled:

They learnt those phrases beautifully! And they used those phrases all the time. We had [non-Muslim teacher's name], we had [non-Muslim teacher's name], and lots of others. They came in on teaching practice, and they learnt those phrases and they used them appropriately, they taught the children those phrases. And they didn't find that difficult or contradictory to anything they wanted to do anyway... And the children take to it, and the teachers take to it, and it becomes normal, it becomes habitual.

The non-Muslim staff members' daily use of Arabic in some form and to some degree allowed them to lead children by example in their everyday experience of Islamic provision. The discussion of the use of Arabic, the use of Arabic among non-Muslim staff and the importance of language in leading children by example demonstrates some complex interrelationships across elements of Islamic provision in different settings.

Profile of Staff at Al-Iman: Structural Changes and the Voluntary-Aided Sector

As the main providers of both Islamic and educational content, the profile of staff at Al-Iman represented an important factor in the school's character. Furthermore, some of the anxieties about the displacement of teaching staff at Medina were arguably in the process of being realised as Al-Iman made the transition into the voluntary-aided sector. At the time of the final on-site interview, there were a very small number of non-Muslim National Vocational Qualification (NVQ) level 3 trainees, and the rest of the class teachers or teaching assistants were Muslim. The fact that most of the staff *was* Muslim whilst in the independent sector had been an important factor for sustainability in the case of Al-Iman owing to the extent of the financial constraints the school had endured. Echoing the conviction of the head at Medina Primary, Nasira stated that 'staff here currently are all Muslims because you have to be fairly committed to work in a school for [a limited] salary!' However, the requirement for all-qualified teachers meant that changes in the body of staff were a key prerequisite in Al-Falah's transition into the voluntary-aided sector, and this would be the same for Al-Iman. The pursuit of voluntary-aided status would necessarily result in a shift towards hiring qualified teaching staff to replace unqualified teachers as had happened in the case of Al-Falah. A long-term objective for the Al-Iman was to utilise the then Graduate Teacher Programme (GTP) with the aim of training graduates in the local community. Through this mechanism, community members could gain QTS through teaching on-site at Al-Iman. A fundamental problem with this plan was the requirement for independent schools to pay to register for the GTP. Owing to financial restrictions, it could not be utilised at Al-Iman to preserve posts for some of their existing unqualified teachers prior to acquiring voluntary-aided status. The necessary prerequisite of employing a fully qualified teaching staff meant that Nasira had 'imported a lot of staff' ahead of the transition to voluntary-aided status. The

THE ROLE OF STAFF IN PROVISION: PROFILES OF STAFF AND IMPLICATIONS...   129

imported staff were predominantly South Asian, and with their arrival, the school had three class teachers with QTS and one with a High-Level Teaching Assistant (HLTA) qualification, which demonstrated sufficient experience to teach, although it was not QTS. Subsequently, interest had also been expressed in the surrounding community with prospective future teachers considering utilising the GTP. Although there had been an influx of qualified teaching staff in anticipation of acquiring voluntary-aided status, Nasira argued that young female graduates in the community

> [have] got to do the GTPs, for the community to have that sort of footing. It's the people from the community that must lead the community and work in the community. That way you get some strength.

From this it is clear that Nasira's vision was to generate interest in local Muslim circles and to reintegrate Al-Iman with the surrounding community through the GTP as part of the process of acquiring voluntary-aided status. Whilst this demonstrates a longer term commitment to rebuilding connectivity between the school and the surrounding community, it raises an important issue around the implications of securing financial stability for the school. State funding did bring financial stability and offered the removal of fees for children and families who would not have previously been able to economically invest in independent denominational schooling for their children. However, whilst the successful transition to voluntary-aided status might represent economic enfranchisement, this was offset with the displacement of teaching staff at both Al-Falah and Al-Iman. This reality arguably reified some of the anxieties about state funding and its implications that were raised at Medina Primary. Whilst economic sustainability is achieved, role models who had been perfectly positioned to reaffirm and deliver the school's distinctive provision in the independent sector became displaced. The active investment of parents as stakeholders at Al-Falah and Al-Iman prior to their transitions into the voluntary-aided sector indicates that the schools represented highly localised manifestations of community need. The transition to voluntary-aided status and the uniform prerequisite of appointing qualified teachers represents something of an anathema, given that the evidence presented here suggests that 'need' within Muslim communities and provision in the independent sector have been mobilised in highly nuanced ways in the interests of diverse and differentiated Muslim groups.

The discussion above provides the foundation for two points that will be developed further as we progress. Firstly, Muslim schools may represent important sites for enfranchisement in terms of equity in the state precisely owing to the fact that needs with particular communities are highly nuanced and variable. CRT identifies that inequalities across marginalised, racialised groups is sustained as a result of the displacement of voices embodying those minority interests from decision-making processes at the policy level. Thus, bottom-up mobilisations such those manifested in independent Muslim schools in particular represent a highly effective way of offering educational enfranchisement for highly diversified communities. Secondly, based on the premise above, it is of paramount importance that any effective strategy for bringing this enfranchisement into mainstream state provision would need to protect the finely tuned and highly nuanced exchange between individual schools and the communities that they serve. In short, the transition from the independent to the state sector would have to be managed in a way which minimises compromise in terms of meeting the needs of existing stakeholders. It is important to note that the discussion below suggests that this *was* the case for Hiqmah School in their transition into the state. However, the discussion above indicates that the highly diverse character of Muslim schools, along with the examples of Al-Falah and Al-Iman, indicate that voluntary-aided structures *can* impose substantive compromises for independent Islamic schools entering the state.

Grant-Maintained or Voluntary-Aided Status: Staff and Intake at Hiqmah School Over Time

The above discussion clearly highlights the importance of the highly nuanced and diversified needs that Muslim schools cater to and also advocates a strategy for enfranchisement through state funding that minimises compromise for Muslim stakeholders. Logically, it does follow that, if the needs of Muslim communities are so varied, nuanced and diverse, there will inevitably be examples where those needs line up effectively with the kind of provision available through the voluntary-aided sector. This was the case with Hiqmah School and was invariably due to the aspiration to offer denominational provision in the independent sector that effectively mirrored that within the state sector. During its lifetime in the independent sector, these aspirations would culminate with Hiqmah already func-

THE ROLE OF STAFF IN PROVISION: PROFILES OF STAFF AND IMPLICATIONS... 131

tioning with many of the prerequisites for state-funded denominational schools in place at the time that they applied for grant-maintained status. Consequently, their transition into the state sector was far smoother at the point of receiving funding, and involved far less 'compromise', than experienced by staff and stakeholders at Al-Falah and Al-Iman.

The central impact that state funding appeared to have had for Hiqmah School was sustainability and growth. When discussing the impact of state funding for the school, the head at Hiqmah emphasised the increased size of the school, more than any other factor, following the transition to voluntary-aided status. According to the head, a mix of Muslim and non-Muslim teaching staff had been employed since the school's inception. The head explained:

> As far as teaching staff was concerned it was virtually 50%, or 60% Muslim, and non-Muslim, because we've always believed in appointing the best person for the job; ultimately it's the children's future that matters and they only have one go with education.

The current profile of staff continued to represent this mix of Muslim and non-Muslim teachers at the time of the research, with around half of the teaching staff being Muslims of South Asian or Arab descent. However, the head explained that among teaching assistants (TAs), a much higher proportion would be Muslims of South Asian or Arab descent.

The tendency to employ a mix of Muslim and non-Muslim staff at Hiqmah School was not seen to clash with the objective of providing an Islamic environment for children and families. The following extract from an interview with the head illustrates the approach to appointing staff at Hiqmah School:

> The first and foremost purpose of the school is a high level of education and so one of the things we do go for is the best person for the job. And at the time of appointment staff who apply for a job at this school are very clear, the school has an Islamic ethos and of course there has to be a willingness to be able to support that. As long as the willingness is there then we go ahead and appoint the member of staff. We train as much as we possibly can, but they're always supported by the senior team and the TAs if they need any help... those established staff who are really committed to the ethos would use the etiquette language throughout the school day, and those who don't wish to, other than *assalamu alaikum* the rest of the etiquettes are very much a matter of choice.

132   7   COMMUNITY, CONNECTIVITY AND NUANCED NEEDS

The appointment of non-Muslim staff at Hiqmah School, along with the encouragement for them to use basic Islamic etiquettes demonstrated approaches to fulfilling objectives of providing a high quality of educational provision whilst retaining Islamic provision.

At the time of the research the intake at Hiqmah School represented a similar cross-section of British Muslims to those represented in Medina Primary's intake, although in different proportions. Interview data indicated that around half the children at the school were of South Asian descent, with the remaining intake comprising pupils of various backgrounds. To quote the head:

> The rest would be a mix of a whole range of different nationalities from pupils of Caribbean descent, those from the African subcontinent such as Somalis, Egyptians and so on. And then we've got pupils from the Arab subcontinent, countries like Syria etc, and we would have some pupils who are mixed heritage, and two or three pupils that come from indigenous English backgrounds who chose Islam as a way of life.

In contrast to experiences at Al-Falah and Al-Iman, the profile of staff at Hiqmah School had remained relatively constant over time. The presence of both Muslim and non-Muslim staff represented a celebrated characteristic of the school. When discussing the influence of non-Muslim staff, the head of teaching and learning explained that the extent to which a given teacher would focus on delivering Islamic content would remain their own personal choice. However, although there were no obligations beyond using basic etiquettes, non-Muslim teachers were encouraged if they showed an interest in broadening their contribution to the Islamic side of provision and environment at the school. Although the modest dress code did not require non-Muslim women to wear the *hijab*, one such staff member did out of choice.

The year 5 teacher, herself a non-Muslim, explained the ways in which she aimed to contribute to the Islamic environment at Hiqmah. Consistent with the convictions of management staff, her interpretation of the purpose of Islamic provision was to promote 'love and peace, that's what we try and instil all the time'. She continued, explaining that providing a good education would leave children with important lifelong skills, although for her providing an Islamic environment where children could comfortably indulge their faith represented an equally important part of provision. Several of the non-Muslim teachers had religious backgrounds including Hinduism and several denominations of Christianity which may explain an overall commitment to contributing to a religious environment. There was a consensus among all interviewees that non-Muslim staff members were keen to contribute Islamic content in relevant lessons and supported the Islamic provision offered at the school. The year 4 teacher summarised that 'like any other religion, everybody says "do good deeds" whether you say it in an Islamic way or you say it in a Christian way it's all the same. So I'm sure [those] teachers are very happy.' There was also a strong conviction that the presence of non-Muslim teachers contributed an important role in children's personal and social development. The influence of non-Muslim staff at Hiqmah was seen to make an important contribution to the school's environment as a whole. The conviction was that the profile of the staff as a mix of Muslims and non-Muslims helped prepare children for life after school. The mixed profile of staff represented an outside influence which played an important role as it reflected the wider society children will be entering on leaving the school.

The transition from independent to voluntary aided saw the intake develop as financial commitments to the school were removed as necessary prerequisites for prospective parents. According to the head of teaching and learning, the school had from the outset attracted parents from districts or towns located several miles from the school, with a very small number of children travelling from a neighbouring city. As an independent school, attendance was based primarily on parents' ability to afford fees, and so only those with the relevant financial resources had access to the school. The transition from independent to grant-maintained status opened up the school to prospective parents who had not previously been able to afford fees. In keeping with the surrounding faith-school community, Hiqmah adopted the same admissions policy as local Church schools (Anglican and Catholic), prioritising children on the basis, firstly, of whether they had siblings in the school, and secondly according to the distance of the family home from the school. As a result, some families who had previously paid fees continued to send their children to the school following the transition to voluntary-aided status, as siblings represented a priority group in admissions policies. Over time, however, families from further afield dwindled as local families took priority under the new admissions system. The current intake largely reflected the composition of the Muslim community immediately surrounding the school with a majority of families of Pakistani descent, but also including Indian, Bangladeshi and Somali families. The head explained that the initial transition from independent to grant-maintained status had changed the profile of intake as a direct result of the requirement for economic commitment being removed.

The above process as documented in the case of Hiqmah represented a scenario that had been considered and met with anxiety at Medina Primary when considering possible implications of state funding. The conviction at Medina was that, whereas the requirement for fees in the independent sector resulted in interest from parents serious enough to make financial commitments regarding their children's education, the lack of fees in the voluntary-aided sector might result in attracting parents who would not have pursued an Islamic education for their children otherwise. For example, it could be argued that parents from further afield who are willing to financially invest in an Islamic education for their children might actually be excluded when their local independent school makes the transition to voluntary-aided status as necessary new admissions policies typically prioritise local families, a proportion of whom will have had no prior dealings with the school. This process of an inevitably changing intake following the acquisition of state funding is consistent with the narratives of Al-Falah and Al-Iman. It is important to recognise here the difficulty in validating whether or not parents who invest economically in an Islamic education for their children are indeed 'more' active or religious in their practice, or simply have more financial resources. When asked if the waiting lists at Hiqmah were full, the deputy head at Hiqmah School responded:

> They are. They [parents] want that Islamic input don't they? As an Islamic school the ethos is all around, they wouldn't get that if they were in another school... RE is Islamic RE, all the subjects from *fiqh*, *aqidah* (belief), *adab*, *sirah* (personal path, scholarship of the life of Prophet Mohammed)... I send my child here because I want him to have both worlds. I mean [Hiqmah] is a very good academic school as well so I send him here so he can have his Islamic knowledge and then he could have his academic, both.

Thus, it was inevitable that the removal of fees would generate more interest on the part of parents who would not otherwise have financially invested in an Islamic school. But the deputy head's convictions challenge the notion that these parents would necessarily be less active in their interest in Islamic schooling for their children. Not only did she emphasise the Islamic content as the key point of interest for parents but she also demonstrated this by having made the personal commitment of sending her own child to the school.

Reconciling Diversity, Muslim Schools and Stakeholder Interests?

The above discussion demonstrates the complexities of provision in Muslim schools and also the extent to which stakeholder groups are highly diversified. This observation, as informed by substantive research findings, has consistencies with critical work on Islamophobia that was explored in the early chapters of this monograph. For example, both Sayyid (2010) and Allen (2010) suggest that one of the key problems with the way in which Islamophobia has been discussed in the public space is the ways in which it's conceptualisation in public political debates has often been simplified (Allen 2010; Sayyid 2010). These simplifications of Islamophobia imply a homogenised experience that does not reflect the realities of anti-Muslim discrimination and the nuanced ways in which this is likely to be experienced by Muslims owing to intersections across factors such as ethnicity, social class, socio-economic status, gender, migration status and nationality. The narratives presented in this chapter clearly provide evidence to substantiate a part of this wider conceptual debate, namely, through the extent to which diversity was manifested within each school and also from school to school. Evidently, enfranchising British Muslims through denominational Islamic schooling is not a process that can be effectively achieved if strategies for state provision either assume that such schools are catering to homogeneous 'needs', or fail to recognise the complexity and diversity of community needs. In line with the application of a CRT lens, failure to recognise the complexity and diversity of needs that Islamic schools cater for, either actively or passively, inevitably results in the sidelining of Muslim interests in strategies for state-funded provision. By way of contrast, the independent sector allows for community-led mobilisations of highly complex and nuanced interests. It is likely that part of the explanation for the substantive over-representation of Muslim schools in the independent sector can be explained through the empty promises and smokescreens offered in the policy narratives that we critically deconstructed in Chap. 3. The discussion presented here suggests that part of the explanation lies in the failure of policy frameworks to adequately recognise the complexity and highly nuanced needs that are manifested in the mobilisation of Muslim schools in the independent sector. This failure is inevitably bound in with the fifth component of the master-narrative identified in Chap. 3: the assumption that Muslim schools are likely to be mono-cultural and, related to this, that the purpose of denominational Islamic schooling for Muslim communities is to satisfy broadly homogeneous 'needs'.

The above discussion does raise important questions around the ability for existing strategies for state-funded provision to mirror and extend the kind of enfranchisement manifested in independent Muslim schools. However, it is important to clarify here that this is not the same as arguing that existing state-funded Muslim schools do not cater for the needs of their local communities. Rather, the argument is that those schools such as Hiqmah School, Al-Falah and Al-Iman have overcome particular barriers in order to secure financial sustainability. These schools have all found ways of catering to the needs of their stakeholders through successfully utilising policy frameworks that allow little in the way of recognition for how diversified and nuanced those needs are. Rather than straightforward enfranchisement, these schools have made financial gains in the face of adversity and 'against the odds'. As we have seen in the cases of Al-Falah and Al-Iman, these odds can be such that arguably substantive sacrifices are required. Clearly, the pursuit of state funding can leave Muslim schools facing a predicament over whose needs are ultimately sustained. Whilst admissions policies may eventually displace parents who have historically demonstrated commitment through travel and financial investment, a whole new community of Muslims become potentially enfranchised through the removal of fees. Whilst the frameworks around free schooling may appear to represent a one-size-fits-all solution (e.g. through the accommodation of unqualified teaching staff), admissions policies are still likely to impact in similar ways. In addition, of course, recent history has demonstrated the ways in which free schools, and Muslim free schools in particular, have been positioned in public political debates around faith schooling (see Chap. 3 for a detailed discussion). Chapter 8 will draw on more detailed research insights to explore the characteristics of provision in both independent and voluntary-aided settings.

References

Allen, C. (2010). Islamophobia: From K.I.S.S. to R.I.P. In S. Sayyid & A. Vakil (Eds.), *Thinking Through Islamophobia: Global Perspectives* (pp. 51–64). London: C. Hurst & Co Publishers.

Sayyid, S. (2010). Out of the Devil's Dictionary. In S. Sayyid & A. Vakil (Eds.), *Thinking Through Islamophobia: Global Perspectives* (pp. 5–18). El Paso: Cinco Puntos Press.

CHAPTER 8

Manifesting Educational and Islamic Interests in Independent and State-Funded Contexts

As noted in Chap. 7, the ability to provide for a highly nuanced set of needs is of paramount importance for Muslim schools. This chapter will continue to draw on the voices of participants in line with a Critical Race Theory (CRT) tradition and will lay the final foundations for the substantive analysis presented in Chap. 9. One phenomenon that was referred to consistently by staff at each of the schools in the study was 'ethos' and how this was manifested through provision. This term has been referred to intermittently up until this point, but it is important to establish a meaningful definition of 'ethos' for the purposes of this chapter, and the remainder of the monograph. The concept of ethos can be difficult to clearly identify and analyse because it is often akin to, and described in terms of, related notions such as 'ambience', 'atmosphere', 'climate', 'culture' and 'ethical environment' (McLaughlin 2005: 308–309). For the purposes of the research that informs this monograph, ethos was interpreted as a school environment within which collective human behaviour takes place and moods that characterise the environment (Allder 1993: 64); the product of a school culture (Solvason 2005: 87); a prevalent or characteristic tone, spirit or sentiment informing an identifiable entity involving human life and interaction (McLaughlin 2005: 311); a plurality of values which may characterise a given social setting, and to the cumulative effects of the above that can be identified by outcomes or intentions to be distinctive. This chapter will explore some of the key factors which staff felt contributed to ethos in their schools in both independent and voluntary-aided contexts.

© The Author(s) 2018
D. Breen, *Muslim Schools, Communities and Critical Race Theory,*
DOI 10.1057/978-1-137-44397-7_8

137

Practices and Values

At Medina Primary, one aspect of provision that was identified as central to informing ethos at the school was the instilling of appropriate values in pupils. This was seen as integral to developing the Islamic identity of the child. The sustained emphasis on values also played a key role in the provision of an Islamic environment at the school. The Qur'an teacher explained that values were promoted with a particular focus on manners. He also stated that, although inherently bound to an Islamic environment in their own particular context, the values promoted were 'fairly universal'. In discussing values promoted at Medina Primary, he explained that those of importance included

> manners, self-control, being tolerant, really stuff that, in a general sense every school tries to portray. I mean these are universal behaviour management techniques, and we call them values as well because if you realise that your behaviour has consequences in the wider society then you become more reflective, and hopefully more measured in your impulses and so on. I suppose that is what we're doing, but putting it in an Islamic context, or seeing that as something which ultimately isn't just a social benefit, [but] has a spiritual benefit as well.

There was also a general consensus among teaching staff that the 'spiritual benefit' of values promoted at the school, including manners, self-control, tolerance and openness with one another, went beyond the individual and represented an inherent characteristic of the Islamic environment of the school. In a statement typical of the above consensus, a year 1 teacher stated:

> With the children, we instil in them the values, so I realise that now their behaviour, they realise what it depends on. So basically, it's all to do with their faith. I feel the environment is, because of their faith, much more positive... In general I think things like respect, even behaviour like how to respect your elders, how to respect teachers, how to respect the head teacher. And we [help] them learn how to be good Muslims outside of the school as well.

These values may well have 'universal relevance' for schools. But the promoting of values with the objective of offering not only a spiritual benefit but also a social benefit, through approaching Islam as a lived way of life, clearly represented the driving force behind prioritising the development of values in the individual child at Medina Primary (see Halstead 2004; Hanson 2001). This point will be developed further towards the end of the chapter.

Consistent with the above, the ways in which values and practices were promoted at Al-Falah represented one of the distinctive elements of the school's ethos that had been retained after entering the state sector as a voluntary-aided school. On describing the specific values and practices that she felt characterised the school throughout its history, Nasira outlined a strong emphasis on prayer, on practising faith rather than simply learning about it, and on developing the *adab* (general appropriate behaviour in accordance with Islamic principles) of the children. Nasira offered the well-oiled argument that for Muslims teaching in the state sector, praying at the appropriate times was difficult owing to the lack of provision and understanding within non-denominational settings. Even if there were a level of provision in a non-denominational school (or indeed a denominational school of a religious tradition other than Islam), Muslim children would still have to step away from the wider group to pray in a small area allocated to them. For Nasira, as with any Muslim school, a central part of the provision at both Al-Falah and Al-Iman was to provide an environment where children and staff could carry out appropriate practices, including prayer, at appropriate times without the need to fracture the wider group.

Provision extended to assemblies within which the focus was on the *dua*s (prayers of supplication) and the *surah*s (chapters in the Qur'an) that the children were learning. Nasira illustrated that the lived Islamic ethos at both Al-Falah and Al-Iman represented an applied way of life. The children lived their religion throughout the day reciting or remembering the specific *dua*s at appropriate times:

> When you enter the bathroom there's a particular *dua*, when you start to eat there's a *dua*, when you finish eating there's a *dua*, when you walk into a room there's a *dua*, when you leave the room there's another *dua*, so all the time you are thanking your Creator for making you what he's made you. And therefore they learn them, they say them, so they become second nature. When you meet an adult there's a certain greeting, when you meet another child there's a certain greeting, when you sneeze there's a particular *dua* etc, so the ability to learn and practise them all the time so they become second nature, I think is what the ethos was. Joint prayer in the afternoon and then, actually, understanding the *adab* and their application, the rulings and what they mean in life.

As with Medina Primary, Al-Falah and Al-Iman, developing children's ability to practise represented a central necessary part of the Islamic ethos at Hiqmah School. Hiqmah School had a purpose-built mosque on-site visually demonstrating the importance of prayer for the school. Consistent with Medina Primary, children were expected to have developed basic levels of practising by the age of ten years. When asked specifically which practices were encouraged in the children, the head of teaching and learning explained:

> Learning how to pray definitely and the ablution [*wudu*] leading on to the prayer. Giving the opportunity to observe fasting and so on. Letting them know about *zakat* and charity, Hajj pilgrimage, making them aware of what it is and why it's so important and so on. Basically teaching the five pillars... We encourage key stage 2 to fast [during Ramadan] and that's an option, it's not enforced. Key stage 1 we do try and discourage really, but if they want to fast and practise for half a day, or two hours, that's fine.

In everyday terms, children would start the day by doing an *adab* which would involve reading a prayer before registration. In addition, 'circle time' on Mondays would be organised around discussing religious texts which took the form of '*hadith* of the week' or 'Qur'an of the week'. The way that these allocated practices informed everyday behaviours was demonstrated on my arrival each day with children being encouraged to welcome visitors using *salam* greetings encompassing elements of etiquette and *adab*. *Salam* greetings were also used by children when teachers entered classrooms and during assemblies where the deputy head would address children as a group, and they would return the greeting. When asked to describe the school in terms of values, the head of teaching and learning outlined the central broad aim as 'providing an Islamic education in an environment which will develop the child both emotionally and academically'. More specifically, the deputy head outlined key values, such as promoting a caring attitude, respect for one another, respect for other faiths, respect for all teachers 'because we don't just have Muslim teachers as you've noticed, tolerating each other and, really, caring. It's all of those aspects really'. The deputy head acknowledged that whilst the values outlined might be present in non-faith schools, the rationale behind developing such values at Hiqmah was for children to develop as good Muslims. In relation to prayer, children were primarily taught necessary practices in the on-site Mosque at Hiqmah School. Approaches to prayer would also be

ISLAMIC PRACTICE IN PROTECTED SPACES   141

discussed in everyday classes, with most classrooms containing displays demonstrating how to pray, and children would also learn from peers outside of school.

ISLAMIC PRACTICE IN PROTECTED SPACES

Insights at both Medina Primary and Hiqmah School revealed that practices and values were highly integrated with practices acting as a necessary mechanism for demonstrating values in the Islamic context. In particular, there was a consensus among staff at Medina Primary that the facilitating of necessary practices for Muslims was important for them as individuals and the school as a whole. Context and environment fundamentally impact on the extent to which religious practice is *accepted* within working environments for Muslim educational professionals. These *protected spaces* may share parallels with the kind of separatism advocated by Du Bois and Garvey (see Chap. 2), even though the defining character of the space is primarily religious. The politics around Muslim schools as *protected spaces* reveals some of the complexities around the ways in which anti-Muslim discrimination can be operationalised in non-Muslim spaces. In Chap. 2 we established ways in which British Muslims are subjected to processes of racialisation, whereby there is an initial identification of the Islamic or Muslim, followed by the discursive positioning of the identified phenomena as other to Britishness or Englishness. This process is demonstrated in the experiences of a year 3 teacher at Medina Primary, who had previously experienced what she identified as 'alienation' when working in a non-Muslim state school. The experience recounted below occurred almost immediately after the attacks in New York on 11 September 2001. Reflecting on this experience, the year 3 teacher explained the reasons why working in a Muslim school had become so important for her:

> I didn't have a good experience, but there are good schools and there are plenty of Muslims who work in good state schools and have a really good time… For non-Muslim children to be taught by an Islamic teacher, I think it really builds up community relations. But I didn't have a very positive experience. There were one or two Asian children in the school but no one wearing the headscarf, no one practising, and also September the eleventh just happened at the time I was working there and I got a very negative reaction from not only pupils but staff. So I decided to come out of the state sector and work in an Islamic environment that really supported me

practising. And also the problems with the prayer time, I had a real issue with that and, if me wearing the headscarf was causing a fuss imagine if I asked someone to come to take my lesson for five minutes!

Whilst the above represents the experiences of a single staff member, it also provides a crucial example of storytelling and counter-story which is important for empowering Islamic voice in discussions around religion and practice in educational institutions. The implications here are twofold. Firstly, the above account clearly identifies, by way of contrast, that Medina Primary provided a safe environment within which Islamic practices would be accepted as the norm rather than an exception. Whilst subtle, this example raises questions about power and privilege in the workplace and also about how notions of neutrality and tolerance function in educational institutions. The year 3 teacher at Medina emphasises that both engaging in prayer and the wearing of the *hijab* were important aspects of practice for her. Whereas the setting of Medina Primary provided a *protected space* within which these aspects of practice were welcomed, attempts to articulate her Islamic identity freely in non-denominational state settings was met with resistance. Tensions around Muslim women in the education sector and Islamic dress seem likely to persist given OFSTED chief Sir Michael Wilshaw's recent guidance for inspectors that schools can be rated as inadequate in cases where wearing Islamic face veils are a barrier to learning (Coughlan 2016). Secondly, this example also demonstrates an interesting example of the dynamics of 'race' and religion in anti-Muslim discrimination. It is worth identifying that the year 3 teacher was a white British revert. Yet her experience clearly demonstrates the ways in which her identification as Muslim served to displace any white privilege in this particular instance. Whilst being 'white' and British would otherwise imply an absence of racialised discrimination in contemporary Britain, our year 3 teacher found herself positioned at the fringes of whiteness when working in a mainstream non-denominational educational institution. The point here is not to generalise, but the insight is nevertheless valuable. Furthermore, whilst being 'white' in terms of her own ethnicity, her reference to 'Asian children' appears to imply a sense of religious identification across 'racial' lines. The stigmatisation around Islam and religious practices that might, for non-Muslims, seem disruptive to the school day, represents a clear example of the marginalisation of Islamic interests within mainstream non-denominational schooling. Therefore, for some Muslim educational professionals the freedom of having practices incorporated into the school day represents a liberty that stands in stark contrast to the stigmatisation and marginalisation demonstrated above.

ISLAMIC VOICES, AUTONOMY AND EMPOWERMENT

The identification of need is also relevant when considering the importance of practice in the daily lives of actively religious Muslims. Again, the positioning of Islamic voices in denominational Muslim schools is of central importance with regard to provision. A central argument in established bodies of work on CRT is the problem around empowering marginalised minorities within a power dynamic where relevant minority voices are absent in decision-making processes. The resultant dynamic facilitates proposed solutions as they appear to an already enfranchised majority, rather than actual solutions that are fit for purpose to marginalised minorities. Consequently, decision-making in policy (whether at the institutional or systemic level) cannot effectively empower minority groups unless it is organised with those relevant minority voices at the centre. Muslim schools represent an almost perfect example of the mobilisation of local Muslim community needs, and the embedding of practices into the school day represents a prime example of local empowerment. One of the ways this was demonstrated in the case of Medina Primary was through the level of autonomy that the school had in not only facilitating practices but also in adjusting the structure of the school day at various points in the academic year. The school day was organised to incorporate at least one daily prayer at lunchtime, and this was obviously a distinctive characteristic within the school's religious provision. However, it is not only the ability to incorporate prayers that is important for empowerment here. Medina also had the autonomy to restructure the school day around prayers according to seasonal changes from summer to winter, and also in response to the annual change to 'British Summer Time'. This would result in the school day being restructured to accommodate an earlier lunchtime prayer, and a prayer at the end of the school day. The Qur'an teacher explained in detail how the structure of the school day incorporated the practice of prayer:

> The midday prayer being the one we do throughout the year... We're doing it at the equivalent of nearly two o'clock now whereas last week we were doing it at half one. We do that throughout the year, and we try and fit that into lunch period. And it means basically that children have less time running round the playground because otherwise the day has to be lengthened

too long because twenty minutes is taken up in prayer. We also shorten the afternoon curriculum in mid-November because then we have to pray the afternoon prayer as well sometimes because it gets very close to sunset, so that's another fifteen minutes off the end of the school day.

Consistent with the above, prayers were also incorporated into the school day at Al-Falah, and teaching would be restructured around this. Nasira explained:

The prayer times change, if the prayer times change the whole curriculum changes, so instead of having this thing, this lesson in the afternoon we have it in the morning. If you need to pray later; it just sort of fluctuates through the day as you need to do it.

Exercising the autonomy to restructure teaching around prayer times that fluctuate over the year is clearly empowering in terms of facilitating religious practice. However, in contrast to Medina Primary, the wider teaching responsibilities of operating as a voluntary-aided school meant that the school day would need to be extended in length at Al-Falah. Whilst autonomy in restructuring the school day around requirements for prayer across the year was demonstrated in both settings, Medina Primary clearly had a greater level of autonomy. This is inherently related to the responsibilities that Al-Falah has as a voluntary-aided school. Whilst it was possible to facilitate prayers at varying times, this would have to be accounted for and offset with additional time being added to the school day, therefore requiring additional time investment from staff.

Learning Practices by Example

The autonomy with which prayer was facilitated at Medina Primary had particular implications for staff and pupils. The implication for staff was that they could carry out necessary obligations within the working environment, but there were also important implications for pupils. As they witnessed staff fulfilling their obligations, pupils were led by example whilst simultaneously learning the act of prayer through taking part. In addition to being led by example, the youngest pupils were explicitly taught how to pray through emulating the behaviour of adults. The head described the process:

Year one and two will come in sometime in the afternoon, and do their own prayer. One of the boys will be Imam, and the teachers will be around watching them...normally, on the midday prayer the recitation is silent. The same with the mid-afternoon prayer, but we tell them to recite out loud so that (a) we can hear them reciting and (b) that the kids can recite and it's not so tempting for them to mess around. So that's how we teach them, through actually letting them do it.

The process above illustrates ways in which children are led by example both passively and actively. Passive leading is informed by an all-Muslim staff acting as role models coming together and exercising their common experiences as Muslims. In doing so children are passively led by example. In addition to the above, children are also led by example actively in being encouraged early on to emulate adults through leading their own prayers. Practices thus form an effective vehicle for leading children by example both passively through role models and actively through ensuring that they emulate Muslim adults. The logistics of facilitating this kind of provision in terms of worship and religious practice within a mainstream non-denominational educational environment would be arguably impossible.

The notion of leading by example was also emphasised at Al-Falah. Referring to children learning about the Qur'an and its delivery to the Prophet Mohammed Nasira explained:

> They learn in everyday life because their parents are doing it, they're told at the mosque, they're told at the school, and when you teach the Qur'an, you don't need to go from one to thirty. It's not like a book with chapters in that sort of sense because they were delivered at different times, and the compilation is different to the order of delivery, and you try and tie it into what you are doing.

The above description of the many contexts in which children at Al-Falah may have learned about the Qur'an by being led by example is consistent with the concept of ethos outlined above. Ethos at Al-Falah can be seen to have been characterised not only by practices and values promoted within the school but also by older Muslim peers in wider social networks. This experience was echoed at Hiqmah School, as the deputy head explained how children were taught to pray, and the way that lunchtime was divided to accommodate daily prayers:

> Depending on the year group some will be shown, some will be doing it maybe with a tape recorder having someone showing them. It could be older people showing them, and a lot is done in the mosque. I'm there or

> I will train somebody to do that element as well. So they'll pick that up as they go, and they'll also do it if they do it at home…there's a timetable where they rotate different activities so they play, they have lunch and then they go to the mosque as well.

Each of the schools in the study demonstrated ways in which Islamic provision was connected with and informed by relations with communities connected to the school. As children are led by example both inside and outside of the school, they consequently contribute to the ethos themselves by bringing experience of Islamic values in from outside. The school then serves as a site for exploring varied interpretations of values and practices. Whilst the outcomes of this exchange will be specifically localised, this further demonstrates the extent to which provision is likely to be highly nuanced in both independent and state-funded settings.

AUTONOMY IN DENOMINATIONAL PROVISION: DELIVERING ISLAMICALLY FOCUSED CONTENT

The explicit delivery of Islamic content at Medina Primary was largely broken down into three subjects: the Qur'an, Islamic studies and separate Arabic lessons. A key part of the school day at the school was the morning sessions of Qur'an. Key stage 2 (years 4, 5 and 6) would have a collective lesson in the prayer room (*masjid*) between 8:50 a.m. to 9:30 a.m. Just before the end of the key stage 2 Qur'an lesson, key stage 1 (all children from foundation 2 up to year 3) would filter into the *masjid* for a whole-school assembly. Once assembly was over, the key stage 2 group would leave the *masjid*, and key stage 1 would have their Qur'an lesson. Verses from the Qur'an would be written on the dry-wipe board by the Qur'an teacher (referred to by the children as '*ustad*' meaning teacher or master) using the Arabic *abjad*. The children would then collectively recite the passage aloud in Arabic whilst following the teacher's guidance across the dry-wipe board one line at a time. The teacher would then stop the recitation and explain the meaning behind each particular line of the passage. Children were then asked to volunteer and explain what they understood each line of the recitation to mean in English. The Qur'an, taken as the word of God delivered through the Prophet Mohammad (s.a.w.), is intended to be read aloud as it was received in Arabic. The children are therefore encouraged to recite in a particular tone (or *tajwid*) which was musical to the ear and had a clear repetitive phrasing. Within this approach children are learning how to read the Arabic *abjad*, how to recite using the *tajwid* and the meaning behind recitations.

The primary objective of the morning lessons was to teach the Qur'an and demonstrate to children how to recite appropriately. A significant secondary function however was that children learned Arabic through learning *how* to recite appropriately. Although there were explicit supplementary Arabic classes at Medina Primary, Arabic was primarily taught through the Qur'an lessons. Teaching Arabic and Qur'an in this integrated way originated from approaches employed by a visiting *sheik* (also described by the Qur'an teacher as a scholar of the *sacred sciences*), who previously taught Qur'an at the school. Reflecting on this technique, the current Qur'an teacher explained that the *sheik* would teach Arabic through teaching verses in the Qur'an, translating them, discussing the Islamic content and meaning whilst also discussing grammar and vocabulary. This was done as an integrated process, and the current Qur'an teacher had adopted and continued the technique. The ways in which the format and delivery of Islamic provision at Medina was bound to spiritual practice is of central importance for the ethos of the school. It is therefore fundamental to what makes provision at the school distinctive, and full waiting lists indicate that this particular approach to provision was in demand among Muslim parents expressing an interest in Medina Primary. As with the embedding of values and practices discussed above, the centrality of Qur'an lessons in the curriculum, their positioning at the start of each day and the attention to correct religious practice by staff provides for an educational environment that clearly adheres to the notion of Islam as a 'lived way of life'. Again, the identification of these approaches as manifestations of need would be impossible without *both* the centrality of Muslim voices and the autonomy facilitated within the independent sector. The voices of participants, along with discussions around autonomy in this and Chap. 7, will be synthesised through the counter-narrative presented in Chap. 9.

In addition to the Qur'an at Medina Primary, separate Arabic lessons were also given periodically and were taught by the Qur'an teacher in year group classrooms. These lessons did not explicitly draw on the Qur'an but had a more general theme such as the naming of fruits, or months of the year in Arabic and English. These periodic lessons, in addition to the daily 40-minute Qur'an lessons for all pupils above foundation 1, demonstrated that a large proportion of Medina Primary's curriculum was dedicated to teaching Qur'an and Arabic. Alongside the Qur'an and Arabic lessons, there were also dedicated Islamic studies lessons at Medina. The content of the curriculum for Islamic studies was primarily developed by the assistant head. However, teachers would also contribute to the content when delivering the subject in the classroom. According to the assistant head, Islamic studies lessons at Medina Primary were equivalent to Religious Education (RE) lessons, and so they did contain a comparative dimension concerning other faiths, although the primary objective was to teach children about Islam and how to practise it. It is worth noting that in Qur'an lessons and assemblies in the morning, references to other faiths around festival times such as Christmas were made. In addition, references to other faiths in passages in the Qur'an then provided the basis for instruction in some of the morning lessons. Although specific lessons concerning other faiths were not part of the curriculum, Judaism and Christianity were often referred to in Islamic studies lessons. These references would include explaining consistencies between the faiths and also historical connections between them. An hour and thirty minutes of Islamic studies was integrated throughout weekly class timetables. The year 1 teacher at the school explained that as children left the nursery, they were still accustomed to play-based learning, and so the assistant head had advised initiating a slow transition during the autumn term, incorporating national curriculum objectives into play-based learning. Meeting Qualifications and Curriculum Authority (QCA) national curriculum requirements was a key theme in the curriculum at Medina Primary, and the assistant head, along with other staff members, had developed content to meet those requirements through an almost entirely Islamicised curriculum (to be discussed in detail later on in this chapter). The year 1 teacher summarised what the content of Islamic studies in her class would involve:

> We have objectives to follow, and when they're this young it's just the basics, the main pillars of Islam. So during the month of Ramadan we learn about that, when it's *hajj* time we learn about that, we teach them how to wash before we pray and we make them learn how to perform the *salah*... it's very simple at this level.

At Hiqmah School, Islamically focused content was primarily delivered through Religious Education (RE) and Islam, Qur'an and Arabic (IQA) lessons. RE was focused on providing denominational Islamic content throughout the year with a week set aside to focus on other faiths. It provided a mechanism for teaching children about their faith and the history of the Islamic tradition. Teaching about a faith and teaching a faith in a school with a distinctive religious character and an all-Muslim pupil intake is necessarily a complex and inter-related one. The head of teaching and learning summarised the overall approach to RE at Hiqmah:

> Building up the faith is very important so that children learn the basics of their own faith and then, yes, they are able to relate to other faiths as well, that there aren't only Muslims around, and there are people of other faiths around, and you need to respect those as well. Therefore, we have 'religions around us week', where they go and visit other places of worship, they've been to a Synagogue, they've been to the Church across the road, a Hindu temple we've been to, so I feel it's important that they do get those experiences.

The head of teaching and learning continued to explain that RE was focused on understanding elements of the Islamic faith such as the five pillars of Islam, the life of the Prophet Mohammed (s.a.w.), the history of the faith including the lives of prophets and more general narratives rooted in the historical tradition of Islam. She also explained that the 'other faiths week' was a necessary RE requirement which the children found enjoyable particularly when it came to visiting places of worship. The content of RE week would include lessons focused on Christianity, Hinduism, Judaism and Sikhism and included activities whereby children would work from activity books about each faith and make displays for the school following visits to places of worship which had included Anglican Churches and, most recently at the time of the research, a Hindu temple.

In addition to RE, Islamic provision was also facilitated through dedicated IQA lessons. Although the teaching staff at Hiqmah School represented a near 50–50 mix of Muslims and non-Muslims, the specialist IQA teachers were all Muslims with a specialisation in the Qur'an. The teachers were specifically assigned to IQA, and classes would be rotated during the day. Whilst the lesson itself was supplementary, the staff were not peripatetic as they taught sessions throughout the whole day. The timetable for IQA was for each group of children to have a daily 30-minute session in dedicated IQA rooms, a number of which were located in a large atrium area comparable to an indoor courtyard at the centre of the school. Interviews with the deputy head and the head of teaching and learning revealed the content of the sessions as focusing on reciting appropriately and memorising the Qur'an with an emphasis on children understanding the underlying meaning behind recitations and also learning Arabic as a language. Consistent with narratives of Qur'an lessons at Al-Falah and Al-Iman, there was also an emphasis on vocalisation and teaching children the correct intonation (referred to as *tajwid* by Nasira) when reciting. IQA sessions also focused on Arabic vocabulary independent of citations from the Qur'an. In teaching children how to read Arabic, to memorise citations from the Qur'an and their underlying meanings and how to recite aloud with the correct intonation, the IQA sessions were focused on equipping children with skills required to explore their own faith. Subsequently children would be able to read the Qur'an in Arabic, to understand the content and to correctly recite aloud in accordance with good practice. Although slightly different in their form, the aims and objectives of IQA lessons at Hiqmah School seem to be consistent with those of the Qur'an lessons observed at Medina Primary.

ARABIC IN EVERYDAY SCHOOL LIFE

In addition to the focus on Arabic in taught lessons, the use of Arabic language between staff members and also between staff and children played an important role in leading pupils by example at Medina Primary. As with the example around recitations given above, this primarily took the form of staff leading children by example through habitual behaviour. For example, Arabic was used abundantly in everyday communication with phrases such as *insh'Allah*, *al-hamdu lil-lah*, *masha'Allah* being used frequently. The use of Arabic phrases could be seen to reaffirm the Islamic context for children. The year 3 teacher held the conviction that this process was an integral part of children's identity development stating:

> They do other things like the Qur'an lesson that you wouldn't get in the state school, the teaching and the language like *insh'Allah*, *al-hamdu lil-lah* (praise be to God); it's like the language is there and that's a constant reminder, and you wouldn't get that with a non-Muslim teacher.

The constant process described above reaffirms to children that they are in an Islamic environment, contributing to the development of their Islamic identity and their practice of Islam. It also reaffirms the emphasis placed on having an all-Muslim staff leading children by example at Medina Primary as discussed in Chap. 7. Arabic was also used in communication in many and varied contexts within the school, and represented a key facet of ethos at Medina. For example, the Qur'an teacher would often play '*ustad* says'

ARABIC IN EVERYDAY SCHOOL LIFE   151

(a variation on 'Simon says') in Arabic with the children before Arabic or Qur'an lessons. Registers were called with teachers addressing children *'assalamu allaikum* [child's name]' and children replying *'walaikum salam'* and on my arrival to classrooms children would often sing *salam* greetings. At the end of the school day children would be encouraged to make a recitation from the Qur'an when lined up in their classrooms. At the end of whole-school assemblies, the head would on occasion ask the school for a big *'Allahu akbar!'* to which the children would enthusiastically oblige. It is also worth noting that the four 'house names' under which children collected house points were represented by the Arabic names: *Farooqi* (blue), *Alawi* (yellow), *Siddiqui* (green) and *Uthmani* (red).

Through the use of Arabic in everyday aspects of school life staff were exercising commonalities, between themselves and with children, inherently derived of their own experiences of living 'Islam as a way of life' (Hussain 2004: 322). In addition to the general use of Arabic in interaction, teachers were also addressed in Arabic by children and each other as either *ablah* for female teachers or *ustad* for male teachers. This repeated behaviour reaffirmed to children that they were in an Islamic environment, contributing to the development of their Islamic identity and their eventual practice of Islam as a lived way of life. The use of Arabic in this way complemented the formal learning of Arabic in the classroom. The provision of an Islamic studies curriculum, in addition to Qur'an and Arabic classes, further demonstrates the role that curriculum played in creating an Islamic ethos at Medina Primary. Although Qur'an, Arabic and Islamic studies demonstrate the explicit ways in which curriculum focused on Islamic provision, most of the remaining curriculum also included some Islamic content.

Overall, the ways in which Arabic language was manifested at Hiqmah School was distinctive from that at Medina Primary, although there were some similarities. The general use of Arabic in the school included referring to male and female staff members as *'ustad'* and *'ustada'* respectively and using phrases such as *insh'Allah* and *masha'Allah* in everyday school life. The bulk of this occurred in interactions between children and staff. Some of the ways in which Arabic was incorporated into daily routines mirrored approaches employed at Medina Primary. For example, whenever the register was taken for a given class at Hiqmah School, the teacher would read out names alphabetically with *'assalamu alaikum'* preceding each name, with children replying *'walaikum salam'*. The year 4 teacher at Hiqmah explained that the Arabic phrases and their importance for provision at the school lie in the ability to make consistent references to God in everyday communication. For example, the phrase *jazak'Allah* would be used in place of 'thank you' so that the two phrases would be largely interchangeable and an everyday phrase takes on a more spiritual meaning. He explained:

> When something good happens, we link it to God, *jazak'Allah*: thank you to God. *Masha'Allah* is "God provided you strength to do this", it's like "well done". And for me the meaning of *assalamu alaikum* is "may God wish you happiness, well-being". So that's what we say [in place of] "hello" to each other, that's all combined in a word *assalamu alaikum*. And if you say *assalam wa rahmatullah-i-wa barakatuhu* that is the complete: "may God be with you, with his blessings and his kindness". So these kinds of things for me are very important for a child.

When discussing the use of Arabic among non-Muslim staff members the head summarised:

> Those established staff who are really committed to the ethos would use the etiquette language throughout the school day, and those who don't wish to, well that's a choice. Other than *assalamu alaikum*, the rest of the etiquettes are very much a matter of choice.

Drawing on experiences of conducting ethnographic research at Medina and Hiqmah, the use of Arabic between staff members and staff and children was a little less apparent at Hiqmah School than observed at Medina Primary. One explanation for this could be the profile of staff. Although non-Muslim staff members did employ Arabic in certain areas of school life, it might have been less likely for Arabic to be used impulsively in everyday communication. Among Muslim staff at Hiqmah, the use of Arabic appeared to be far more prevalent in everyday communication and was not confined to interactions with other Muslims (on several occasions Muslim staff members were observed using Arabic phrases when talking to non-Muslim staff).

APPROACHES TO PROVIDING AN 'ISLAMICISED CURRICULUM': THE INDEPENDENT CONTEXT

The 'Islamicisation' of the curriculum (a term repeatedly used by participants) as a whole was an important facet of ethos at Medina. The feeling communicated by staff, and through experiences conducting observation in classes, was that the curriculum was itself derived from a sense of Islamic obligation. The assistant head explained that

> if you look at a lot of Islamic rulings, look at *hadith* books, the first couple of sections are all about seeking knowledge and how it's an obligation. And seeking knowledge is not just religious knowledge because, in Islam everything is Islamic.

The assistant head went on to point out that meeting national curriculum requirements was important for children at Medina Primary because their educational experience would ultimately culminate in GCSE examinations. This was achieved through careful consideration of how content could be taught 'Islamically'. She went on to argue that Islamic education needed to go beyond dress codes and language, and that children 'need to learn throughout their day, through the curriculum, the concepts of Islam'. In practice, this approach to the curriculum had a significant influence on not only lesson content but also delivery in the classroom. For example, the Qur'an teacher, discussing his approaches to teaching art, emphasised that the content had focused on Islamic art, calligraphy and the architecture of mosques around the world. Consistent with the above, the year 3 teacher informed me:

> In every subject you try your best to bring something in. I was doing light and shadow in science, and then there's an *ayat* in the Qur'an saying if Allah wanted to, he would have kept the shadows still, but it's a sign of God, the fact that the shadows move. And so you're reminding them, even if it's just something very simple like that. And just getting them to think about how amazing is the creation of Allah! How big, how magnificent, everything's, this perfect clock and all the planets going round the Sun, isn't it amazing? So you're constantly bringing it back.

She continued by giving an example of how a geography lesson concerning weather would be approached. Discussions about rain would be brought back to an Islamic point of reference simply through referring to it as the work of Allah. Similarly, teaching about floods afforded the year 3 teacher the opportunity to review the story of Nuh (*Noah* in Christian theology) and the great flood. Questions would then be raised as to why floods happen and whether they represent a test from God, the aim being that children would have learned simultaneously about natural events and their faith. The above approach to Islamicising the curriculum is similar to that documented in Berglund's research on Islamic Religious Education (IRE) in three Muslim schools in Sweden. In all three schools IRE featured the teaching of Islamic history through the telling of religious narratives (Berglund 2009: 199). Furthermore, in the case of one school, content from the Qur'an was also used to support theories of modern science (Berglund 2009: 199). It was also typical of class teachers at Medina Primary in general to use Islamic names in exercises in addition to the non-Islamic names which more typically featured in existing resources. The year 6 teacher illustrated the ways in which the entire curriculum was delivered within an Islamic framework stating

> Islam is obviously a total way of life, so we try to make them see that Islam is not just a religion that you practise… For example, when I'm teaching something like probability, in Islam that is something that we don't believe in. So if I'm teaching that in a maths lesson, I'll go into the Islamic teachings which apply to it, and we can understand it. However, we don't shy away from teaching them; it's more like a learning platform for them because then they know what it is that they have to understand in the society and what it is you have got to understand as a Muslim and how they are going to relate and be able to deal with it.

The above demonstrates not only the approach to Islamicising the curriculum at Medina but also the underlying objectives. Through this approach, the staff expressed that they were exercising their obligations as Muslims. The conviction that the pursuit of knowledge is obligatory for Muslims and so their pupils were encouraged to learn as part of the development of their own Islamic identity. Following from this, the process of learning was consistently informed with references to the Qur'an, and so staff not only Islamicised their educational resources in terms of their own sense of purpose but also Islamicised materials through the use of Muslim names in classroom exercises. The implications and objectives of the above are that (a) the mechanism for Islamicisation allows for any topic to be approached and taught because Islam is a lived way of life; (b) the concept of the obligatory pursuit of knowledge for Muslims informs the meeting of national curriculum requirements; (c) children not only develop their own Islamic identity but in doing so within the educational context become skilled to function in wider society; thus (d) Islamicisation offers both a spiritual and social benefit.

Islamicising the Curriculum: The State-Funded Context

A key theme in the narrative of Al-Falah and Al-Iman is an Islamicising of curriculum subjects not inherently related to Islamic provision, that is national curriculum subjects which are present in all state schools regardless of whether the school has a religious character. Evidence has been presented in Chaps. 2 and 3 that clearly demonstrates the ways in which Islam has been constructed as 'other to' Britishness and Englishness in master-narratives around Islam in the public space (see Chap. 3 for definitive conclusions). Whilst independent Muslim schools have a good deal of flexibility in terms of educational provision, voluntary-aided schools are bound to follow the national curriculum more rigidly. Consequently, if the master-narratives are to be left unchallenged, we might expect there to be some tension between meeting the requirements of the national curriculum and providing Islamicised curriculum content in state-funded Muslim schools. In stark contrast to this, Nasira described an easy union between Islamic ethos and national curriculum subjects. Her conviction was that bringing the two together presented no problems owing to an inherent flexibility in the requirements of the national curriculum:

> It doesn't say how things need to be taught; it says what children need to learn. Some of it is skill based, some of it is knowledge based. The skill based is dead easy. The knowledge based, you can teach from an Islamic perspective. You can say some people believe in the theory of evolution, so you teach it as a perspective. But of course, we know that *Allah Subhana Wa Tala* tells us through the Qur'an that this happened and that happened.

Nasira felt that reaffirming the Islamic perspective when teaching such elements of the curriculum removed any complications in delivering the national curriculum in the classroom. The above could give the misleading impression that Islamicising the curriculum simply refers to clarifying when science and Islam clash. In the case of teaching evolution, this was certainly possible and even probable, but in many cases science could be entirely incorporated into an Islamic perspective without 'clashing'. Nasira explained:

> Being able to refer back to the Qur'an...1400 years ago, *Allah Subhana Wa Tala* told us through the Qur'an that in the sea there are two seas running,

there's a salty sea and a non-salty sea, sweet water and salty water, and these two seas never mix. And now scientists have discovered that it's to do with the density of the water and the heat etc., and you can refer back... so they're recognising that the Qur'an is a source of information and knowledge not just *dua*s and *surah*s that you learn through repetition.

Islamicising the curriculum then refers to grounding elements of science and others in the Islamic perspective, so allowing the easy union in Nasira's account. This approach resulted in the children learning about their faith in a continuous process, rather than leaving it at the door when learning elements of science. Nasira's account illustrated that, as is consistent with the conviction that Islam is a lived way of life, the experience of learning in Al-Falah was filled with an overlap of inter-related factors, but with each giving some point of reflection on Islam. In describing the nature of the Qur'an and the ways in which learning about it could fulfil the requirements of the national curriculum, Nasira explained:

So we're going to learn *surah naba* [The Tidings, Qur'an 078]... There's the historical context, or there's the scientific context or, there's something you're looking at in geography, you're looking at an area, you're looking at mountainous regions and you say the people of the mountain etc., etc., and this is what happened. Or, they looked at Egypt for instance and you were looking at the arid conditions and the river Nile and it bringing [sic], and you look at what that tells you and where it is. So it's sort of a cross-linked... mish-mash (laughs) but a lovely mish-mash!

Thus, according to Nasira's account, Islamicising the curriculum could dissolve a perceived gap between Islamic ethos and elements of the national curriculum. Approaches to Islamicising the curriculum were also observed at Hiqmah School and followed a similar strategy to that described by Nasira. When asked how the national curriculum was integrated into Islamic provision, the deputy head at Hiqmah explained:

We have the basis of the national curriculum and what we do is we try and put an Islamic input into that. So we look at the topic and we see what Islamic input ...like [the] Earth, Sun and Moon, they could be looking at a Creator, God made them and so they might look at a [Qur'anic] verse which is related to that. So that's how we would integrate.

The process of integration itself was highly organised and took the form of workshops where managerial and teaching staff would brainstorm ideas for including Islamic input when delivering the national curriculum. The deputy head explained that whatever the curriculum is, you could adapt it as long as you achieve the objectives. [As regards] the resources—you could use anything.

Consistent with approaches at Al-Falah, staff at Hiqmah described an easy union between the national curriculum and Islamic input in the classroom. The year 4 teacher argued that integrating religion into processes of meeting educational objectives represented a progressive approach within the school. He explained that he had an advantage in having read the Qur'an and thus had developed his own system to offer Islamic input on a list of curriculum topics. He summarised:

> They learn about science, but then they see what Qur'an says about a particular topic, things like pollution or the water cycle. In the Qur'an, there are many places it mentions [that]... Within the staff as well, sometimes we have meetings and those who are more familiar with Qur'an, they can help [other teachers] and say "OK your topic is linked with that topic", so I think it's a great philosophy.

The year 4 teacher's account above provides one example of how a Muslim staff member was able to draw on personal experiences to inform approaches to Islamicising the curriculum. However, initiatives around integrating Islamic content were not confined to Muslim members of staff. The year 5 teacher provided an example of how non-Muslim staff adopted an applied approach to Islamicising the curriculum. She explained that, whilst integrating Islamic input into the curriculum was a new experience for her, the methods she employed reflected those of the year 4 teacher. Like the year 4 teacher, the year 5 teacher described that the process used by staff in integrating Islamic provision into the curriculum involved referring back to the Qur'an as a resource, often referring to stories or citations. Although unfamiliar with the Qur'an and new to the approach of Islamicising the curriculum, the year 5 teacher indicated her keenness as a non-Muslim to contribute to the ethos of the school as a whole and argued that Muslim children should feel comfortable with their religious identity in an environment where they were being taught the national curriculum.

MUSLIM SCHOOLING AND CONNECTIONS TO COMMUNITY

As alluded to in the discussion around learning practices by example, a recurring theme in each of the schools studied was the ways in which relations were manifested and sustained with communities connected to the school. For example, at Medina Primary, one of the ways in which the ethos of the school extended beyond the school building was through relations with parents. In addition to the role that the school played in Islamic provision, the commitment of parents in providing continuity between school and home environments was seen as an important explanatory factor in the school's educational success. As well as being active economic stakeholders, parents were also active in engaging with Medina Primary outside of school hours. Attendance at Friday prayers in the *masjid* at the end of the school day was a regular occurrence, with a visiting Imam leading the prayer. In addition, parents, friends of parents and Muslim members of the surrounding community would attend. The Qur'an teacher explained that part of the rationale for community involvement on a Friday was the requirement for a valid congregation to include at least four men (in addition to the Imam) for Friday prayer. As the majority of the staff at Medina were women, a visiting Imam, along with encouragement for men in particular to attend, would increase the chance of having a valid congregation. In the event that fewer than four men were present, the format for prayers remained the same as daily prayers during the week. For the Qur'an teacher, attendance for Friday prayers represented one of the ways in which parents and the surrounding community 'fed back' into the ethos of the school. He explained:

> You see people regularly, and they're definitely contributing and taking part... It's nice for them to come in and see the school and see what we're doing.

The wide diversity of ethnic and cultural backgrounds at Medina Primary informed an institutional commitment to remaining free of affiliation with any one particular mosque. The head explained that this approach had been intentional from the school's inception. The aim was to avoid being labelled as an exclusive extension of any one particular community, mosque or Islamic school of thought. This approach allowed the school to draw connections with families across a broad range of ethnic and cultural backgrounds. Whilst there were clear benefits, the head explained that there were limitations, namely that there was no one community or mosque which could be approached during fund-raising exercises.

Whilst more localised, a similar connection with the surrounding Muslim community was observed at Hiqmah School. The on-site mosque was frequented by parents and local community members that had connections with the school. Whilst community involvement in prayers represented a significant bridge between the schools as educational institutions and their stakeholders, at Medina Primary, there were other ways in which parents and community members were active in the school. At the time of the research, Medina had recently secured an allotment nearby. The Qur'an teacher described the location as being such that a class of children could walk there within five minutes. However, the size of the plot secured would also facilitate a 'community plot' (Qur'an teacher), in addition to a plot set aside for classes. There was a recurring emphasis on the importance of connections between the school and families and communities connected to it. These connections and the involvement of parents and community members in school-led activities necessarily had an influence on the character of the school. For staff, the position of parents as active stakeholders (in an economic sense, but also terms of the continuity of values and practices between home and school), the diversity of intake and the active nature of relations between a broadly dispersed community and the school all represented important influences for ethos at Medina Primary. The two-way nature of the relationship between parents and members of the surrounding community with Medina Primary demonstrated the school's commitment to Islamic provision that reflected a way of life that did not simply cease at the intersection between the outside world and the school walls.

In Conclusion: In What Ways Do the Above Examples of Provision Serve the Interests of Muslim Stakeholders?

Arguably the most apparent answer to this question may appear to be related to parental preferences about the environment within which their children are schooled. Throughout this chapter and Chap. 7, we have seen a series of examples of distinctive denominational provision. Whilst approaches are nuanced across schools, there is a broadly common rationale inherently informed by a shared understanding of Islam as a 'way of life'. Again, the nuances of how this is facilitated are distinctive from school to school, but there is significance in the fact that local communities have variable needs and aspirations for what is desirable in denominational Islamic provision. Against the backdrop of all of the processes of marginalisation explored through the CRT lens outlined in Chaps. 2 and 3, denominational schooling represents an effective site for enfranchising/reenfranchising Muslims as stakeholders in the nation-state. But there is also bigger picture here which inherently raises questions about the position of Muslims and their limited access to equity in *non-denominational* education. Approaches to denominational teaching and learning detailed in this chapter thus far had positive implications for *academic performance*. Consistent with trends in both independent and faith schools, Medina Primary had a good reputation in terms of performance in Standard Assessment Tests (SATs). The head's conviction was that this was directly derived from the Islamic ethos of the school. He elaborated that although secondary schools wanted good key stage 2 results from children at Medina Primary:

> That's not what drives us. We believe, again with varying degrees of success, that with a good Islamic education that will follow (see Dangor 2005; Halstead 2004).

The head went on to discuss the performance of the school as follows:

> [School performance can be affected] in a couple of ways. One is that parents who generally choose a Muslim school have an interest in their kid's education, and especially [in the case of] independent schools, they are making a financial investment over and above their taxes. So it's in their interests that the child does well. They keep us on our toes, and they keep their kids on their toes, because they make sure that homework is done and so forth.

The conviction above was echoed in the narratives of provision at Hiqmah School. The head explained that, as a former teacher, her approaches to the curriculum were her main area of expertise when starting the school. The fundamental aim of the curriculum at Hiqmah School had been to educate children 'in a well-rounded way' (head, Hiqmah), with a key objective being that children would have a chance of being likely candidates for Higher Education. The emphasis on educational objectives at Hiqmah School can be clearly contextualised when considering educational equity among British Muslims more generally. For example, two of the largest minority ethnic groups represented among Britain's Muslim communities, those of Pakistani and Bangladeshi background, are the two ethnic groups with the highest proportions of individuals possessing no educational qualifications (Lymperopoulou and Parameshwaran 2014). Census data from 2011 shows that British Bangladeshis are the

IN CONCLUSION: IN WHAT WAYS DO THE ABOVE EXAMPLES OF PROVISION... 161

most disadvantaged in this regard with 28% possessing no educational qualifications, followed by British Pakistanis (26%). The proportion of those with no educational qualifications who are white British is 23%, and whilst this gap may appear to be small, it was far greater just 10 years previously. Census data from 2001 shows that 47% of British Bangladeshis had no qualifications alongside 41% of British Pakistanis compared with 29% of those who were white British (Lymperopoulou and Parameshwaran 2014). Whilst the gap appears to be closing, it is still evident that Bangladeshi and Pakistani groups are the most disadvantaged in terms of possessing educational qualifications, and that at the time of the research, these groups were likely at a far greater proportional disadvantage than they are today. It is important to note here that these are insights from only two ethnic groups within which there is significant Muslim representation, and this chapter and the preceding one have clearly demonstrated the extent of ethnic diversity in the schools researched for this monograph. Yet, this does not detract from the observable educational inequity across two predominantly Muslim groups in Britain.

Whilst the above indicates educational inequity within Pakistani and Bangladeshi groups as a whole, the picture becomes more complex if we go beyond the total representation of educational qualifications and focus on educational attainment among school-age children. DfE figures from 2014 indicate that, whilst only 51.4% of Pakistani children are achieving 5 A*–C including English and Maths relative to the national average of 56.6%, for Bangladeshi children this figure is 61.3%, clearly higher than the national average (DfE 2014). Whilst this might seem to challenge the argument that Muslim groups are currently experiencing educational inequality and inequity, the above findings can be contextualised when looking at educational trends across religious group. National figures on attainment by religious grouping are not currently available through the DfE. However, a report for the National Equality Panel in 2009 offers some insight into trends in educational attainment among British Muslims. The report identifies that Muslim children have the lowest rates of attainment at key stage 2 and key stage 3 relative to children classified as Christian, Buddhist, Hindu, Jewish, Sikh, 'Other' and finally those of no faith (Burgess et al. 2009: 16). Only 50% of Muslim boys achieved 5A*–C at GCSE level which was lower than boys in all other groups (Burgess et al. 2009: 17). The proportion for Muslim girls achieving 5A*–C at GCSE was 66%; this was lower than girls in all other groups except those of no faith (60%) (Burgess et al. 2009: 17). The proportion of Muslim boys achieving 5 GCSEs at A*–C including English and Maths is the lowest for all groups at 36%. Proportions of boys achieving 5A*–C at GCSE including English and Maths in all other groups were as follows: Christian (49%); Buddhist (44%); Hindu (63%); Jewish (62%); Sikh (54%); Other (45%) and boys of no faith (41%) (Burgess et al. 2009: 17). The proportion of Muslim girls achieving 5A*–C including English and Maths was 45%, the only other group with a smaller proportion being girls identified as 'Other' (44%). Proportions of girls achieving 5A*–Cs at GCSE including English and Maths for the remaining groups were as follows: Christian (56%); Buddhist (50%); Hindu (74%); Jewish (72%); Sikh (59%) and girls of no faith (48%) (Burgess et al. 2009: 17). The above trends in educational attainment across religious grouping allow us to conclusively identify that British Muslims are clearly the most consistently disadvantaged group in terms of educational equity manifested in qualifications—the only exception being two instances where Muslim girls marginally avoided being the lowest achieving group. Given the evidence above, part of the rationale behind Muslim schools lies in providing an environment which will allow Muslim children to transcend the inequalities and inequity evidenced in education more widely. This sense of purpose was clearly manifested in the emphasis on both the Islamic environment and academic performance at Medina Primary and Hiqmah School.

When asked if one of the key objectives at Hiqmah School had been to 'level the playing field' for Muslim children the head responded:

> One can put it like that. One of my fears as an educator, is that children who do sacrifice their own identities do have problems as they grow up, because clarity of identity is so important for confidence, and to do well in life. To me it is so fundamental for children to be able to understand who they are, and of course like all human beings, we're all curious about where we've come from and where we are going.

In addition to these objectives the head placed equal emphasis on the social benefit that the school could offer Muslim children as they 'need to be prepared for a world which is multicultural, multifaith, and they need to be confident people in themselves' (head, Hiqmah). This objective echoes Berglund's analysis of IRE as a mechanism for providing connectedness between children, Islamic identity and the wider context of Swedish society (Berglund 2009: 200). Consistent with the conviction at Hiqmah,

IN CONCLUSION: IN WHAT WAYS DO THE ABOVE EXAMPLES OF PROVISION... 163

we saw earlier that the approach to promoting values at Medina Primary was informed by the objective of offering a spiritual but also a social benefit. The commitment to approaching Islam as a 'lived way of life' was clearly articulated as a strategy of social and spiritual empowerment for children, which is again consistent with Berglund's observations. It is important to situate this against the third component of master-narrative identified in Chap. 3: the notion that British Muslims have access to an equitable stake within democratic politics in contemporary Britain. Discussion of this component of master-narrative has been confined to the conceptual level in Chaps. 2 and 3. However, within those discussions it was argued that wider public political climates (in particular, anxieties around national security and Islam in the public space) impact on Muslims in ways that stifle public political engagement in ways that do not (currently) apply for other ethnic or religious groups. Against this backdrop, the 'social' benefit manifested in provision at Medina Primary and Hiqmah School appears to resemble an institutionalised strategy for the public political enfranchisement of Muslims as a broadly marginalised group. In addition to this 'social benefit', at Hiqmah School there was also a practical commitment to providing a school for Muslim children that offered better educational opportunities than those present in the state sector. As a result, at the core of the school's objectives, there has been a consistent commitment to improving educational attainment as a strategy for addressing an 'uneven playing field'. The particular emphasis on educational attainment in the case of Hiqmah was arguably demonstrated with the school having already acquired an all-qualified teaching staff at the time of securing state funding. Thus, at Hiqmah, an integral part of the purpose of the school has historically been focused on educational empowerment.

The above further demonstrates that, for the staff at Hiqmah School and Medina Primary in particular, offering a good Islamic education was inherently related to facilitating improved opportunities for educational attainment. Most importantly, for all of the schools in the study, educational attainment was seen to be, albeit to varying degrees, inherently connected with the wider Islamic provision manifested in ethos. Therefore, it is the totality of educational experience in an Islamic setting, manifested according to highly nuanced local needs, which informs these tailored strategies for educational enfranchisement. These insights are particularly noteworthy given the trend for faith schools to consistently perform better than non-faith schools. In fact, this trend was part of New Labour's political rhetoric around the expansion of state-faith school provision, a rhetoric which has played out with marginal gains in the way of state funding for British Muslim schools. Whilst there might not be sufficient evidence to generalise how Muslim schools are operating more widely, each of the schools in this study was demonstrably committed to providing distinctive Islamically centred strategies for educational enfranchisement. It is important to note here that there is a vital need for further research on British Muslims and educational attainment both in denominational and non-denominational settings. However, the evidence here does suggest that an effective strategy for improved educational enfranchisement and equity for British Muslims lies in the further expansion of Islamic schools within the state sector. The extent to which these schools are able to autonomously develop their own models of provision is crucial in not only facilitating the needs of pupils, staff and communities but also in providing greater educational and political enfranchisement for Muslims as a marginalised group in contemporary Britain.

REFERENCES

Allder, M. (1993). The Meaning of School Ethos. *Westminster Studies of Education, 16*, 59–69.

Berglund, J. (2009). *Teaching Islam: Islamic Religious Education at Three Muslim Schools in Sweden.* Uppsala: Universitetstryckerie.

Burgess, S., Greaves, E., & Wilson, D. (2009). *An Investigation of Educational Outcomes by Ethnicity and Religion: A Report for the National Equality Panel.* Centre for Market and Public Organisation, University of Bristol

Coughlan, S. (2016, January 26). OFSTED Can Downgrade Schools for Islamic Veils. *BBC News.* Available at: http://www.bbc.co.uk/news/education-35411518. Accessed 1 Dec 2016.

Dangor, S. (2005). Islamization of Disciplines: Towards an Indigenous Education System. *Educational Philosophy and Theory, 37*(4), 519–531.

DfE. (2014). *GCSE and Equivalent Attainment by Pupils Characteristics, 2013–14 (Revised).* London: Department for Education.

Halstead, J. M. (2004). An Islamic Concept of Education. *Comparative Education, 40*(4), 517–529.

Hanson, H. Y. (2001). *Lambs to the Slaughter.* California: Ihya Productions.

Hussain, A. (2004). Islamic Education: Why is There a Need for it? *Journal of Beliefs and Values, 25*(3), 317–323.

Lymperopoulou, K., & Parameshwaran, M. (2014). *Dynamics of Diversity: Evidence from the 2011 Census.* ESRC Centre on Dynamics of Ethnicity (CoDE), University of Manchester/Joseph Rowntree Foundation.

McLaughlin, T. (2005). The Educative Importance of Ethos. *British Journal of Educational Studies, 53*(3), 306–325.

Solvason, C. (2005). Investigating Specialist School Ethos... Or Do You Mean Culture? *Educational Studies, 31*(1), 85–94.

CHAPTER 9

In Conclusion: Distilling an Effective Counter-Narrative Around British Muslim Schools

This chapter draws on the insights presented in the research findings as a strategy for contesting several of the components of the master-narrative identified in Chap. 3. Initially, the discussion will focus on tacit intentionality and interest convergence before moving on to revisit policy structures around state funding for Muslim in the light of the findings presented in Chaps. 6, 7 and 8. The chapter will then discuss the diversity and nuanced needs manifested in Muslim communities as stakeholders in Islamic schooling. Finally, substantive conclusions will be drawn around the role that Muslim schools could play in the educational and political enfranchisement of British Muslims as stakeholders in the state.

MUSLIM SCHOOLS, TACIT INTENTIONALITY AND INTEREST CONVERGENCE

The concluding argument in this monograph is the conviction that expanding the numbers of Muslim schools would serve as an effective way of extending the political equity of Muslim communities in Britain as stakeholders in the state. Master-narratives around Islam and the public space suggest that increased Islamic influence is 'risky', and the result of this is the restriction of opportunities to negotiate Muslim interests in mainstream democratic politics in the British public sphere. The implications here are cyclical: if we adhere to such master-narratives, the 'reasonable' course of action results in the displacement of Muslim interests from the public space. This consequently ensures that the political equity British

© The Author(s) 2018
D. Breen, *Muslim Schools, Communities and Critical Race Theory*,
DOI 10.1057/978-1-137-44397-7_9

167

Muslim groups are able to negotiate as stakeholders in the nation-state remains constrained at the margins of tolerability (Breen 2016). In order for this argument to be explored to the fullest, it is important to draw the connection here between education and political enfranchisement. State funding for denominational Muslim schools is significant because it represents state investment in partnerships with Muslim communities. Given the economic gains at stake, state-funded Islamic schooling is important for Muslims as stakeholders in the state. Within this reasoning, education is political. This claim would not mean much if there was little evidence to suggest that Islamic schooling is important for British Muslims. However, Muslim communities have demonstrated with their actions the importance of denominational faith schooling through the ever-growing numbers of Muslim schools in the independent sector. Furthermore, the lengthy processes in applying for state funding detailed in the research findings presented here, but also in the case of schools such as Islamic Primary and Feversham College detailed elsewhere (see Tinker 2009: 540), further demonstrates the extent to which efforts have been made from within Muslim communities to bring Islamic denominational schooling into the mainstream education sector. The secondary and primary analysis presented in the monograph has clearly demonstrated that Muslim schools which have successfully entered the voluntary-aided sector between 1998 and 2010 undeniably did so against substantive odds. These 'odds' were manifested within a system which was technically capable of facilitating denominational Muslim schools but ultimately served to offer minimal gains as a mechanism for constructing a smokescreen that obscured the difficulties for Muslim communities in actually securing effective outcomes. The outcome allows for the state to present itself as liberal and open to making economic investment in Muslim schools, with proven examples where a small number of schools are successful, but without committing to any substantive model of enfranchisement through denominational Islamic education. These insights are revealing in their own terms, but they take on more sinister overtones when positioned against the first and second components of the master-narrative identified in Chap. 3:

1. The notion that Islam can only ever exist in tension with Britishness or Englishness and;
2. The discursive implication that substantive Islamic influence or mobilisation in the public space should be met with suspicion and concern and therefore needs to be policed, restricted or closely monitored.

When you position the outcomes for Muslim schools in the voluntary-aided actor against the backdrop of these two components of the master-narrative around Muslim schools, then the difficulties in making substantive gains starts to look like the strategic result of a calculated effort, or tacit intentionality, to minimise enfranchisement for British Muslims. Furthermore, in line with the second component of the master-narrative identified above, where there have been gains in the voluntary-aided sector, meeting the necessary regulations has sometimes required changes that have fundamentally impacted on stakeholders in those schools. For example, in the case of both Al-Falah and Al-Iman, the benefit of securing state funding was offset by the displacement of unqualified teaching staff. Whilst the requirement for teachers to be qualified is presented as a reasonable prerequisite for acquiring state funding, this requirement impacts for Muslim communities in specific ways and has racialised outcomes. Although the Academies Act 2010 has led to a shift in policy away from the requirement that teachers in academies and free schools carry Qualified Teacher Status (QTS), the proportion of teachers with QTS remains very high at over 96% (UK Government 2014: 6). Thus, even in the light of the relaxing of regulations around teaching qualifications, the high proportion of teachers with QTS invariably means that competing effectively within this employment market ultimately requires carrying formal teaching qualifications. So, whilst QTS is no longer formally required to teach in academies or free schools, market forces operate to ensure that holding formal teaching qualifications remains as an industry benchmark across the state education sector against which prospective teachers are measured. But this becomes even more of a cause for concern when considering numbers of teachers with minority ethnic backgrounds that are present in high proportions among British Muslim groups. For example, census data from 2011 identifies that 4.8% of the population of England and Wales identify as Muslim (ONS 2011b). The Muslim Council of Britain has broken this data down further and identifies that those who identify as 'Asian or Asian British' make up 67.6% of all Muslims in England and Wales (MCB 2014: 24), and 43.4% of those who are Asian or Asian British are Muslim (MCB 2014: 25). The same category of Asian and Asian British makes up 7.5% of the population of England and Wales (ONS 2011a). Whilst this measure is far from ideal, it does allow us to draw some conclusions about the representation of minority ethnic groups across staff in the education sector. Unfortunately, national-level data on teachers is broken down across broader census ethnicity classifications which do not allow us to see exact proportions of, for example, Pakistani and Bangladeshi teachers. However, we can identify that the largest proportional ethnic group amongst Muslims in England and Wales would fall into the category of 'Black and Minority Ethnic' (BME) often used in large-scale research on ethnicity. Whilst there is no national-level data which provides finer-scale minority ethnic categories, data on representations of BME teachers more generally is a cause for concern. The Department for Education's School Workforce in England (2014) report identifies that 88% of all teachers in state-funded schools are white British, with the remaining ethnic groups comprising of 2% white Irish, 3% any other white background, 2% Indian, 1% black Caribbean and 4% 'other' (DfE 2014: 8). Whilst these categories undoubtedly mean that much meaningful data is lost here, the proportions that are recorded are still a cause for concern with regard to the representation of Muslims within the teaching profession. Most notably, it appears that even the broader minority ethnic category of Asian or Asian British, a group of which 43.4% are Muslim, is not represented, yet the category 'Indian' is represented individually. Whilst this picture is far from clear, the inference here is that those 'Asian or Asian British' who are Muslim are likely to be dramatically underrepresented among teachers in the state-funded sector. Given that over 96% of teachers hold QTS, the requirement for voluntary-aided schools to appoint qualified teachers has very specific implications for Muslim schools. This is especially significant when considering the likely massive under-representation of Muslims among qualified teachers in England and Wales. At the systemic level, at least between the years of 1998 and 2010, the prerequisite for qualified teaching staff under voluntary-aided status played out in ways that disadvantaged unqualified Muslim teachers who have established themselves in the independent sector. The outcome has been a framework around faith schooling which permits some marginal gains for Muslim schools pursuing state funding but only where provision is regulated systemically in a way that dramatically increases the chances of non-Muslim teachers being appointed.

Of course, it is important to recognise that non-Muslim teachers at Hiqmah School and Al-Falah were highly valued at those schools. The argument here is not that non-Muslim teachers are problematic for Muslim schools—the cases of both Hiqmah School and Al-Falah demonstrate the very opposite. But there is a systemic restriction to the autonomy that Muslim schools have to appoint teachers which is not present in the independent sector. For example, at Medina Primary, there was a central emphasis on an all-Muslim staff leading children by example. For Medina then, this restriction would arguably result in the displacement or erosion of Muslim-centred voices in stakeholdership over Muslim interests in their particular model of provision. The argument here is that Muslim schools should have autonomy to appoint teachers based on the localised needs of stakeholders in Muslim communities. For some schools, such as Hiqmah, their chosen institutional strategies for meeting local needs will mean that a high value is placed on appointing a balance of Muslim and non-Muslim teachers. However, other schools may prefer to have a higher proportion of Muslim teachers—a target which is difficult under voluntary-aided status given the likely under-representation of Muslims among qualified teachers in England and Wales. The above arguments have more sinister overtones when situating them within the broader current political climate around Islam in the British public space. For example, when taking account of the second component of the master-narrative identified above, the way that the voluntary-aided framework has played out for Muslim schools appears to reinforce the notion that substantive Islamic mobilisations in the public space should be met with concern, and regulated or monitored; and in this case, through increasing the chances of non-Muslim influence within the staff body. It is argued here that this invariably represents a significant example of tacit intentionality that has persistently sidelined Muslim interests from denominational faith schooling in the voluntary-aided sector.

STRATEGIES AND SMOKESCREENS

As argued above, the ability for governments to present cases where Muslim schools have successfully secured state funding serves as a smokescreen to obscure the difficulties and challenges faced by Muslim communities looking to enter into partnerships with the state through denominational Islamic schooling. The political rhetoric detailed in Chap. 3 clearly saw the New Labour government constructing itself as 'open' to partnerships with Muslim communities whilst minimising access to substantive gains. In more recent years, following the Academies Act of 2010, we have seen the Coalition and Conservative governments offering 'free schooling' as a universal strategy for communities to establish schools that serve local needs. If we return to the points raised above around teaching staff, the Academies Act of 2010 and its aftermath has seen a shift away from the requirement for teaching staff to carry QTS status. On the surface then, this new and emergent system may initially appear to solve some of the difficulties that Muslim schools have faced when considering state funding through the voluntary-aided system. But whilst we have actually seen the expansion of Muslim schools through free schooling, the mechanism is fraught with difficulties that again can be identified as embodying tacit intentionality (this point is developed further later on; also see Chap. 3). Central to the argument here is the notion of the autonomous Muslim school—that is, advocating the gradual nationalisation of Muslim schools as they exist in the independent sector. These mobilisations represent the purest embodiment of institutionalised British Muslim interests and as such represent an excellent reference point for policy makers looking to enfranchise those communities. This process should represent a mutual investment where the state volunteers substantive support and shared responsibility, and local Muslim stakeholders take responsibility for ensuring that the denominational Islamic character of the school appropriately reflects the highly nuanced needs of local communities. The disproportionate accountability placed on individual free schools undermines the possibility of this kind of partnership. The voluntary-aided system has worked for the interests of specific Muslim communities in certain contexts, such as those served by Hiqmah School. However, the sacrifices endured at Al-Falah and Al-Iman alongside the highly nuanced nature of provision in the independent sector suggests that this is only one model. Furthermore, this model, and the potential compromises that it might require, may very well have led many independent Muslim schools prior to 2010 to avoid the process of applying for state funding. Coupled with the ways in which tacit intentionality within policy structures have explicitly operated and continue to operate for Muslim schools seeking state funding, anxieties around the possible and associated risks detailed above may explain why there is such a disproportionate representation of Muslim schools in the independent sector (158) compared with the state-funded sector (21). Clearly, the discussion above embodies a counter-narrative which challenges the fourth component of the master-narratives around Muslim schools: the conviction that policy has provided Muslim communities with ample opportunities for denominational educational enfranchisement in the public space.

Muslim Schools, Diversity and Community Needs

The next objective to address here is to challenge the fifth component of the master-narratives around Muslim schools: the assumption that Muslim schools are likely to be monocultural and therefore will serve broadly homogeneous needs. Whilst the accounts of provision at Medina Primary,

Al-Falah, Al-Iman and Hiqmah School do indeed have commonalities, Chaps. 6, 7 and 8 have also demonstrated the complexities of meeting local needs for each school. The landscape is far from homogeneous, with the interests of both localised and fragmented communities being met. At the very basic level, the profile of intake at each school was characterised by ethnic diversity, with this being particularly manifested at Medina Primary—the one school in the study that continued to operate within the independent sector. For example, the ethnic backgrounds represented at Medina Primary included South Asian with a small majority of Gujarati Indian or Indian-Ugandan children, Bengali, Somali, African-Caribbean, French and dual-heritage with English, Gujarati, Arabic, Bengali, Italian, Punjabi, Somali, Tamil and Urdu being identified as languages spoken within the school. Similarly, the intake at Hiqmah School was also far from monocultural with families represented across South Asian, black Caribbean, Somali, Egyptian, Syrian, dual-heritage and white British revert backgrounds. The trend continued at Al-Falah, which catered to the needs of notable numbers of Pakistani, Gujarati, Bengali and Somali families with approximately 24 languages being spoken among children across the whole school. Finally, the intake at Al-Iman included families from Somali, African-Caribbean, dual-heritage, Algerian, Irish, white British, Chinese and revert families. Clearly the evidence presented here provides part of a counter-narrative to contest the notion that Muslim schools are necessarily monocultural. But these insights can be situated within existing research to provide a more substantive evidential base for the counter-narrative. The findings discussed above are consistent with those of Tinker (2009), who interviewed stakeholders in Muslim school-ing across four main groups: politicians from leading political parties; representatives of Muslim, Christian and secular or humanist organisations; head teachers at Muslim and non-Muslim schools, both state funded and independent; and Muslim parents who send their children to the various schools identified in the penultimate group (Tinker 2006a: 76–77). Tinker contests the misconception that non-denominational state schools are more ethnically diverse, whereas faith schools are broadly monocultural, which is held by many critics of faith schools. She argues that in some areas of Britain, particularly in northern towns and cities, there are Church of England and non-faith community schools that contain only Muslim pupils, and that this pupil population can be entirely from a particular settled migrant community (Tinker 2006b: 15). Conversely, some denom-inational Muslim schools, particularly in London, have pupils of many different nationalities, languages, ethnicities and cultures, brought together *only* by their belief in Islam (Tinker 2006b: 15). Tinker gives an example, recalling that on visiting the London-based Islamia Primary School in 2003, it contained pupils of 23 different nationalities (Tinker 2006b: 15). She concludes arguing that the suggestion that faith schools fail to prepare their pupils for life in a multicultural society is based on inaccurate perceptions of both faith and mainstream state schools (Tinker 2006b: 15). Thus, even if we only look at concerns around ethnic diversity and Islamic schooling, the available evidence provides a firm foundation from which to contest the fifth component of the master-narratives around Muslim schools: the assumption that Muslim schools will be monocultural and therefore meet broadly homogeneous needs.

This leads us to the final part of the counter-narrative presented in this monograph—the extent to which the needs of Muslim communities have been met and mobilised through highly nuanced models of provision among the Muslim schools in the study. Chapters 6, 7 and 8 have detailed the highly nuanced models of provision that have been manifested at Medina Primary, Hiqmah School, Al-Falah and Al-Iman. One of the key themes throughout the monograph has been the extent to which needs within Muslim communities have been catered for by Muslim schools. The strategies of provision are invariably related to the position of each school as either independent or voluntary aided. Commonalities in provision have included efforts to 'Islamicise' curriculum content to varying degrees, facilitate practices in everyday school life and to emphasise the use of Arabic in everyday interaction. However, and in line with the insights provided around ethnic diversity above, these strategies have evolved and are implemented to serve very specific needs across diverse Muslim communities in each case. Whereas Medina prioritised an all-Muslim staff leading children by example, Hiqmah School and Al-Falah emphasised the importance of the influence of non-Muslim staff for pupils. For Hiqmah School, a model was adopted early on, which saw the school already reflecting the prerequisites for state funding well before it was finally achieved. Therefore, that transition to grant-maintained (and later voluntary-aided) status was an organic and natural progression, albeit hard fought. For Al-Falah, and more so Al-Iman, state funding was about economic survival for schools which were struggling to continue in the independent sector. In both cases, the emphasis was on securing state funding to alleviate the financial burden of fees for local Muslims with an interest in Islamic schooling for their children. By way of contrast, at Medina

Primary state funding was not considered a realistic option for the school precisely because of the implications that this might bring for the nature of provision. Related to this, voluntary-aided status would also require the school to affiliate itself with a mosque, a process which had been avoided so that the school could continue to provide for the interests of many differing interpretations of Islam rather than promoting one dominant reading of the faith. So whilst we might be able to identify some commonalities, the needs that are being catered or prioritised in each case are highly nuanced and invariably intertwined with interpretations of need in Muslim communities served by each school. Such a complex picture provides the proverbial 'nail in the coffin' for the second part of the fifth component of the master-narratives around Muslim schools: that Muslim schools cater to broadly homogeneous needs.

A Note on the Future for State-Funded Muslim Schools

In line with the conclusions drawn in this chapter, what we need to see, if British Muslims are to be effectively educationally and politically enfranchised through state-funded denominational schooling, is a system that facilitates autonomous Muslim schools. Free schooling appears to offer this, but there are serious limitations around the lack of state involvement and support for communities that lack experience in the formal processes around founding and maintaining schools in the state sector. Either policy makers are aware of these factors and they are actively ignored, or there is a lack of awareness of these factors and their implications for Muslim communities looking to develop state-funded Islamic schools from the ground up. Whether the interests of Muslim communities are actively ignored or passively overlooked, the outcome still positions Muslim stakeholders at a position of disadvantage. Comparing existing figures of independent and state-funded Muslim schools demonstrates a wealth of experience in denominational Islamic schooling in the independent sector versus limited experience in the state-funded sector. Whilst the recent emergence of free schooling appears to solve the issue in principle, the discussions in Chap. 3 and in this chapter have demonstrated some of the key risks that are specifically faced by Muslim free schools. Furthermore, the framework also represents a near-perfect model of interest convergence. Not only do many other already enfranchised groups also stand to make gains, but where gains are made with the establishment of Muslim free schools, they function under a highly racialised microscope of concern and anxiety. No other group that stands to make gains through free schooling faces that prospect. Furthermore, where there are concerns around practices, provision or organisational or management processes in Muslim free schools, the emphasis is on the 'Muslim' character of the school, rather than its status as a free school or the lack of state responsibility built into that system that inevitably disadvantages Muslim communities owing to their limited experience in denominational state-funded schooling. This process is cyclical and is informed by a tacit intentionality that serves to ensure that there is a sustained public concern about the Islamic in the British public space. The result is that we have a system which is set up to ensure that mobilisations of Muslim interests in denominational state schooling are permitted to exist only under a scrutiny that sustains wider tensions around Islam in the British public space. This reality sits in stark contrast to the strategy for enfranchising British Muslims advocated in this monograph— to increase numbers of state-funded autonomous Muslim schools as a strategy for increasing public political equity for Muslims. This process requires an active investment on the part of the state in terms of offering both support and volunteering shared responsibility for the successful expansion of state-funded autonomous Muslim schools. It is argued here that this would increase the stake held by Muslims as British citizens in polity and the nation-state, in effect contributing to the process of eroding the various Islamophobias that exist (and which current policy ensures are sustained) around Muslim schools in the state-funded education sector.

In Conclusion: So What?

So why does any of this matter? It matters because independent Muslim schools represent perfectly nuanced models of what particular British Muslim communities want for the educational enfranchisement of their children. Incorporating these institutions into mainstream educational provision with minimal change and maximum state support would therefore represent one of the clearest ways for offering public political enfranchisement for British Muslims from the ground up. Free schools in theory offer part one of this model (state money for schools with highly nuanced characteristics), but a CRT analysis reveals that this is offset against massively increased risk of public accountability where inexperience or a lack of state or professional support results in a problem. An approach that facilitates a space in mainstream publicly funded education with minimal compromise and increased professional support would result in the establishment of truly 'ground up' and highly nuanced manifestations of public political equity for British Muslims. So why should this approach be advocated? Well, Chaps. 2 and 3 have demonstrated the ways in which demonstrating legitimate dissent has become risky for Muslims in Britain. In the worst-case scenarios, those expressing political dissent can be lumped in with those actually posing a risk for national security. This clearly stands in contrast to third component of the master-narrative identified in Chap. 3: the notion that British Muslims have access to an equitable stake within democratic politics in contemporary Britain. The wider discursive effects of this are far more subtle and constricting than they may initially appear. From a CRT perspective, the all-important political voices of Muslims become displaced from mainstream public political spaces as a result of the conflating of legitimate democratic dissent with religiosity. In short, perspectives embodying dissent from those who are easily identifiable as Muslim become dismissed as simply being informed by too much religious influence. But a strong identification with Islam should not come at the cost of being displaced from legitimate public political discussion. It is against this backdrop that Muslim schools become so important. Independent Muslim schools already exist and have done for longer than state-funded Muslim schools have. Therefore, there is no logic for arguing that, in the current system, these highly nuanced schools should not exist. Existing policy clearly facilitates their existence in the independent sector. Bringing those schools into the mainstream educational system in the ways specified above would offer British Muslims significant stakeholdership in terms of polity and the state. Offering these spaces in a way that meets the varying needs of Muslim communities would do much to enfranchise British Muslims as stakeholders in British educational and political equity. The proposition here is that this would represent one approach that would start to erode the many discursive forces discussed in this monograph that ensure the continued racialised marginalisation of Muslims in Britain. Existing independent Muslim schools represent such near-perfect models of need that the mainstreaming of provision as it currently exists in the independent sector, along with appropriate professional support for those schools through partnerships with the state with shared responsibility and accountability, represents an ideal opportunity to enfranchise a marginalised group through substantive gains in educational and political enfranchisement.

REFERENCES

Breen, D. (2016). Critical Race Theory, Policy Rhetoric and Outcomes: The Case of Muslim Schools in Britain. *Race Ethnicity and Education*, published online 8 Nov 2016. Available at: http://www.tandfonline.com/doi/abs/10.1080/13613324.2016.1248828

DfE. (2014). *School Workforce in England: November 2013*. London: Department for Education.

MCB. (2014). *British Muslims in Numbers: A Demographic, Sociology-Economic and Health Profile of Muslims in Britain Drawing on the 2011 Census*. The Muslim Council of Britain's Research and Documentation Committee, London, Muslim Council or Britain.

ONS. (2011a). *Ethnicity and National Identity in England and Wales: 2011*. London: Office for National Statistics.

ONS. (2011b). *Religion in England and Wales 2011*. London: Office for National Statistics.

Tinker, C. (2006a). Islamophobia, Social Cohesion and Autonomy: Challenging the Arguments Against State Funded Muslim Schools in Britain. *Muslim Educational Quarterly, 23*(1&2), 4–19.

Tinker, C. (2006b). *State Funded Muslim Schools? Equality, Identity and Community in Multi-Faith Britain*, Unpublished PhD Thesis, University of Nottingham Library.

Tinker, C. (2009). Rights, Social Cohesion and Identity: Arguments for and Against State Funded Muslim Schools in Britain. *Race, Ethnicity and Education, 12*(4), 539–553.

UK Government. (2014). *Types of School: Free Schools*, UK Government Website. Available at: https://www.gov.uk/types-of-school/free-schools. Accessed 3 Jan 2015.

GLOSSARY OF ISLAMIC TERMS

Ablah:	Perfectly formed
Adab:	General appropriate behaviour
Abjad:	Arabic alphabet
'Adl:	Justice
Alayhi salam:	Upon him/her be peace, abbreviated to 'a.s.' after a prophet's name
Al-hamdu lil-lah:	Praise be to God
Allah:	God
Allahu 'Akbar:	Allah is great
Al-Masjid an-Nabawi:	The 'Mosque of the Prophet', located in Medina, Saudi Arabia
Aqidah:	Belief
Assalamu alaikum:	Greeting meaning 'peace be upon you'
Assalam wa rahmatullah-i-wa barakatuhu:	May God be with you, with his blessings and his kindness
Ayat:	Evidence or miracles, also verses of the Holy *Qur'an*
Bismillah:	In or with the name of *Allah*
Din:	The faith
Dua:	Prayer of supplication
Eid:	Festival. Usually refers to *Eid ul Fitr*, which marks the end of Ramadan. Also refers to *Eid al Adha*, the festival which

© The Author(s) 2018
D. Breen, *Muslim Schools, Communities and Critical Race Theory*,
DOI 10.1057/978-1-137-44397-7

180 GLOSSARY OF ISLAMIC TERMS

	marks Ibrahim's (a.s.) willingness to sacrifice his son as an act of obedience to God
Fitra:	Innocence
Hadith:	The traditions of the Prophet Mohammed (s.a.w.)
Hajj:	Pilgrimage to Mecca
Hijab:	Headscarf worn by Muslim women to cover the head
Hikira/hiqmah:	Wisdom
Insan kamil:	The perfect human being
Insh'Allah:	God willing
Jazak'Allah:	Thank you
Madrassa:	Supplementary Islamic school
Masha'Allah:	Used for 'well done' to acknowledge appropriate behaviour
Masjid:	Mosque or prayer room
Nashid:	Islamic song, often sung without musical accompaniment
Niqab:	Veil worn by some Muslim women to cover the face
Qur'an:	The Holy Book revealed to Prophet Mohammed (s.a.w.) by Allah
Salah/salat:	Prayer
Sallallahu alayhi wa salam:	Abbreviated to 's.a.w.' following reference to Prophet Mohammed. Means 'may the peace and blessings of Allah be upon him'
Salam:	Peace
Sirah:	The biography/scholarship of the life of Prophet Mohammed (s.a.w.)
Subhana Wa Tala:	Glorious and exalted is He. Follows reference to Allah
Sunnah:	Ways and laws of Prophet Mohammed (s.a.w.)
Surah:	Chapters of the Holy Qur'an
Tajwid:	Appropriate intonation for recitation
Ustad:	Master/teacher (masculine)
Ustada:	Master/teacher (feminine)

GLOSSARY OF ISLAMIC TERMS   181

Walaikum salam:	And upon you be peace. Used in response to *assalamu alaikum*
Wudu:	Ablution made before *salah*/prayer in the manner as described in the Hadith
Zakat:	The obligation to contribute to charity, literally means 'purification'

Notes on the Use of Arabic

In the text, Arabic terms are in italics. Islamic terms were often pluralised, both by interviewees and in the writing of the thesis. In these instances, a non-italicised 's' is added at the end of an Islamic word in the text, e.g., *surah*s, *dua*s, etc.

© The Author(s) 2018
D. Breen, *Muslim Schools, Communities and Critical Race Theory,*
DOI 10.1057/978-1-137-44397-7

ISLAMIC ARABIC DEFINITIONS ARE TAKEN FROM

Qazi, M. A. (2000). *A Concise Dictionary of Islamic Terms.* New Delhi: Kitab Bhavan.

References

Adams, R. (2013). Government Shuts Free School Amid Claims Taxpayers' Money Was Wasted. *The Guardian*. Available at: http://www.theguardian.com/education/2013/dec/13/government-shuts-free-school-discovery-west-sussex

Agar, M. H. (1996). *The Professional Stranger: An Informal Introduction to Ethnography* (2nd ed.). London: Academic Press Limited.

Ali, S. (2005). Why Here, Why Now? Young Muslim Women Wearing Hijab. *The Muslim World, 95*, 515–530.

Allder, M. (1993). The Meaning of School Ethos. *Westminster Studies of Education, 16*, 59–69.

Allen, C. (2010a). Islamophobia: From K.I.S.S. to R.I.P. In S. Sayyid & A. Vakil (Eds.), *Thinking Through Islamophobia: Global Perspectives* (pp. 51–64). London: C. Hurst & Co Publishers.

Allen, C. (2010b). Fear and Loathing: The Political Discourse in Relation to Muslims and Islam in the British Contemporary Setting. *Politics and Religion, 4*(2), 221–236.

AMS. (2014). Data from the Association of Muslim Schools UK. Website as of 6 October 2014. Available at: http://ams-uk.org/muslim-schools/

BBC. (2013a). *Woolwich: Michael Adebolajo Charged with Lee Rigby Murder.* Available at: http://www.bbc.co.uk/news/uk-22743438. Accessed 1 June 2013.

BBC. (2013b). Al-Madinah Free School in Derby Labelled 'Dysfunctional' by OFSTED. Available at: http://www.bbc.co.uk/news/uk-england-derbyshire-24548690. 17 October 2013.

Beckett, A. (2012). Bradford Free School Fiasco: The Hard Lessons Learned. *The Guardian*. Available at: http://www.theguardian.com/education/2012/sep/10/bradford-free-school-fiasco-lessons

188 REFERENCES

Bell, D. (1980). Brown and the Interest-Convergence Dilemma. In D. Bell (Ed.), *Shades of Brown: New Perspectives on School Desegregation* (pp. 90–106). New York: Teachers College Press.

Bell, D. (1990). After We're Gone: Prudent Speculations on America in a Post-racial Epoch. *St Louis Law Journal*, reprinted in R. Delgado & J. Stefancic (eds.) 2000: *Critical Race Theory: The Cutting Edge (second edition)* (pp. 2–8). Philadelphia: Temple University Press.

Berglund, J. (2009). *Teaching Islam: Islamic Religious Education at Three Muslim Schools in Sweden*. Uppsala: Universitetstryckerie.

Bhopal, K. (2000). Gender, 'Race' and Power in the Research Process: South Asian Women in East London. In C. Truman, D. M. Mertens, & B. Humphries (Eds.), *Research and Inequality* (pp. 67–79). London: UCL Press.

Bigger, S. (2006). Muslim Women's Views on Dress Code and the Hijaab: Some Issues for Education. *Journal of Beliefs and Values, 27*(2), 215–226.

Bignall, P. (2013, May 23). 'He Was Always Smiling': Lee Rigby Named as Woolwich Victim. *The Independent*. Available at: http://www.independent.co.uk/news/uk/crime/he-was-always-smiling-lee-rigby-named-as-woolwich-victim-8628583.html. Accessed 1 Dec 2016.

Bolton, P. (2013). *Converter Academies: Statistics*, 12 June 2013, House of Commons Library.

Bonnett, A. (1997). Constructions of Whiteness in European and American Anti-racism. In P. Werbner & T. Modood (Eds.), *Debating Cultural Hybridity: Multi-cultural Identities and the Politics of Anti-racism* (pp. 173–192). London: Zed Books.

Borger, J., & MacAskill, E. (2016, December 20). Truck Attacks in Berlin and Nice Reflect Change in Islamic State Tactics. *The Guardian*. Available at: https://www.theguardian.com/world/2016/dec/20/truck-attacks-in-berlin-and-nice-reflect-change-in-isis-tactics. Accessed 21 Dec 2016.

Breen, D. (2009). A Qualitative Narrative of the Transition from Independent to Voluntary-Aided Status: A Problem for the Concept of the Muslim School. In A. A. Veinguer, G. Deitz, D. Jozsa, & T. Knauth (Eds.), *Islam in Education in European Countries – Pedagogical Concepts and Empirical Findings* (pp. 95–112). Münster: Waxmann.

Breen, D. (2013). State-Funded Muslim Schools: Stakeholders and Legitimacy in the UK Context. In J. Miller, K. O'Grady, & U. McKenna (Eds.), *Religion in Education: Innovation in International Research* (pp. 41–57). London: Routledge.

Breen, D. (2014). British Muslim Schools: Institutional Isomorphism and the Transition from Independent to Voluntary-Aided Status. In R. Race & V. Lander (Eds.), *Advancing Race and Ethnicity in Education* (pp. 32–46). Hampshire: Palgrave Macmillan.

Breen, D. (2016). Critical Race Theory, Policy Rhetoric and Outcomes: The Case of Muslim Schools in Britain. *Race Ethnicity and Education*, published online

8 Nov 2016. Available at: http://www.tandfonline.com/doi/abs/10.1080/1 3613324.2016.1248828

Burgess, R. G. (1988). Conversations with a Purpose: The Ethnographic Interview in Educational Research. In R. G. Burgess (Ed.), *Studies in Qualitative Methodology: Conducting Qualitative Research* (Vol. 1, pp. 137–156). London: JAI Press.

Burgess, R. G. (2000). Some Issues and Problems in Cross-Cultural Case Study Research. In C. J. Pole & R. G. Burgess (Eds.), *Studies in Qualitative Methodology Vol.6: Cross-Cultural Case Study* (pp. 43–52). New York: Elsevier Science.

Burgess, S., Greaves, E., & Wilson, D. (2009). *An Investigation of Educational Outcomes by Ethnicity and Religion: A Report for the National Equality Panel.* Centre for Market and Public Organisation, University of Bristol

Carspecken, P. F. (1996). *Critical Ethnography in Educational Research: A Theoretical and Practical Guide.* New York: Routledge.

Carvajal, D. (2002). The Artisan's Tools: Critical Issues When Teaching and Learning CAQDAS. *Forum Qualitative Sozialforschung/Forum: Qualitative Social Research, 3*(2), article 14, [47 paragraphs], http://nbn-resolving.de/ urn:nbn:de:0114-fqs0202147. Accessed 1 Aug 2010

CES. (2012). *Collecting Data on Catholic Schools and Colleges.* Catholic Education Service. Available at: http://www.catholiceducation.org.uk/news/ces-blog/ item/1000075-collecting-data-on-catholic-schools-and-colleges. Accessed 24 May 2013.

Chadwick, P. (2012). *The Church School of the Future Review.* Church of England Archbishop's Council – Education Division.

CofE. (2013). *Church Schools and Academies in England and Wales,* Church of England, Copyright: Archbishop's Council. Accessed at: http://www. churchofengland.org/education/church-schools-academies.aspx, 23 May 2013.

Corbin, J., & Strauss, A. (2008). *Basics of Qualitative Research* (3rd ed.). Thousand Oaks: SAGE.

Coughlan, S. (2007, May 14). Education, Education, Education. *BBC News.* Available at: http://news.bbc.co.uk/1/hi/education/6564933.stm

Coughlan, S. (2016, January 26). OFSTED Can Downgrade Schools for Islamic Veils. *BBC News.* Available at: http://www.bbc.co.uk/news/education-35411518. Accessed 1 Dec 2016.

Crenshaw, K. (2002). *The First Decade: Critical Reflections, or "A Foot in the Closing Door".* In F. Valdes, J. McCristal Culp, & A. Harris (Eds.), *Crossroads, Directions and a New Critical Race Theory* (pp. 9–31). Philadelphia: Temple University Press.

Crenshaw, K., Gotanda, N., Peller, G., & Thomas, K. (Eds.). (1995). *Critical Race Theory: The Key Writings that Formed the Movement.* New York: Free Press.

190   REFERENCES

Dangor, S. (2005). Islamization of Disciplines: Towards an Indigenous Education System. *Educational Philosophy and Theory, 37*(4), 519–531.

DCSF. (2007). *Faith in the System: The Role of Schools with a Religious Character in English Education and Society*. London: Department of Children Schools and Families.

Delgado, R. (1997). Rodrigo's Fifteenth Chronicle: Racial Mixture, Latino-Critical Scholarship, and the Black-White Binary. *Texas Law Review, 75*, 1181–1201.

Delgado, R., & Stefancic, J. (2000). *Critical Race Theory: The Cutting Edge (Second Edition)*. Philadelphia: Temple University Press.

DfE. (2014a). *GCSE and Equivalent Attainment by Pupils Characteristics, 2013–14 (Revised)*. London: Department for Education.

DfE. (2014b). *School Workforce in England: November 2013*. London: Department for Education.

DfE. (2015). *The Prevent Duty: Departmental Advice for Schools and Childcare Providers*. London: Department for Education.

DfE. (2016). *Registration of Independent Schools: Departmental Advice for Proprietors and Prospective Proprietors of Independent Schools in England*. London: Department for Education.

DfEE. (2001). *Schools Building on Success: Raising Standards, Promoting Diversity, Achieving Results*. Norwich: Her Majesty's Stationary Office.

DfES. (2002). *Regulatory Reform (Voluntary-aided Schools Liabilities and Funding) (England) Order 2002*. London: Department for Education and Skills.

DfES. (2005). *Registration of Independent Schools: A Guide for Proprietors on the Statutory Requirements for Registration*, Independent and Education Boarding Team.

Dodd, V., & Addley, E. (2015, June 8). Leytonstone Knife Attack: Man Convicted of Attempted Murder'. *The Guardian*. Available at: https://www.theguardian.com/uk-news/2016/jun/08/leytonstone-knife-attack-man-convicted-of-attempted. Accessed 10 Aug 2016.

Dooley, P. (1991). *Muslim Private Schools*. In G. Walford (Ed.), *Tradition, Change and Diversity*. London: Chapman.

Du Bois, W. E. B. (1897). *The Conservation of Races*. Washington, DC: American Negro Academy.

Du Bois, W. E. B. (1903). *The Souls of Black Folk*. Cambridge: University Press John Wilson & Son.

Duncan, G. A. (2005). Critical Race Ethnography in Education: Narrative, Inequality and the Problem of Epistemology. *Race Ethnicity and Education, 8*(1), 93–114.

Fanon, F. (1963). *The Wretched of the Earth*. New York: Grove Press.

Fekete, L. (2004). Anti-Muslim Racism and the European Security State. *Race & Class, 46*(3), 3–29.

REFERENCES   191

Fontana, A., & Frey, J. H. (2005). The Interview: From Neutral Stance to Political Involvement. In N. K. Denzin & Y. S. Lincoln (Eds.), *The SAGE Handbook of Qualitative Research* (pp. 695–727). Thousand Oaks: SAGE.

Freedman, J. (2004). Secularism as a Barrier to Integration? The French Dilemma. *International Migration, 42*(3), 5–25.

Garvey, M. (1927). Garvey Recalls History of His Career in United States in Ward Theater Speech, 18 December 1927. In R. A. Hill, B. Bair, E. Johnson, & S. De Sal (Eds.), *1990: The Marcus Garvey and Universal Negro Improvement Association Papers Vol. VII November 1927–August 1940* (pp. 46–63). London: University of California Press.

Gavins, R. (2016). *Buffalo Soldiers. The Cambridge Guide to African American History.* New York: Cambridge University Press.

Gillborn, D. (2005). Education Policy as an Act of White Supremacy: Whiteness, Critical Race Theory and Reform. *Journal of Education Policy, 20*(4), 484–505.

Gillborn, D. (2008). *Racism and Education: Coincidence or Conspiracy?* London: Routledge.

Glaser, B. G., & Strauss, A. L. (1967). *The Discovery of Grounded Theory.* Chicago: Aldine Publishing.

Go, J. (2013). Fanon's Postcolonial Cosmopolitanism. *European Journal of Social Theory, 16*(2), 208–225.

Halstead, J. M. (2004). An Islamic Concept of Education. *Comparative Education, 40*(4), 517–529.

Hammersley, M., & Atkinson, P. (1995). *Ethnography: Principles in Practice* (2nd ed.). London: Routledge.

Hanson, H. Y. (2001). *Lambs to the Slaughter.* California: Ihya Productions.

Helm, T., Taylor, M., & Davis, R. (2011, February 5). David Cameron Sparks Fury from Critics Who Say Attack on Multiculturalism Has Boosted English Defence League. *The Guardian.* Available at: http://www.guardian.co.uk/politics/2011/feb/05/david-cameron-speech-criticised-edl. Accessed 21 July 2014.

Henley, J., & Chrisafis, A. (2015, November 14). Paris Terror Attacks: Hollande Says ISIS Atrocity Was "Act of War". *The Guardian.* Available at: https://www.theguardian.com/world/2015/nov/13/paris-attacks-shootings-explosions-hostages. Accessed 2 Dec 2016.

Henley, J., & Willsher, K. (2015, January 7). Charlie Hebdo Attacks: "It's Carnage, a Bloodbath. Everyone is Dead. *The Guardian.* Available at: https://www.theguardian.com/world/2015/jan/07/charlie-hebdo-shooting-paris-magazine-target-raid. Accessed 21 Aug 2015.

Hirschmann, N. J. (1998). Western Feminism, Eastern Veiling, and the Question of Free Agency. *Constellations, 5*(3), 345–368.

Housee, S. (2012). What's the Point? Anti-racism and Students' Voices Against Islamophobia. *Race Ethnicity and Education, 15*(1), 101–120.

Hussain, A. (2004). Islamic Education: Why is There a Need for it? *Journal of Beliefs and Values, 25*(3), 317–323.

192 REFERENCES

Hussain, Y., & Bagguley, P. (2012). Securitised Citizens: Islamophobia, Racism and the 7/7 Bombings. *The Sociological Review, 60*(4), 715–734.

John, P., Margetts, H., Rowland, D., & Weir, S. (2006). *The BNP: The Roots of its Appeal,* Democratic Audit. Human Rights Centre, University of Essex.

Kelle, U. (1995). Introduction: An Overview of Computer-Aided Methods in Qualitative Research. In U. Kelle (Ed.), *Computer-Aided Qualitative Data Analysis: Theory, Methods and Practice* (pp. 1–17). London: SAGE.

Kershaw, I. (2014). *Investigation Report: Trojan Horse Letter – Report of Ian Kershaw of Northern Education for Birmingham City Council in Respect of Issues Arising as a Result of Concerns Raised in a Letter Dated 27 November 2013, Known as the Trojan Horse Letter.*

Kundnani, A. (2009). *Spooked – How Not to Prevent Violent Extremism.* London: Institute of Race Relations.

Laborde, C. (2005). Secular Philosophy and Muslim Headscarves in Schools. *The Journal of Political Philosophy, 13*(3), 305–329.

Ladson-Billings, G. (1998). Just What is Critical Race Theory and What's it Doing in a *nice* Field Like Education? *International Journal of Qualitative Studies in Education, 11*(1), 7–24.

Ladson-Billings, G., & Tate, W. F. (1995). Towards a Critical Race Theory of education. *Teacher's College Record, 97*(1), 47–68.

Leonardo, Z. (2002). The Souls of White Folk: Critical Pedagogy, Whiteness Studies, and Globalization Discourse. *Race Ethnicity & Education, 5*(1), 29–50.

Lomotey, K., & Staley, J. (1990). *The Education of African Americans in Buffalo Public Schools.* Paper Presented at the Annual Meeting of the American Research Association, Boston.

Lymperopoulou, K., & Parameshwaran, M. (2014). *Dynamics of Diversity: Evidence from the 2011 Census.* ESRC Centre on Dynamics of Ethnicity (CoDE), University of Manchester/Joseph Rowntree Foundation.

Mac an Ghaill, M. (1988). *Young, Gifted and Black.* Oxford: Alden Press.

Malagon, M. C., Huber, L. P., & Velez, V. N. (2009). Our Experiences, Our Methods: Using Grounded Theory to Inform a Critical Race Theory Methodology. *Seattle Journal for Social Justice, 8*(1), 252–272.

MCB. (2014). *British Muslims in Numbers: A Demographic, Sociology-Economic and Health Profile of Muslims in Britain Drawing on the 2011 Census.* The Muslim Council of Britain's Research and Documentation Committee, London, Muslim Council or Britain.

McLaughlin, T. (2005). The Educative Importance of Ethos. *British Journal of Educational Studies, 53*(3), 306–325.

Meer, N. (2007). Muslim Schools in Britain: Challenging Mobilisations or Logical Developments? *Asia Pacific Journal of Education, 27*(1), 55–71.

Meer, N. (2009). Identity Articulations, Mobilization, and Autonomy in the Movement for Muslim Schools in Britain. *Race Ethnicity and Education, 12*(3), 379–399.

REFERENCES 193

Meer, N., & Breen, B. (forthcoming). Muslim Schools in Britain: Between Mobilisation and Incorporation. In M. Abu Bakar (Ed.), *Living the Faith Engaging the Mind: Rethinking Madrasah Education in the Modern World*.

Meer, N., & Breen, D. (2017). Muslim Schools in Britain: Between Mobilisation and Incorporation. (Forthcoming).

Meer, N., & Modood, T. (2009). Refutations of Racism in the 'Muslim Question'. *Patterns of Prejudice, 43*(3–4), 335–354.

Modood, T. (1994). Political Blackness and British Asians. *Sociology, 28*(4), 859–876.

Modood, T. (1998). Anti-essentialism, Multiculturalism and the 'Recognition' of Religious Groups. *The Journal of Political Philosophy, 6*(4), 378–399.

Modood, T. (2005). *Multicultural Politics: Racism, Ethnicity and Muslims in Britain*. Edinburgh: Edinburgh University Press.

Modood, T. (2008). A Basis for and Two Obstacles in the Way of a Multiculturalist Coalition. *The British Journal of Sociology, 59*(1), 47–52.

Modood, T., & Werbner, P. (1997). *The Politics of Multiculturalism in the New Europe: Racism, Identity and Community*. Hampshire: Palgrave Macmillan.

ONS. (2011a). *Ethnicity and National Identity in England and Wales: 2011*. London: Office for National Statistics.

ONS. (2011b). *Religion in England and Wales 2011*. London: Office for National Statistics.

Parekh, B. C. (2000). *The Future of Multi-ethnic Britain: Report of the Commission on the Future of Multi-ethnic Britain*. London: Profile Books.

Parker-Jenkins, M., Hartas, D., & Irving, B. A. (2005). *In Good Faith, Schools, Religion and Public Funding*. Hampshire: Ashgate Publishing.

Pole, C., & Lampard, R. (2000). *Practical Social Investigation: Qualitative and Quantitative Methods in Social Research*. London: Prentice Hall.

Preston, J., & Chadderton, C. (2012). Rediscovering 'Race Traitor': Towards a Critical Race Theory Informed Public Pedagogy. *Race Ethnicity and Education, 15*(1), 85–100.

Roberts, K. A., & Wilson, R. W. (2002). ICT and the Research Process: Issues Around the Compatibility of Technology with Qualitative Data Analysis. *Forum Qualitative Sozialforschung/Forum: Qualitative Social Research, 3*(2), article 23, [52 paragraphs], http://nbnresolving.de/urn:nbn:de:0114-fqs0202234. Accessed 1 Aug 2010.

Runnymede. (1997). *Islamophobia – A Challenge for Us All*. Runnymede Trust.

Said, E. W. (1978). *Orientalism*. New York: Pantheon Books.

Said, E. W. (1985). Orientalism Reconsidered. *Cultural Critique, 1*, 89–107.

Sayyid, S. (2010). Out of the Devil's Dictionary. In S. Sayyid & A. Vakil (Eds.), *Thinking Through Islamophobia: Global Perspectives* (pp. 5–18). El Paso: Cinco Puntos Press.

Sayyid, S. (2014). A Measure of Islamophobia. *Islamophobia Studies Journal, 2*(1), 10–25.

194   REFERENCES

Scheurich, J. J. (1995). A Postmodernist Critique of Research Interviewing. *Qualitative Studies in Education, 8*, 239–252.

Shah, S. (2004). The Researcher/Interviewer in Intercultural Context: A Social Intruder! *British Education Research Journal, 30*(4), 549–575.

Sian, K. P. (2015). Spies, Surveillance and Stakeouts: Monitoring Muslim Moves in British State Schools. *Race Ethnicity and Education, 18*(2), 183–201.

Singh, G. (2003). Multiculturalism in Contemporary Britain: Reflections on the "Leicester Model". *International Journal on Multicultural Societies (IJMS), 5*(1), 40–54.

Solorzano, D. G., & Delgado-Bernal, D. (2001). Examining Transformational Resistance Through a Critical Race and LatCrit Theory Framework: Chicana and Chicano Students in an Urban Context. *Urban Education, 36*(3), 308–342.

Solorzano, D. T., & Yosso, T. (2002). Critical Race Methodology: Counter-Storytelling as an Analytical Framework for Education Research. *Qualitative Inquiry, 8*(1), 23–44.

Solvason, C. (2005). Investigating Specialist School Ethos… Or Do You Mean Culture? *Educational Studies, 31*(1), 85–94.

Stanley, C. A. (2007). When Counter Narratives Meet Master Narratives in the Journal Editorial-Review Process. *Educational Researcher, 36*(1), 14–24.

Strauss, A., & Corbin, J. (1997). *Grounded Theory in Practice*. London: SAGE.

Swann, M. (1985). *Education for All: The Report of the Inquiry into the Education of Pupils of Children from Ethnic Minority Groups*. London: HMSO.

Terrill, R. E. (2001). Protest, Prophecy and Prudence in the Rhetoric of Malcolm X. *Rhetoric & Public Affairs, 4*(1), 25–53.

Thomas, P. (2009). Between Two Stools? The Government's 'Preventing Violent Extremism' Agenda. *The Political Quarterly, 80*(2), 282–291.

Tinker, C. (2006a). Islamophobia, Social Cohesion and Autonomy: Challenging the Arguments Against State Funded Muslim Schools in Britain. *Muslim Educational Quarterly, 23*(1&2), 4–19.

Tinker, C. (2006b). *State Funded Muslim Schools? Equality, Identity and Community in Multi-Faith Britain*, Unpublished PhD Thesis, University of Nottingham Library.

Tinker, C. (2009). Rights, Social Cohesion and Identity: Arguments for and Against State Funded Muslim Schools in Britain. *Race, Ethnicity and Education, 12*(4), 539–553.

UK Government. (2005). *The Schools White Paper: Higher Standards, Better Schools for All*. London: Her Majesty's Stationary Office.

UK Government. (2014). *Types of School: Free Schools*, UK Government Website. Available at: https://www.gov.uk/types-of-school/free-schools. Accessed 3 Jan 2015.

UK Parliament. (1998). *School Standards and Framework Act*. London: Her Majesty's Stationary Office.

UK Parliament. (2003). *Designation of Schools Having a Religious Character (Independent Schools) (England) Order 2003*. London: Her Majesty's Stationary Office.

UK Parliament. (2010). *The Academies Act*. London: HMSO.

Walford, G. (2003). Muslim Schools in Britain. In G. Walford (Ed.), *British Private Schools: Research on Policy and Practice* (pp. 158–176). London: Woburn Press.

Warmington, P. (2012). A Tradition in Ceaseless Motion': Critical Race Theory and Black British Intellectual Spaces. *Race, Ethnicity and Education, 15*(1), 5–21.

Yin, R. K. (2003). *Applications of Case Study Research* (2nd ed.). Thousand Oaks: SAGE.

Index

A

academies, 41, 50–2, 98, 99, 126, 169
  conversions to academy status across
    denominational group, 45, 51
Academies Act 2010, The, 4, 41,
    44–6, 50–2, 97, 98, 169, 171
Al-Falah (pseudonym), 67, 68, 79, 82,
    99, 105, 116, 118–23, 127,
    129–32, 134, 136, 139, 140, 144,
    145, 150, 155–7, 169, 170, 172–4
Al-Iman (pseudonym), 67, 68, 79, 99,
    103, 105, 107–9, 116, 119, 123,
    128–32, 134, 136, 140, 150,
    155, 169, 172–4
Allen, Chris, 21, 22, 24, 25, 29, 30,
    35, 135
anti-Muslim
  discrimination, 9, 12, 20–2, 25–8,
    30, 115, 135, 141, 142
  marginalisation, 12
  racism, 26, 38, 63
anti-semitism
  and anti-Muslim racism, 30
  and Islamophobia, 23
Arabic

in everyday school life, 150–2, 174
  use among non-Muslim staff, 127,
    128, 152
  use among pupils, 72–4, 147–9
  use between Muslim staff, 152
Association of Muslim Schools UK
    (AMS), 19, 47, 50, 52, 61, 101
attainment
  educational attainment by religion,
    161, 162, 164
  educational equity among Pakistani
    and Bangladeshi groups, 160
  Muslim schools as a strategy for
    improved educational
    attainment, 163
autonomy, 68, 95, 125, 127, 143,
    144, 146, 147, 170, 171

B

Bell, Derek, 13, 16
'Black' separatism
  Du Bois, W. E. B., 12, 13
  Garvey, M., 12
  Nation of Islam, 12, 13

© The Author(s) 2018
D. Breen, *Muslim Schools, Communities and Critical Race Theory*,
DOI 10.1057/978-1-137-44397-7

198 INDEX

British National Party (BNP), 2, 24–6, 29, 39
Britishness, 25, 30, 41, 54, 141, 155, 168

C
colonialism, 9, 11
counter-narratives, 4, 19–21, 32, 36, 61–5, 70, 87, 91
counter-storytelling, 19, 21, 26, 62, 64, 87
counter-terror, 27, 28, 36–9, 54
Critical Race Theory (CRT)
   and African American groups, 4, 5
   application to British Muslims, 9–32, 35–57
   legal discourse, 4
   in the UK context, 5, 20, 31
   in the USA context, 5
curriculum
   Islamicised curriculum, 148, 152–5
   national curriculum, 96, 97, 103, 104, 111, 153, 155, 156

E
educational enfranchisement
   Muslim schools as mobilisations for, 46, 47, 56, 130, 163, 164, 172, 176
empathetic interviews, 81, 82, 87, 91
empowerment
   educational, 43, 142, 143, 163
   political, 32, 43, 143, 144
English Defence League, 2, 25, 29, 30, 39
Englishness, 25, 29, 30, 54, 141, 155, 168
equity/inequity
   civic, 16, 20, 28, 36, 62, 162

educational, 16, 37, 51, 56, 130, 160–2, 164
nation state, 39, 160, 168, 176
political, 35, 37–9, 54–6, 167, 176, 177
polity, 15, 176
ethnicity
   and diversity in Muslim schools, 1, 35–7, 70–2, 100, 118, 122, 123, 158, 161, 173, 174
   staff/intake at Al-Falah, 119–22
   staff/intake at Al-Iman, 120, 122
   staff/intake at Hiqmah School, 100–1
   staff/intake at Medina Primary, 71, 100, 118, 119, 123
ethnography
   audio diaries, 84
   empathetic interviews, 81, 82, 91
   participant observation, 63, 68, 69, 79, 84–7, 91
   semi-structured interviews, 68
ethos, 104, 105, 131, 134, 137–40, 145–7, 150–2, 155–60, 163

F
faith schooling
   numbers of Catholic schools in the state and independent sectors, 45, 47, 48, 99
   numbers of Church of England schools in the state and independent sectors, 45–7, 173
Fanon, Frantz, 9–11
Fekete, Liz, 38, 39
financial instability, 47, 50
free schools, 3, 4, 19, 41, 44, 50–3, 56, 57, 61, 97–9, 125, 126, 136, 169, 171, 172, 175, 176
fundamental British values, 39–41, 97, 98

INDEX 199

G

Gillborn, David, 15–18, 20, 36, 62, 64

grant-maintained schools, 42, 48, 49, 100, 104, 105, 116, 130–4, 174

grounded theory, 62, 63, 87–91

H

Hiqmah School (pseudonym), 66–8, 74, 79, 80, 83, 84, 86, 87, 99, 100, 103–5, 111, 112, 116, 120, 123, 130, 136, 140, 141, 145, 148–52, 156–8, 160, 162, 163, 170–4

I

independent schools, 2, 3, 7, 19, 41–3, 46–51, 55, 61, 63, 66, 67, 74, 80, 95–9, 101–5, 107, 108, 110, 111, 115–17, 121, 122, 124, 125, 128–30, 133–6, 155, 160, 168, 172–7

insider/outsider positionality
and ethnicity, 70–2
and gender, 72–3
male non-Muslim, 71, 75
researcher as a white, 70–2

interest convergence, 6, 16, 17, 20, 32, 35, 62, 167, 175

Islam in the public space, 1, 6, 54, 57, 155, 163

Islamic dress
media narratives around the *hijab/niqab*, 52
policy responses around the *hijab/niqab*, 73, 74
wearing the *hijab* in educational settings, 72, 84, 101, 124, 132, 142

wearing the *niqab* in educational settings, 72–4, 86, 87, 101, 124

Islamic extremism, 2

Islamic identification, 18

Islamic provision, 105, 111, 119, 127, 128, 132, 133, 146, 147, 149, 151, 155–9, 163

Islamophobia, 2, 4, 9, 18, 20–8, 30, 55, 70, 135, 176
critical notions of, 25, 115
Runnymede Trust 1997, 21, 35

K

Kundnani, Arun, 37, 38

L

Ladson-Billings, Gloria, 4, 5, 13, 17, 18, 64, 65

learning by example, 144–6

Leonardo, Zeus, 17

Lomotey, K.
Buffalo County, 17

M

master-narratives
ample opportunities for state-funded Muslim schooling, 55
British Muslims as having an equitable stake in democratic politics, 55, 163, 177
concern or policing around increased Islamic influence in the public sphere, 38
Islam as existing in tension with Britishness/Englishness, 54
Muslim schools as monocultural thus satisfying broadly homogenous needs, 172, 174, 175

media narratives, 1, 24, 26, 38, 52–4

200 INDEX

Medina Primary (pseudonym), 66–8,
71, 73, 79, 80, 82–7, 99–105,
109–11, 116, 123–9, 132, 134,
138–44, 146–8, 150–4, 157–60,
162, 163, 170, 172–4
Meer, Nasar, 27, 28, 39, 40, 44–7, 49
Modood, Tariq, 27, 28, 44
Muslim communities
assumptions about Muslims as a
homogeneous group, 29, 30,
118
and diversity within Muslim
communities, 1, 26, 119, 123
Muslim Council of Britain, 169
Muslim schools
as mobilisations of nuanced needs,
95–112
numbers in the independent sector,
3, 19, 47, 48, 50, 56, 61, 67,
96–111, 121, 125–9, 135, 168,
170, 172–4, 177
numbers in the state sector, 1, 2, 42,
43, 45, 47–9, 67, 105, 106,
121, 125, 126, 130, 131, 139,
163, 164, 175
in the post-2010 era, 51–3, 56, 125
as a response to community need,
55, 56, 122, 129, 135, 143,
172–5
under New Labour, 19, 41–3, 46,
48, 49, 56, 61, 164, 171

N

Nasira (pseudonym), 66–8, 79, 82,
99, 105–9, 120–2, 127–9, 139,
144, 145, 150, 155, 156

O

Orientalism, 10, 11

P

participant observation, 68, 84, 90
political enfranchisement, 36, 163,
164, 167, 168, 176, 177
marginalisation of Muslim voices in
democratic politics, 28
Preston, John, 15, 18, 26, 62
prevent strategy
guidelines, 40
implications for political dissidents, 39
statutory duty, 39

Q

Qur'an, 73, 74, 110, 123, 124,
138–40, 143, 145–51, 153–9

R

race, 4, 5, 9, 12, 13, 15, 16, 24–8, 31,
35, 36, 44, 64, 65, 70, 71, 142
racialisation
racialised discrimination, 70, 142
racialised marginalisation, 177
racism, 4, 9, 12–15, 17–24, 26–31,
35, 38, 61–5, 72
radicalisation, 37
religious identification, 142
religious practice/practise, 84, 106,
107, 110, 126, 127, 139–42,
144, 145, 147, 148, 154
religious values, 140

S

Said, Edward, 10, 11
Sayyid, Salman, 23, 24, 26, 30, 35, 135
School Standards and Frameworks Act
1998, The, 41
semi-structured interviews, 68, 82, 83,
85

INDEX 201

smokescreens, 14, 49, 135, 168, 171, 172
stakeholders
  families, 116–19
  intake, 115–19, 159
  parents, 80, 111, 129, 158, 159
  staff, 115, 116, 169
Staley, J.
  Buffalo County, 17

T
tacit intentionality, 6, 15, 16, 19, 28, 32, 49, 167–72, 176
teachers
  in the independent sector, 124, 125, 129, 170, 173
  Muslim teachers, 140, 170, 171
  non-Muslim teachers, 127, 131–3, 150, 170, 171
  qualified status QTS, 124–6, 128, 129, 169–71
  unqualified, 128
terrorism
  Charlie Hebdo and attacks in Paris 2015, 1, 54
  European truck attacks, 1
  Leytonstone station 2015, 1

London bombings 7th July 2005, 1, 21, 25, 44, 80
Rigby, Lee, 1, 25
September 11th 2001, 1, 21, 25, 141
2017 Westminster attack, 2
Tinker, Claire, 6, 35, 42, 46–9, 168, 173, 174
Trojan Horse letter, 6, 44

V
voices, 13, 19, 27, 35, 38, 39, 54, 62–6, 69, 70, 72, 75, 87, 88, 90, 96, 115, 116, 130, 137, 142–4, 147, 171, 177
voluntary-aided schools, 41, 42, 44–6, 50–2, 56, 97, 99, 100, 105, 109, 116, 139, 144, 155, 170

W
whiteness
  as a racial discourse, 17
  white people, 4, 17, 18, 20, 62
  and white privilege, 15, 18, 20, 26, 32, 62, 65, 142
  white supremacy, 12–15, 17, 72